ELDON J. EPP

FROM DEATH TO LIFE

ROBERT MARTIN–ACHARD

FROM DEATH
TO LIFE

A STUDY OF THE DEVELOPMENT OF THE DOCTRINE OF THE RESURRECTION IN THE OLD TESTAMENT

Translated by
JOHN PENNEY SMITH

OLIVER AND BOYD
EDINBURGH AND LONDON
1960

OLIVER AND BOYD LTD
Tweeddale Court
Edinburgh 1

39A Welbeck Street
London W1

A translation of *De la Mort à la résurrection, d'après l'Ancien
Testament,* by R. Martin-Achard, first published by
Delachaux & Niestlé S. A. in the Bibliothèque
Théologique at Neuchâtel and Paris 1956

ENGLISH EDITION
First published 1960

Printed in Great Britain for Oliver & Boyd Ltd
by T. and A. CONSTABLE LTD, Hopetoun Street
Printers to the University of Edinburgh

TRANSLATOR'S FOREWORD

This book is an examination of the Old Testament passages which illustrate the emergence of the Doctrine of the Resurrection in Ancient Israel and Early Judaism. Its author, Professor R. Martin-Achard, D.Theol., is Professor of Old Testament Language and Theology in the Universities of Geneva and Neuchâtel.

In this translation, the Scriptural quotations and the citations in the footnotes have been conformed, as to chapter, verse and text, to the Revised Standard Version of the Bible, copyrighted 1946 and 1952 by the Division of Christian Education of the National Council of the Churches of Christ in the United States of America, and are used by permission. Where the author's French rendering or his exegesis has made it necessary to depart from the R.S.V. text, this has been indicated by italicising.

For the transliterations from the Hebrew, the system adopted in *The Old Testament and Modern Study*, edited by Professor H. H. Rowley, Oxford 1951, has been followed, except that פ has been transliterated by *q*.

The translator's thanks are due to the Rev. R. J. Ehrlich, B.D., Ph.D., Leith, and to the Rev. Professor James Barr, New College, Edinburgh, for their help and advice; he is also much indebted to the author for his guidance on many points.

J. P. S.

CONTENTS

Translator's Foreword v

Introduction ix

PART I

LIFE AND DEATH IN OLD TESTAMENT TEACHING

I.   The Meaning and Nature of Life 3

II. The Meaning and Nature of Death 16

PART II

THE VICTORY OVER DEATH

I.   Yahweh kills and makes alive 52

II. The Proclamation of the Resurrection and of the Destruction of Death 74

III. "Nothing can separate us . . ." 147

PART III

FROM DEATH TO RESURRECTION

I.   Possible Foreign Influence on the Formation of the Old Testament Belief in the Resurrection of the Dead . . 186

II. Old Testament Belief in the Resurrection of the Dead a Consequence of the Revelation of the Living God to His People 206

Conclusion 223

Bibliography 231

List of Abbreviations 239

INTRODUCTION

THE starting-point of this study is death, which comes intimately close to our life in the pastoral work of the ministry.

To-day, as at other times, the most confused ideas prevail on the subject of the Beyond. There is no doubt that many of our contemporaries share the contradictory opinions of the Hebrews on the lot of the dead, on the one hand endowing them with more than living capacity, on the other condemning them to a pitiful existence. We commonly conceive of the dead as knowing, if not all things, at least much that is beyond our ken, yet at the same time we wonder with Bossuet whether "to die is not to become I know not what, nameless in any tongue," since nothing follows death. In short, we are continually oscillating between spiritualism and materialism, to make use of convenient terms, not knowing exactly to what we should hold in face of the ineluctable fact of death.

We must return to the fountain-head and open our Bibles again, and find there the grounds of the Christian hope in the hour when a human life comes to its close. The Gospel, without answering all our questions and especially those that the passing of our own beloved brings tells us enough to bid us believe in the resurrection of the dead. Thereafter, the Church confesses that Jesus Christ, dead under Pontius Pilate, descended into Hell, was raised on the third day, and sees His destiny as the pattern and pledge of our living again. The way for these declarations was prepared in the Old Testament. So it seemed useful to us to study the Scriptures of the People of God to find how belief in the resurrection arose and gradually established itself in Israel. For is not Easter the shining vindication of that hope which is the consummation of the Old Covenant?

We have restricted ourselves to the study of Old Testament texts, in the hope that some day a similar study of the New Testament may be undertaken and a definite statement of its teaching made, in the light both of the ancient documents, among which a whole apocryphal literature must not be disregarded, and also of the appearances of the Risen Christ to His disciples within hours of His death. Our main purpose has been to bring to the notice not only of specialists who know them well, but also of Christians unskilled in placing them in their Scriptural context, some Old Testament passages by means of which we can see the believer arriving, step by step, at this overwhelming discovery: death is not the end of human life, the closing chapter of our story; we are not doomed to die, God is calling us to life; we go on beyond the grave to the life everlasting in union with Him. This certainty, far from diminishing the significance of our earthly career, as we sometimes imagine, endows it, as a careful study of the Scriptures shows, with an inestimable worth, since, according to the whole of the Bible, it is here below that our ultimate destiny is determined; in some very real sense the Beyond makes no difference at all but merely makes manifest what we truly are.

In writing this study with the aid of the most eminent Old Testament specialists, we have not forgotten the parish in which we are at present ministering, and especially the families stricken by the death of some loved one, and we trust that, like the believers among the Chosen People, we and they together shall find in the Word of God the assurance that, in life as in death, <u>we belong to the Living God who is the God of the living.</u>

In concluding this introduction, we have to thank all those who in any way have helped us in the preparation of this work, the many teachers who have given us the guidance of their counsel and the stimulus of their encouragement, among whom we particularly mention Professor G. Nagel of Geneva, who for years has been interested in our study of the Old Testament, and also the members of the Reformed Church at Nancy who helped to read the proofs; and we express our gratitude to the University of Geneva for the generosity that has made this publication possible.

NANCY, Holy Week, 1955.

PART I

LIFE AND DEATH IN OLD TESTAMENT TEACHING

WE cannot discuss the resurrection without making a statement, however brief, of the meaning life and death have for the Old Testament; so we shall begin our study by recalling how the Israelites understood them both. Naturally, what follows in these pages is only an outline.

Hebrew conceptions in this sphere have often been likened to Mesopotamian, Egyptian or even Greek ideas. The comparison is legitimate, the resemblances observed by the specialists being numerous. A perusal of the works of L. Dürr, A. Bertholet, A. Lods, and E. Dhorme, to cite only these, is enough to carry conviction.[1] Writers such as J. Pedersen and H. Wheeler Robinson and others have made a point of stressing the parallels that may be traced between the psychology of the Israelites and that of primitive peoples; many Old Testament

---

[1] L. Dürr, *Die Wertung des Lebens im A.T. und im antiken Orient*, 1926-7; A. Bertholet, *Die israelitischen Vorstellungen vom Zustand nach dem Tode*, 2nd edn., 1914; A. Lods, *La croyance à la vie future dans l'antiquité israélite* 1906; E. Dhorme, "Séjour des morts chez les Babyloniens et chez les Hébreux," in *Rev. bib.*, 1907, pp. 5 ff.

Among more recent studies we may also cite: C. Barth, *Die Errettung vom Tode in den individuellen Klage- und Dankliedern des A. T.*, 1947; A. Heidel, *The Gilgamesh Epic and Old Testament Parallels*, 1946, etc. In the bibliographies of these works the writers make particular mention of the studies on Mesopotamia made by: A. Jeremias, *Die babylonisch-assyrischen Vorstellungen vom Leben nach dem Tode*, 1887, and *Hölle und Paradies bei den Babyloniern*, 1903; E. Ebeling, *Tod und Leben nach den Vorstellungen der Babylonier*, vol. I, 1931; and K. Tallqvist, *Sumerische und Akkadische Namen für die Totenwelt*, 1934; and special reference to those on Egypt by: A. Erman, *Die Religion der Aegypter*, 1934; H. Kees, *Totenglaube und Jenseitsvorstellung der alten Aegypter*, 1926; A. Gardiner, *The Attitude of the Ancient Egyptians to Death and the Dead*, 1935; and A. Sander-Hansen, *Der Begriff des Totes bei den Aegyptern*, 1942.

For further details of many of the works cited in these footnotes, see the Bibliography, pp. 230-6; and for a list of the abbreviations used both in Bibliography and footnotes, see pp. 237-8.

texts shine with a new light when we restore them to a framework of thought more akin to the mentality of the African or
the South Sea Islander than to our own.[2] In short, in face of
life or death, the Hebrew reacted in very much the same way
as once the Babylonian and the Egyptian did, or as the Kanaka
and the Hottentot do now. The comparison of Old Testament
texts with the writings of antiquity, as with the expressions
employed by the Negroes today, is full of interest. Nevertheless, we see no need to discuss the subject here again, but shall
restrict ourselves to a few pages of review of the Chosen
People's own conception of life and death.

[2] J. PEDERSEN, *Israel*, VOLS. I-II, 1926, and III-IV, 1940; H. WHEELER
ROBINSON, "The Hebrew Conception of Corporate Personality," in *Werden
und Wesen des A. T.*, in Beitr. z. Wiss. vom A. N. T., 1936, pp. 49 ff.; A. R.
JOHNSON, *The Vitality of the Individual in the Thought of Ancient Israel*, 1949;
G. PIDOUX, *L'homme dans l'A. T.*, 1953.

Also to be noted are G. VAN DER LEEUW, *Religion in Essence and Manifestation, a Study in Phenomenology*, 1938; M. ELIADE, *Traité d'histoire des
religions*, 1953.

Chapter I

The Meaning and Nature of Life

The Israelite loves life; he meets it with optimism; he sees it as a gift of God. Existence at its most physical and concrete shows forth the bounty of Yahweh; thus the believer does not long to escape from this world, but rather to have length of days in it; he desires, not to be lifted up above earthly chance and change into some intemporal spiritual state, but rather to enjoy all the resources the Creator offers him in His creation. His ideal finds its expression in the portrait of Job, satisfied with honours and substance, a perfect and upright man, fabulously rich, a model of piety and generosity (Job I. 1 ff.; XXIX. 2 ff.; XLII. 10 ff.); it is also revealed (Ps. CXXVIII) in the prosperity promised to the man who "fears the LORD and walks in his ways":

> You shall eat the fruit of the labour
> of your hands;
> You shall be happy, and it shall be
> well with you.
>
> Your wife will be like a fruitful vine
> within your house;
> Your children will be like olive shoots
> around your table.
> Lo, thus shall the man be blessed
> who fears the LORD.
>
> The LORD bless you from Zion!
> May you see the prosperity of
> Jerusalem
> all the days of your life!
> May you see your children's children!
> Peace be upon Israel!

These are the prayers of a peasant people: to live long on the land inherited from the fathers, to have many sons at one's side to ensure the stint of the day, to see the fruit of one's toil, the abundance of one's reaping and gathering, the increase of one's flocks, and finally to share these blessings with a whole people and, especially, with the City of God.

We find this theme almost everywhere in the Old Testament, and it is particularly prominent in the Psalms and the Proverbs, which are faithful reflexions of the mind of the Chosen People as a whole.

Israel has a wholesome and positive outlook on life and does not regard it as a mocking and bitter game, and cannot subscribe to J. P. Sartre's saying, "The story of any life whatsoever is a story of failure"; [1] on the contrary, it considers success to be possible and normal, and failure accidental. Existence is not irrational, but significant; being a gift of God and not a product of chance, it leads to an end and is part of a plan whose essential elements Yahweh has revealed to His People. Over against the romanticism that would find the essence of things in death, the Israelite considers life to be the supreme reality, and would never have agreed with G. Frommel, who writes: "To die is not to cease to be, it is to cease to be seen." [2] The divine blessings are not mere semblance, sheer illusion; what has been termed the "eudaemonism" of the Old Testament recalls that God is no stranger in the world He has made by His Word, and that His purpose is to reign in it, absolutely and everywhere. The Israelite is no mystic longing to lose himself in an inexpressible rapture and to be absorbed in the deity in the extinction of his carnal and personal self; throughout all his life in this world he meets with the God of Abraham and of Isaac and of Jacob, and under His guidance goes forward with his brethren.

Human life is thus delivered from disorder and chance and develops in a setting appointed by Yahweh Himself. Along with his life every Israelite receives a family to whose common interests he is tightly bound, a land in which he may and must live, and a people whose destiny he shares, and all these depend alike on the Living God and condition a life which is the gift of Yahweh; should any of these essential elements of his existence happen to be missing, then the Israelite ceases to live.

[1] J. P. SARTRE, *L'être et le néant*, Paris 1943, p. 561.
[2] Cited by C. GENEQUAND, *Vers l'invisible*, Geneva 1940, p. 90.

LIFE IS A FORCE

Life, for the Israelite, is not simply existence. It is an active force, an operative power. חַיִּים, *ḥayyîm*, "life," is plural in form, which must be to stress its intensive character. "The verb חָיָה, *ḥāyâ*, 'to live,' seems in the Semitic languages originally to have the sense of muscular contraction, in contrast with death, whose verbal root signifies to be stretched out, to be relaxed." [1]

To live is more than to be. The Israelite defines life not conceptually, but functionally, he knows it in its manifestations. Thus it is identified with the blood or the breath, without which it is inconceivable. "The blood is the life", declares Deuteronomy (XII. 23), because it conditions it and is its vehicle.[2] Life is also confused with breath; after the creation of man, Yahweh breathed a "breath" of life into the nostrils of the being that He had fashioned, and only then did Adam begin to live (Gen. II. 7).[3] The breath is thus one of "the aspects that life can assume." [4]

Thus life is primarily a force; indeed it is precisely what the expression "vital force" brings to our minds; its nature is to express itself, to act, to move, to fulfil itself; therefore it involves mobility, spontaneity, and development; it must grow, flourish, and accomplish its end; the absence of movement, freedom, or future is tantamount to its negation.[5] As a power it may decrease or increase, its intensity varies from moment to moment and being to being, from the Living God or the King to the humble Israelite, or again to the sick, or even the dead; sickness (II Kings VIII. 8, 10, 14; XX. 1, 7), weariness (Gen. XXV. 30, 32), sleep (Is. V. 27), and death are enfeebled forms of life, a sort of life slowed down because bereft of all its potentialities. "To be awakened," "to be healed," "to be raised," means to recover every faculty, to be once again in possession of all the power involved in the life given by God to His creature.[6]

---

[1] F. MICHAELI, in *Voc. bib.*, p. 302.
[2] Cp. also Gen. IX. 4; Lev. XVII. 14; Ps. LXXII. 14; etc.
[3] Job XXVII. 3, XXXIII. 4, XXXIV. 14, etc.
[4] PIDOUX, *op. cit.* (above, p. 2, n. 2), pp. 49 ff.
[5] C. BARTH, *op. cit.* (above, p. 1, n. 1), pp. 22 ff.
[6] PIDOUX, *op. cit.*, pp. 53 ff.

B

LIFE IS A GOOD, THE SUPREME GOOD

In a general way, life is seen by the Israelite as a "good," as the "supreme good" on which all the others depend, the most precious of blessings, surpassing riches and honour (Prov. III. 16); [1] Satan understands the mind of Israel well when he declares: "All that a man has he will give for his life" (Job II. 4). As the Israelite aspires to long life for himself, so on the day of the enthronement of his King, in whom the people's lot is bound up, he cries (I Sam. x. 24): "Long live the king!" or "Live for ever!"—meaning "May his reign be long!" [2]

The ideal is to die in fulness of years, abounding in days and possessions, to depart in peace after a long and blessed old age. This was especially the privilege of Abraham (Gen. xv. 15), Jacob (Gen. xxxv. 29), and Job (XLII. 17). [3]

Tradition claims that the antediluvian generations lived to exceptional ages; this favour had been granted them because they had lived closer to God than their descendants. [4] Ecclesiastes expresses the mind of his people well when he declares (IX. 4) that even "a living dog is better than a dead lion," meaning that life is worth more than all else. [5]

Therefore to die prematurely, to depart in the midst of one's days, that is to say before having fulfilled one's being and

---

[1] G. VON RAD, s.v. ζωή, in KITTEL, VOL. II., pp. 844 f.; J. LINDBLOM, *Das ewige Leben*, 1914, pp. 9 ff., etc.

[2] II Sam. XVI. 16; I KINGS I. 31; Ps. XXI. 4; and also Neh. II. 3; Dan. II. 4, III. 9.

[3] Cp. the expressions בְּשֵׂיבָה טוֹבָה (*beśēbâ ṭôbâ*, "in a good old age" (Gen. XV. 15), and זָקֵן וּשְׂבַע יָמִים, *zāqēn ûśebaʿ yāmîm*, "old and full of days" (Gen. XXXV. 29); and also Pss. XCI. 16, CXXXIII. 3; Tob. XIV. 3, 13 ff.; II Macc. VI. 23; etc.

[4] DÜRR, *op. cit.* (above, p. 2, n. 1), pp. 13 ff., who in support of his position cites some Egyptian texts, considers that, according to Israelite conceptions, the minimum length of human life would be 110 years: in point of fact, both Joseph and Joshua died at that very age (Gen. I. 26; Josh. XXIV. 29; Jg. II. 8); moreover, at the time of the Flood, the life-span of man was still 120 years (Gen. VI. 3), and under the conditions of the new creation it is going to exceed 100 (Is. LXV. 20).

[5] Cp. EURIPIDES, *Iph.*: "A lowly life is better than death." See HOMER *Od.*, XI. 489-491, where Achilles says: "I would rather be living a serf bound to some churl of scanty means than lord it over the perished dead."

exhausted the resources of life, is a great evil, a dire punishment (Ps. CII. 23 f.) [6]

The prolongation of life is a recurrent theme in the teaching of Deuteronomy which is re-echoed in the message of the prophets: "Seek the LORD and live. . . ," proclaims Amos to his people, "Seek good, and not evil, so that you may live." [7]

The Fourth Commandment connects duty to parents with duration of life not only for the individual but also for the People in the Holy Land (Exod. XX. 12).[8] In the same way, for Deuteronomy, "to remain alive" has the special meaning of entering into possession of the land of Canaan and keeping it (Deut. IV. 40).[9] Israel is confronted with a curse or a blessing, that is the chance of living in the land Yahweh gives it or the constraint of being exiled or even extirpated (Deut. XXX. 16 ff.) [10] In his turn the Israelite is called to dwell in the Holy Land or else to disappear (Prov. X. 30; Is. LVII. 13; Ps. XXXVII. 10, etc.) Thus to live is to subsist on the soil that the Living God has chosen for Himself.

In the Old Testament the believer does not yearn for the end of his existence, he does not sing the praise of "sweet death" like some J. S. Bach, but rejoices in living as long as he can.

Rarely is an Old Testament voice heard calling for death; Job's imprecations against life (Job III. 3 ff.),[11] and Jeremiah's maledictions (Jer. XX. 14 ff.) remain exceptional and border on blasphemy; they reveal the depths of despair into which these two Old Testament men have fallen. By such bitter and disillusioned assertions as that "the day of death" is better "than the day of birth," Ecclesiastes (VII. 1; cp. IV. 2 f.) diverges in this respect, as in others, from the true tradition of Israel. Balaam, strictly speaking, does not ask for death, but desires that the end of a righteous man, that is to say, of a member of the Chosen People, may be granted to him, even to him, a heathen; he seems quite simply to be wishing

---

[6] Gen. XLVII. 9; Is. XXXVIII. 10; Jer. XVII. 11.

[7] Am. V. 4, 14. Cp. also Ezek. XVIII. 23, 31 f., XXXIII. 11; Hab. II. 4; etc.

[8] DÜRR, *op. cit.*, pp. 23 ff.

[9] Deut. VI. 18, 24, VIII, 1, XI. 8 f.; etc.

[10] Deut. IV. 26 f.; Lev. XXVI. 31 ff.; II Sam. VII. 10 f.; I Kings IX. 7; Jer. VII. 3, 7; Jer. XXXV. 15; etc.

[11] Job VII. 15, X. 1; XVII. 13 ff.

for a long life (Num. xxiii. 10; Ps. cxvi. 15).[12] The words of the psalmist, "Thy steadfast love is better than life" (Ps. lxiii. 3), reveal a quite specific conception of existence; for the believer, physical life here is no longer an absolute good; supreme blessing consists in communion with Yahweh, and to abide in irrefrangible relationship with Him is the grace beyond grace.[13]

Thus, in a general way, life, to the Chosen People, is the greatest of goods, the foremost of blessings.

LIFE AND ITS VARIOUS MANIFESTATIONS

Life is a boon; it is identical with blessing; it is compounded of force and fulness; it implies abundance, peace, and prosperity. According to W. von Baudissin,[1] the word חַיִּים, *ḥayyîm*, has the twofold meaning of "life" and "blessing," especially in the Wisdom literature; life becomes a reward, the fruit of obedience or of wisdom, happiness; thus we read in the Book of Proverbs (viii. 35): "He who finds me finds life," which means that whoever finds wisdom finds blessing. Israel thus accords positive attributes to human existence, considering it to be bound up with a harmonious development of all its resources, with the complete realisation of all its potentialities. The Old Testament is little concerned to distinguish between "spiritual values" and "material realities," for there is a danger that the former may become no more than pure abstractions, and the latter may be separated from the sovereign rule of Yahweh; in its various aspects, life, like creation, is one; it forms a whole, and expresses itself in righteousness and abundance alike, in power as in piety.

For Israel, therefore, life presupposes success, stability, and security, and makes itself manifest in joy, light, and victory. It involves the existence of normal relationships in the midst

---

[12] F. Baumgärtel, *Die Eigenart der alttestamentlichen Frömmigkeit*, 1932, p. 37, n. 50.

[13] Von Rad, "Gerechtigkeit und Leben in der Kultsprache der Psalmen," in *Festschrift A. Berthelot*, 1950, pp. 431 f.

[1] W. von Baudissin, "Alttestamentliches 'Hajjim' 'Leben' in der Bedeutung von Glück," in *Festschrift E. Sachau*, 1915.

of the community and with the God of Israel; righteousness
is one of its essential conditions.   The individual does not
flourish except in contact with the Holy Nation and in
communion with Yahweh;   thus loneliness, suffering, and
failure, quite as much as sickness, separation, and sin, prejudice
the life that God gives to His creature and to the Chosen
People, disturb the order established by Yahweh, which the
Old Testament calls peace, and threaten to bring chaos into it.[2]

Again, the Hebrews, like the Babylonians and the Egyptians,
associate life with light or with water, on both of which it
depends.   This, for the Israelites, is more than a mere matter
of symbolism.   In point of fact, there is no real life in the shadows
or in the wilderness.

It is not fortuitous, observes C. Barth,[3] that God creates light
first, for light is the condition of all life.   It is not necessary to
mention here all the Old Testament texts in which these two
elements are compared or even identified, and in which they
involve blessing, salvation, and health all at once.[4]   Let us
point out two striking parallelisms (Job III. 20 and Ps. xxxvi. 9):

> Why is light given to him that is
>   in misery,
>   and life to the bitter in soul? . . .
>
> For with thee is the fountain of life;
>   in thy light do we see light.

Upon the People that is walking in the shadows of the
Exile a light is shining to bring it deliverance and open the
way to a new life (Is. IX. 2);   to see light means to live.[5]   When
Yahweh causes His face to shine on His People, He blesses
it and shows Himself to it as gracious and willing to save
(Num. vi. 25;   Ps. LXVII. 1).   The believer prays his God
"to lift the light of His countenance upon him," that is to
say, to save him (Pss. IV. 6, xxxi. 16),[6] or "to grant him
light," which means to restore him his strength (Ps. XIII. 3).[7]

---

[2] C. BARTH, *op. cit.* (above, p. 1, n. 1), pp. 24 ff.
[3] C. BARTH, *op. cit.*, p. 34.
[4] M. GIERLICH, *Der Lichtgedanke in den Psalmen*, 1940.
[5] C. BARTH, *op. cit.*, p. 35.
[6] Cp. also Pss. LXXX. 3, CXIX. 135; Dan. IX. 17; etc.
[7] Ps. XIX. 8; Prov. XXIX. 13; Ez. IX. 8.

Water, too, is a necessity for existence, and is naturally associated with life, especially in the Near East, where it is manifest how much nature and men depend upon it. Therefore it is not surprising that rains, wells, springs, rivers, and even dews, have a prominent place in the Old Testament; the lot of Israel is, in point of fact, bound up with the water that Yahweh grants or withholds; its presence means plenty, healing, and salvation, and is a characteristic sign of the blessing of Yahweh. Conversely, drought, with the fruitlessness and famine that it causes, are manifest marks of divine anger and are tantamount to a sentence of death upon the Chosen People.[8]

Thus the land of Canaan, "a land . . . which drinks water by the rain of heaven, a land which the LORD your God cares for," may become a place of perdition for Israel should it forsake its God (Deut. XI. 11-12, 17).[9] Rivers flow in the places where God dwells: the Garden of Eden (Gen. II. 10 ff.), the City of Zion (Is. VIII. 6; Ps. XLVI. 4), the New Jerusalem (Ezek. XLVII. 1 ff.; Joel III. 18); water likewise plays a principal part during the periods of the Exodus and the Restoration; it is the pledge of the Israelites' salvation and testifies to Yahweh's care for His People.[10]

According to a striking saying, the believer is "like a tree planted by streams of water, that yields its fruit in its season, and its leaf does not wither" (Ps. I. 3; cp. Jer. XVII. 17 f.) This picture portrays a blessed life, prospering in all things, continually flourishing—in short, life indeed.

Let us also note the expression "fountain of life" which occurs especially in the Wisdom literature; thus in Prov. XIV. 27 we find: "The fear of the LORD is a fountain of life." [11]

Let us observe, moreover, that water, which in all antiquity,

---

[8] E. DISERENS, s.v. "Eau," in *Voc. bib.*, pp. 77 ff.

[9] Gen. XXVII. 28; Deut. XXXIII. 13 f., 28; Lev. XXVI. 19; 1 Kings VIII. 35, XVII. 1 ff.; Jer. XIV. 1 f.; Hag. I. 9 f.; Mal. III. 10, etc.

[10] Ex. XV. 22, XVII. 1 ff.; Num. XX. 2 ff.; Ps. LXXVIII. 15 f.; and Is. XLI. 17 ff., XLIII. 19 f.; XLV. 8, LV. 1 ff.; etc.

[11] Cp. also Prov. IV. 23, X. 11, XIII. 14, XVI. 22; P. KLEINERT, "Zur Idee des Lebens in A. T.," in *Th. St. Kr.*, LXVIII (1895), p. 713, draws attention to the "living waters" theme: Ex. XV. 22 ff.; Is. XII. 3; Jer. II. 13; XVII. 13; Prov. X. 11, etc. Doubtless living waters are simply running waters, but they ensure life.

as in the Old Testament, is the symbol and pledge of life,[12] plays a considerable part not only in the destiny of the living, but also in the lot of the dead, since, according to popular belief, the departed have need of it to slake their consuming thirst (Lk. XVI. 19 ff.); the libation of pure fresh water is an essential part of funerary ritual,[13] as A. Parrot has shown.[14]

Finally, let us indicate another symbol which, not surprisingly, is found in a region that is prolific in agricultural cults, because the future of the natives is bound up with the permanence of the vegetation: that of the Tree of Life, of which, according to G. Widengren, we can find traces, not only in the opening pages of Genesis (Gen. II. 9, III. 22 ff.),[15] but also in the Messianic prophecies (Is. XI. 1 ff.; Jer. XXIII. 5; Is. LIII. 2; etc.), or in the cultic accessories (Exod. XXV. 31 f.; Num. XVII. 1 ff.) [16]

Thus for the Israelites, as for their neighbours, or for primitive peoples in general, life assumes a multiplicity of diverse forms, since it is identified with the phenomena it produces or with the relationships it appears to involve; it is power, action, and movement, as well as blood and breath, or similarly, light, water, and vegetation, or again, peace, victory, and communion; it has to do with every sphere of human existence, and all that concerns the People of God serves to express it.

LIFE DEPENDS ON YAHWEH

It is not given to man either to create or to preserve life. For the ancient Near East, as for the Old Testament, the gods

---

[12] Cp. for example A. CAUSSE, "Le jardin d'Elohim et la source de la vie," *R. h. r.*, 1920, pp. 283 ff.

[13] 1 Sam. VII. 6; Jer. XVI. 7; Tob. IV. 17.

[14] A. PARROT, *Le "refrigerium" dans l'au-delà*, 1938; cp. also ELIADE, *op. cit.* (above, p. 2, n. 2), pp. 175 ff.

[15] Cp. also Prov. III. 18, XI. 30, XIII. 12, XV. 4.

[16] G. WIDENGREN, "The King and the Tree of Life in Ancient Near Eastern Religion," *Upps. U. Årsskr.*, 1951; for this writer the Tree of Life is an avatar of an agricultural divinity, and the king was both its guardian and its equivalent. On the signification of the tree, cp. also ELIADE, *op. cit.*, pp. 232 ff.

alone are immortal, they alone have the power to make alive
or to kill (II Kings v. 7).[1]   Life depends on the divinity,
but if, as C. Barth observes,[2] in the heathen faiths the divinity
is, in most instances, ultimately nothing more than a series of
personifications of natural forces, the God of Israel is in no
way identified with life.   He forms it, He renews it, He disposes
of it freely, He is its Lord, and is thus clearly distinguished from
a mere life force.

Yahweh is the Living God, and not only the God of Life,
as others are the gods of war or of death; He is not life deified,
vital force at its highest, a blind and brutal power, an impersonal
being whose vitality can express itself only in haphazard
fashion.   His unwearying energy, His creative power, and
His incessant activity are made manifest in actions that accord
with a plan; Yahweh creates life, sustains it, and restores it,
by His creative and redemptive deeds which are wrought
into the story of world-salvation.   The Old Testament calls
Him the Living God; [3] He reveals Himself as a living Person,
who speaks, acts, sees, and hears, in contradistinction from
a mute and motionless idol.[4]   The expression "Yahweh is
living," חַי־יְהוָה, *ḥay-'yᵉhôwâh*, is a typical formula,[5] doubtless
employed in the swearing of oaths, the abuse of which explains
the Third Commandment; [6] it emphasises an essential
characteristic of the God of Israel just as the words "I am
living," חַי־אָנִי, *ḥay-'ânî*, do when the prophet employs them
to support the statements he makes in Yahweh's name.[7]

The very name of the God of Israel revealed to Moses
(Ex. III. 1 ff.), whose proper pronunciation and exact inter-

---

[1] Cp. also Deut. xxxII. 39; I Sam. II. 6.

[2] C. BARTH, *op. cit.* (above, p. 1, n. 1), pp. 36 ff.

[3] אֵל חַי, *'ēl ḥay*, "the living God" (Josh. III. 10; Ps. XLII. 2; Ps. LXXXIV.
2; Hos. II. 1); אֱלֹהִים חַי, *'ᵉlōhîm ḥay*, "the living God" (II Kings XIX. 4, 16);
אֱלֹהִים חַיִּים, *'ᵉlōhîm ḥayyîm*, "the living God" (Deut. v. 26 (23 M.T.);
I Sam. XVII. 26, 36; Jer. x. 10, etc.); A. R. JOHNSON, *op cit.* (above,
p. 2, n. 2), pp. 105 f.; W. EICHRODT, *Theologie des Alten Testaments*, 1948,
VOL. I, pp. 100 f.

[4] F. MICHAELI, *Dieu à l'image de l'homme*, 1950, pp. 145 f.

[5] I Sam. XIV. 39; Jer. IV. 2, XII. 16, XVI. 14 f., etc.

[6] MICHAELI, *op. cit.* (above, n. 4), p. 146; K.-B., p. 292.

[7] Num. XIV. 21, 28; Deut. XXXII. 40, etc., and esp. Ezek. v. 11, XIV. 16,
18, 20, XVI. 48, etc.

pretation are still unknown in spite of extensive research,[8] suggests that Yahweh is not the Eternal in the philosophical sense of the word, pure being (so dear to the Aristotelian school), a static and non-temporal essence, but the Living God, who ceaselessly intervenes in nature and history, a God of movement and overflowing activity, whose constant action orders the universe, a God with a purpose, who confronts His creatures, and upon whom, each moment and entirely, all that have being depend.[9]

Nevertheless Yahweh is the Holy One of Israel; the life He creates (Gen. II. 7), whose source He is (Ps. xxxvi. 9; Jer. II. 13, xvII. 13), over which He is sovereign (Job xII. 10; Ezek. xvIII. 4), and which He protects and preserves (Pss. xvI. 9, xxv. 20, xxxIII. 19, etc.), remains bound up with that holiness whose ethical character the Prophets particularly stressed, recalling especially that, for the Chosen People, it involved regarding everyone's rights, and respecting other men. The existence of Israel, then, is primarily subject to its knowledge of the divine will; therefore Yahweh speaks to the beings that He calls into existence, He enters into relation with His creature by His Word, by which He nourishes it and sustains it in life (Deut. vIII. 3) and when Yahweh is silent, man dies (Am. vIII. 11 ff.)

Thus the life of the Chosen People is not dependent on magical rites, nor on mystical absorption in the divinity, but on a dialogue in which Yahweh takes the initiative to disclose first of all who He is ("I am . . ."), and thereafter declares what He expects of His People ("Thou shalt . . ."); Israel, by its response, shows whether it is willing to be the Holy Nation, that is, whether it accepts or rejects the existence that the Holy God offers it; therefore life, for the men of the Old Testament, is ultimately identified with obedience to the divine commandments. To live will be to walk in the ways ordained by Yahweh, according to Deuteronomy (xxx. 15 ff.);

[8] Cp. also recent studies by: G. QUELL, s.v. κύριος, in KITTEL, VOL. III., pp. 1056 ff.; K.-B., pp. 368 ff.; M. T. C. VRIEZEN, in *Bertholetfestschrift*, 1950, pp. 498 ff.; P. VAN IMSCHOOT, *Théologie de l'Ancien Testament*, 1954, pp. 7 f.; E. SCHILD, " On Exodus III. 4-14: 'I am that I am'," in *Vet. test.*, 1954, pp. 296 ff.; etc.

[9] KLEINERT, *op. cit.* (above, p. 10, n. 11), pp. 693 ff.

for Amos (v. 4, 14 ff.), to seek good and righteousness; and, according to Jeremiah or Ezekiel (Ezek. XVIII. 23, 32), to return to Yahweh, in short, to accept, in all their forms, the demands of the Holy God, whose interventions in history have opened the way of life for Israel. Thus it is for the People of Israel to abide in the covenant that has been sealed between it and the Living God. Though the life of Israel and of each of its members derives from a creative act of Yahweh, the Old Testament, as G. von Rad observes,[10] is ultimately less concerned with its origin than with its pre- servation, which is definitely bound up with the keeping of the agreement uniting the God of Israel to His People. Apart from Him, there is no salvation, there is no life for Israel.

In the Wisdom literature, life depends primarily on wisdom; the wise man, that is, the man who fears Yahweh, is temperate in all things, he shuns the proud and controls his tongue, and obtains health and blessing.[11] Wisdom is truly a power making for life, ensuring length of days; whoever has found it has found life, and thanks to it his days are multiplied.[12]

One further point will engage our attention: since it is bound up with the Covenant, life has to do with Yahweh's purpose for all mankind, it is part of a plan yet to be fulfilled; it is pledged in a promise that God has made to His People; and therefore, without ceasing to be conditioned by the present, it is prospective.

The religion of the Old Testament is a religion of hope, declares P. Kleinert;[13] this characteristic, the same writer considers, gives Israel's attitude to life its wholesome and balanced quality; the Israelites, in so far as they allow them- selves to be led by the messengers of Yahweh, seem to lapse neither into the cult of life-force nor into contempt for human existence; they accept life, then, in expectation of the fulfilment of the Word of their God, they live in the present, in which they find the tokens of divine graciousness or wrath, without ceasing to look towards the consummation of history. The more the

---

[10] Von Rad, s.v. ζωή, in Kittel, vol. II., p. 846.

[11] Prov. III. 7 f., IV. 4, V. 23, etc.

[12] Prov. III. 16 ff., VIII. 35, IX. 11, X. 17, etc.; J. Lindblom, *Das ewige Leben*, 1914, pp. 40 ff.

[13] Kleinert, *op. cit.*, pp. 11 f.

centuries pass, the more the trials of the Chosen People increase, the more judgment is seen as inevitable, and the more life becomes the good laid up in store for whoever will walk with the Living God, for the faithful and purified "remnant" that will survive the cataclysms to greet Yahweh at His coming to establish His Kingdom on earth. Thus life takes on an eschatological *nuance* and tends to take its ultimate meaning, not from the past, nor from the present, but from the future that God is preparing for His own.

CHAPTER II

THE MEANING AND NATURE OF DEATH

"From whatever angle we approach it, and that of the Biblical tradition is no exception, the question of death is not a simple one," Père Féret justly observes.[1] A mysterious phenomenon, death creates complex and contradictory reactions, and it is an error to try to integrate these at all costs; thus the dead are at once mourned and dreaded; the living lament their strengthlessness, and, at the same time, fear their power; moreover, the departed, it would seem, haunt the places they knew in life, or stay near their tomb, but, at the same time, they are supposed to be gathered together in a nether world whence they cannot escape. Again, it is thought that death strikes the whole being, although something difficult to define escapes the dissolution of the corpse, and persists in precarious yet disquieting existence. In short, it is scarcely possible to reconcile the various beliefs that the sight of death provokes in man.[2]

The Old Testament is not free from this complexity; rather its witness confirms the difficulty felt by mankind in finding a logical explanation of the problem of death; moreover, it is formed by various traditions from different periods, which have been superimposed one on another; and, finally, it depends on a psychology alien to ours, which wholly accepts assertions that to us seem to be mutually exclusive. In these circumstances, it would appear to be hazardous to paint an accurate picture of the development of the Israelite doctrines about the lot of the departed, as A. Lods, for example, has tried.[3]

The contradictory way in which man in general and the Israelite in particular reacts in the presence of death, and not the modification of their beliefs in the course of the centuries under the pressure of various influences, remains the fundamental fact.

[1] P. Féret, "La mort dans la tradition biblique," in *Le mystère de la mort et sa célébration*, 1951, p. 16.

[2] J. T. Addison, *Life beyond Death in the Beliefs of Mankind*, 1933.

[3] A. Lods, *La croyance à la vie future dans l'antiquité israélite*, 1906.

At the outset, the Old Testament informs us that man is not immortal; there is nothing eternal in him. No part of him is immune from death. Thus the Old Testament rejects the belief in the immortality of the soul, brought into prominence by the philosophy of Plato, which is often taken to be a fundamental dogma of the Christian faith; in fact, for the Israelites, the soul is not, in essence, superior to the body, and cannot develop without it; it does not appertain to an uncreated and thus imperishable reality; its destiny depends, not on its nature, but on the Living God.[4]

Thus death is seen as a universal and natural fact that concerns the whole being of man.

Nevertheless, although the departed no longer lives, he none the less continues in existence. He does not entirely vanish away, his existence goes on, but under such conditions as do not deserve the name of life. "It is an enfeebled form of life," writes G. Pidoux, and adds: "Death is not the antithesis, the opposite of life. It is conceived of as a state in which the powers of life are at their lowest ebb, as a sleep from which one may awake." [5] Yet L. Aubert does not exaggerate when he declares that the existence of the departed "differs from absolute nothingness only in that a shade remains, some undefinable and insubstantial vestige of the individual formerly full of force and activity in the land of the living." [6] Thus, sometimes, the state of the departed recalls that of a weary slumbering man, and the contrast between life and death remains relative; sometimes it is such a pale and pitiful reflexion of human existence that it has no longer any reality, and is only a metaphorical expression of non-being.

To this conception, which condemns the dead to a miserable condition, defined in terms of life and by contrast with all that makes life worth while, another, perhaps more primitive, is opposed, according to which the departed are endowed with a

---

[4] Cp., for example: ADDISON, *op. cit.*, pp. 111 ff., 135 ff.; P. MENOUD, *Le sort des trépassés*, 1945, pp. 11 ff., and *L'homme face à la mort*, 1952, pp. 156 ff.; R. MEHL, *Notre vie et notre mort*, 1953, pp. 49 ff.

[5] PIDOUX, *op. cit.* (above, p. 2, n. 2), p. 55; cp. also ELIADE, *op. cit.*, p. 155, "Death is not the extinction of the purpose of life, but a modification of it which is generally temporary . . . death belongs to another category of life."

[6] L. AUBERT, *La vie après la mort chez les Israélites*, 1902, p. 5.

certain divine, or rather demonic, power, with which the living must reckon; whence the numerous funerary rites practised by the Hebrews in conformity with the customs of their neighbours and of primitive peoples in general.

Doubtless these various beliefs, originally more or less independent of one another, were coexistent among the people of Israel; but certain scholars—for example, A. Lods—prefer to regard them as having been consecutive; they hold the truth to be that for centuries Israel had attributed a dreadful power to the dead, then under the influence of Yahwism, it had banished them, at least officially, to everlasting imprisonment in the nether world. It was not until the time of Judaism that the bridges thus broken between the land of the living and Sheol were rebuilt, tentatively at first, as the canonical texts witness, and then with growing confidence, as the pseudepigrapha prove. Though it contains elements of value, this reconstruction of the facts does not appear to us to take sufficient account of their complexity; the Yahweh cultus may have contributed to the lowering of the status of the departed, but the Israelites did not wait until the coming of the Prophets before being impressed, as were the Babylonians and the Greeks, by the strengthlessness of the dead; moreover, notwithstanding official condemnations, the age-old beliefs in the power of the perished persisted throughout the whole of the history of the Chosen People.

But the Old Testament does not restrict itself to making occasional references to the lot of the departed; it reveals the importance of death as such for the living, the threat it holds over those who are alive as well as the dominion it exerts over those who are dead; nevertheless it is aware of the limits that the God of Israel imposes upon death, and culminates at last in the proclamation of its destruction.

DEATH A NATURAL FACT

"Therefore as sin came into the world through one man and death through sin, and so death spread to all men because all men sinned . . ." (Rom. v. 12); "The wages of sin is death . . ." (Rom. VI. 23): These assertions by the Apostle Paul seem to be utterly at variance with a whole Israelite tradition, according to which man is born mortal and his death is regarded as entirely natural. In this no problem is raised, the fact of death is simply noted. Of course the Israelites are far from singing of "our sister, bodily death," for which, according to St Francis, the Lord is to be praised, but they do not postulate any cause and effect relationship between sin and death in this tradition. It is natural that man, Adam, taken from the earth, Adamah, should return to it. Nothing in him is divine, he subsists only by the breath of God, and when that is withdrawn from him he expires.[1]

There is no doubt that this is also the mind of the Yahwistic theologian who wrote the first and second chapters of the Book of Genesis. According to this passage of Scripture (and here the writer is making a simple statement and not proclaiming a punishment), Adam is mortal by nature, and shall "return to the ground, for out of it you were taken; you are dust, and to dust you shall return" (Gen. III. 19*b*, *c*); moreover, if he may become immortal, it is because he was not immortal before (Gen. III. 22 f.). His chastisement changes, not his nature, but his condition, henceforth he must live in a hostile world, on an accursed soil (Gen. III. 19*a*).[2] The three actors in the drama are condemned, not to death, but to live under new conditions in which their existence is to be precarious; the sanctions imposed on them (Gen. III. 14, 16, 19*a*) are signs that their life will be spent far from God, and near to death, under the inevitable law of "Thou shalt surely die" (Gen. II. 16*b*, 17*c*). Before the Fall, between Adam and death, which is part of his natural lot as an element in his human heritage, there stands the Living God; His presence is sufficient to ward death off, to conceal it; Adam, standing before God, is able to ignore it, it is nothing to him, it does not exist. Whatever other significance the existence of the Tree of Life may have, man, in fellowship with his Creator, is unaware of his mortality, in a sense he disdains it, it has no meaning for him, he is alive

---

[1] Ps. CIV. 29 f.; Ecclesiastes XII. 9; Ps. CXLVI. 4; Job XII. 10, XXXIV. 14 f., etc.

[2] P. HUMBERT, *Etudes sur le récit du paradis et de la chute dans la Genèse*, 1940, p. 149: "Death is not the chastisement that God inflicts upon man, the divine curse consists in the 'labour and the days,' the wearisome toil for existence." Cp. also L. KÖHLER, *Theologie des Alten Testaments*, 1947, p. 135 (tr. by A. S. Todd, *Old Testament Theology*, 1957, pp. 148 ff.), etc.

and has no need of further life than that which God gives him. But when God withdraws, nothing is left to Adam but the presence of death, of whose imminence he is constantly reminded by the enmity he encounters everywhere on his way, in the world (Gen. III. 15), in his home (Gen. III. 16), and in his work (Gen. III. 17 ff.) Before, he had simply to live; now, he can only die. Henceforth, "man, living, is living for dying." [3] Man, then, is born mortal, but by his sin he renders death effective; it enters as a reality into his existence; [4] henceforth he lives as one who has heard the capital sentence pronounced against him.[5] He is aware that death is at hand and he cannot escape it. Between the presence of God and the presence of death, he has chosen the latter. By his disobedience, Adam has transformed the human situation into a curse; in this sense, death, through the threatening shadow it constantly throws on his life, is truly the wages of sin. Thus, accidentally, man becomes that "being-for-death" that is at the core of Heidegger's thought.[6]

But, soberly recalling peaceful deaths "falling like ripened fruit," the Old Testament remembers that, neither in His original intention, nor in His purpose of redemption, has the

[3] F. LEENHARDT, "La situation de l'homme d'après la Genèse," in *Das Menschenbild im Lichte des Evangeliums: Festschrift z. E. Brunner*, 1950, p. 23; cp., on this point, HUMBERT, *op. cit.* (esp. Ch. 4, "Mortalité ou immortalité de l'homme primitive"; pp. 117 and 152 with an important bibliography); W. VOLLBORN, "Das Problem des Todes in Genesis ii. und iii.," *Th. Lz.*, 1952, pp. 710 ff.; G. PIDOUX, "Encore les deux arbres de Genèse iii," in *Z. alttest. W.*, 1954, pp. 37 ff.

[4] HUMBERT, *op. cit.*, p. 147: "Mortality is his condition, but nevertheless his death is conditional. His death, *certain* if he disobeys, would therefore be *uncertain* had he obeyed."

[5] VOLLBORN, *op. cit.*, pp. 712 f., cites Hölderlin's words, "The child is immortal for it knows nothing of death"; and adds, "Adam, on the other hand, is now aware that his life has an ending."

[6] E. MOUNIER, *Introduction aux Existentialismes*, 1947, p. 52, suggests the following interpretation of M. Heidegger's thought: "For Heidegger, the finite nature of the human being becomes absolute and essential, every life makes its hopeless way towards death. Death . . . does not come from without . . . it is our paramount possibility. Human existence is *being-for-death*. To die my death is, in point of fact, the one thing that no one else can do for me. My death is my most personal, real, and at the same time irrational possibility. It is not situated at the end of my life, it is anticipated each moment of my life, in my very act of living."

Creator made death necessarily contingent on sin; thus the patriarchs Abraham, Ishmael, Isaac, and Jacob depart in peace after long and blessed old age.[7] Moreover, such serene ending of life fulfilled is not reserved for these alone,[8] it is promised to those who will be living when Jerusalem and the world are renewed (Is. LXV. 20; Zech. VIII. 4).

The Israelite dies, but Israel lives on. Individuals go "the way of all the earth" (Josh. XXIII. 14; I Kings II. 2), but the Chosen People continues to live, and that is the essential matter. It is in fact to Israel that God has given His Word, it is with it that He has covenanted and carries the story of salvation on. "Israelite religion is first national and communal before it is individual and personal . . . the decease of members of the People is not a particularly agonising problem." [9] This is all the more so since, according to certain of their conceptions, the Hebrews consider that death does not entirely separate the departed from the land of the living. The deceased Israelite remains in contact with his People and even in some sense shares in its history. This is doubtless why Rachel weeps for her murdered children in the days of Jeremiah (Jer. XXXI. 15 ff.); it is also the probable reason why Yahweh punishes the children for the sins of their fathers; in visiting them to the third and fourth generation, His aim is to reach the real culprits.[10]

But in order that death may not mean a complete severance of the relationship between Israel and the perished, it is essential that these should have offspring, and in particular a son in whom, in a certain sense, they may continue to live. The Israelite is extremely anxious to have children, especially boys; the birth of a son is an occasion of particular joy; there is something solemn about the intimation that a man-child has been born; [11] on the other hand, sterility embitters a wife, it is shameful.[12]

The history of the patriarchs is bound up with the question

---

[7] Gen. XV. 15, XXV. 8, XXXV. 29, XLIX. 33.
[8] Jg. VIII. 32; II Sam. VII. 12; Job V. 26, XLII. 17; Ps. XCI. 16; etc.
[9] J. J. VON ALMEN, s.v. "Mort," in *Voc. bib.*, p. 184.
[10] Ex. XX. 5; Num. XIV. 18; Ps. CIX. 12; Is. XIV. 21.
[11] Jer. XX. 15; Job III. 3; Is. VII. 14; Ruth IV. 13 ff.; I Sam. IV. 20; etc.
[12] Gen. XXX. 1-24; I Sam. I. 4-17; Is. LIV. 1.

C

of their offspring; Abraham, put to the test by Yahweh, receives in reward for his obedience the unprecedented promise: "I will indeed bless you, and I will multiply your descendants as the stars of the heaven and as the sand which is on the seashore" (Gen. XXII. 17).[13] To have many children is one of the surest signs of divine favour.[14] Thus Israel also prays Yahweh for its own increase; the repopulation of the Holy Land is one of the merciful acts of God.[15]

Conversely, to die without leaving a son is a great misfortune, the mark of the reprobation of the Living God (Gen. XV. 2; Jer. XXII. 30). Mourning for an only son is bitterest of all. "I will make it like the mourning for an only son," the God of Israel threatens (Am. VIII. 10).[16] When a man dies without leaving an heir a whole family is cut off from the land of the living, for it has no "name" left (II Sam. XIV. 7); thus Absalom, who was childless, sets up a memorial to himself during his life-time, "for he said, 'I have no son to keep my name in remembrance'" (II Sam. XVIII. 18). In the last days, Yahweh Himself will give "an everlasting name" to the eunuchs who will keep His laws.[17] Yahweh promises David to bless his posterity and to give him a successor on the throne of Jerusalem for ever,[18] but He swears to exterminate the house of Jeroboam,[19] and that of Ahab, notorious for their idolatries and crimes. To extirpate a man's offspring is a particularly severe punishment.[20]

To perish without leaving male offspring is such a great misfortune that Israelite legislation introduced the Levirate Law: the brother of a man who has died without issue has to marry his widow, and the first-born son of the union is to be considered to be the son of the dead man.[21] The purpose of

[13] Cp. also: Gen. XII. 2, XV. 2 ff., XVII. 2 ff., 15 ff.; etc.
[14] Deut. XXVIII. 11; Pss. CXXVII. 3 ff., CXXVIII. 3.
[15] Is. XXVI. 15, LI. 2; Jer. XXX. 19, XXXIII. 22; etc.
[16] Cp. also Jer. VI. 26; Zech. XII. 10.
[17] Is. LVI. 3 f.; Deut. XXIII. 1; Lev. XXI. 17 ff.
[18] II Sam. VII. 12 ff.; I Kings XI. 36; I Kings XV. 4; II Kings VIII. 19; Ps. LXXXIX. 29 ff.
[19] I Kings XXI. 21 ff.; II Kings X. 6 ff.
[20] II Sam. XIV. 7; Pss. CIX. 13 f., XXXVII. 36 f.; Job XVIII. 19; etc.
[21] Gen. XXXVIII. 6 ff.; Deut. XXV. 5 ff.; Ruth II. 20, III. 9, IV. 1 ff.; Mt. XXII. 23 ff.; etc.

this law imposed upon every male Israelite is to prevent
"his name from being blotted out from Israel."

It has been held that this custom which, as should be borne
in mind, was prohibited by later legislation,[22] and to which
A. Lods [23] has discovered parallels amongst peoples as far
apart as the Hindus, the Gallas, the Afghans, and the Persians,
was observed to ensure the continued maintenance of ancestor-
worship; it is, in point of fact, incumbent upon the son to
render to his forefathers the reverence that is due to them,
which explains why his birth is celebrated as a particularly
happy event.[24]

W. Eichrodt,[25] following J. Frey and K. Gruneisen in
particular, disagrees with this theory, and considers that, in
introducing the Levirate, Israel was primarily concerned to
ensure that the power, the *mana*, attached to a particular
family should not be allowed to disappear, in order that there
should be no weakening of the People as a whole. For the
destiny of the People is bound up with that of each of its
members, and it is to its advantage to ensure the continuance
of a name, so that the blessing that rests upon that name may
be kept.[26]

Finally, whatever may have been the various motives that
originally led the Israelites to institute the Levirate, this must
be noted: Israel found most of its ritual and mythology in the
surrounding paganism; but these, set into the framework of
the revelation of Yahweh, and in the context of the relationship between the Living God and the Chosen People, assumed,
or could assume, a new aspect. Therefore, although the
preoccupation with having male issue may have had some
connexion with ancestor-worship, it must also be placed in the
perspective of Yahweh's purpose for mankind, it is conditioned
by a promise made by God to His People, which, sooner or

---

[22] Lev. XVIII. 16; XX. 21; Num. XXVII. 1 ff.

[23] A. Lods, *Le culte des ancêtres dans l'antiquité hébraïque et ses rapports avec
l'organisation familiale et sociale des anciens Israélites*, 1906, pp. 74 ff.

[24] Lods, *op. cit.*, pp. 62 ff.: "The great misfortune is not so much to live
without children as to die without leaving a son."

[25] Cp. Eichrodt, *op. cit.* (above, p. 12, n. 3), vol. II, pp. 115 ff., on the
question of ancestor-worship.

[26] Cp. also Pedersen, *op. cit.* (above, p. 2, n. 2), vols. I-II, pp. 77 ff.,
495 f., 509 f., etc.

later, must be fulfilled. The whole nation must needs come
to this culmination of its history. Just as it must keep its
portion in the Promised Land, so "every family must attain
to its end" (W. Vischer), for its continuity concerns not Israel
alone, but also the God who has called Israel to life.

For the Hebrews, there is nothing extraordinary in the
thought that a human being continues to exist in his children;
man is not an individual unrelated to his immediate or remote
temporal and spatial environment. On the contrary, the
Israelite forms an integral part of his family past and present,
one body with his ancestors and descendants. His fore-fathers
have part in his life, as he himself will share in his son's
existence. The future and the past of the whole people are
present in the destiny of every member of Israel. The Israelite
is part of a community, which, beginning before and fulfilling
itself after him, is yet his constant concern, his own story opens
with Abraham, or even with Adam, and ends with the
establishment of the kingship of Yahweh.[27]

In these circumstances, death can be accepted as a natural
fact, coming in due course, a normal event to be met with
quiet resignation (II Sam. XIV. 14), in which the predominant
mood is sometimes a sense of thankfulness for a long, happy,
and fruitful existence, the sign of the blessing of God.[28] The
dying Israelite seems to be less concerned about the unknown
world he is entering than about the future of God's People;
that at least is what the traditional accounts of the farewell
speeches of Jacob and Moses (Gen. XLVIII f.; Deut. XXXIII)
appear to suggest.

FUNERARY RITES

The future of the departed, and especially his relationship
with the living, depends, secondly, on a certain number of
practices which seem to be as important for the deceased
Israelite as for his kindred. The funerary rites which are
mentioned more than once in the Old Testament, and which

[27] WHEELER ROBINSON, *op. cit.* (above, p. 2, n. 2), pp. 49 ff.
[28] FÉRET, *op. cit.* (above, p. 16, n. 1), pp. 19 ff.

are confirmed by archaeological discoveries,[1] have occasioned countless discussions, particularly at the beginning of the twentieth century, among Old Testament specialists. These affirm that when a death occurs, the Israelite usages are in fact akin to those of the nations surrounding the land of Canaan, and to those of primitive peoples in general; they seem, on the other hand, to have little in common with the worship of Yahweh; certain scholars, like F. Schwally and A. Lods, infer from them that the mourning customs are evidence of the existence of a cult of the dead in Israel; the kinsmen of the deceased offer him libations, prayers, and even sacrifices, as to a divinity.[2] This opinion is far from being shared by the generality of critics; thus for J. Frey,[3] the funerary rites are inspired by compassion for the dead and humble submission to the will of Yahweh; according to M. J. Lagrange, they must not be described as a worship of the dead but as an office addressed to God on their behalf; H. J. Elhorst, on the other hand, considers that a cult of death, with the acknowledgment of its fearful power by the living, is involved. For his part, J. Scheftelowitz thinks that the mourning ceremonies of the Israelites are primarily an expression of their fear of the dead, their desire to placate them, and to escape them by, for example, disguising themselves; E. Dhorme lays the chief stress on the concern that the Hebrews show, on the one hand, to identify themselves as closely as possible with the departed, by rending their garments, wallowing on the ground, and covering themselves with dust and ashes, and, on the other hand, to give him some particle of vital force by offering him their hair or their

---

[1] E. L. SUKENIK, "Arrangements for the Cult of the Dead in Ugarit and Samaria," in *Mémorial Lagrange*, 1940, pp. 59-65.

[2] F. SCHWALLY, *Das Leben nach dem Tode nach den Vorstellungen des alten Israel*, 1892, and A. LODS, *La croyance à la vie future dans l'antiquité israélite*, 1906.

[3] J. FREY, *Tod, Seelenglaube und Seelenkult im alten Israel*, 1898; M. J. LAGRANGE, *Etudes sur les religions sémitiques*, 1905, pp. 332 ff.; H. J. ELHORST, "Die israelitischen Trauerriten," Beihefte z. *Z. A. W.*, 1914, *Festschrift J. Wellhausen*, pp. 117 ff.; J. SCHEFTELOWITZ, "Der Seelen und Unsterblichkeitsglaube im A. T.," in *Arch. Rw.*, 1916, pp. 210 ff.; E. DHORME, "L'idée de l'au-delà dans la religion hébraïque," in *R. h. r.*, 1941, pp. 112 ff.; A. BERTHOLET, *Die israelitischen Vorstellungen vom Zustand nach dem Tode*, 2nd edn., 1914.

blood. A. Bertholet rightly counsels us to be cautious in interpreting the Old Testament funerary rites; these must have had various meanings in the course of the history of the Chosen People; moreover, confronted by death, man experiences a multitude of contradictory emotions; at one and the same time, the departed inspires him with pity and terror. Psychoanalysis has for long pointed to the ambivalent character of many manifestations of mourning. Thus it is not surprising that the Israelites, like so many other peoples, should have been impressed, at one and the same time, by the dreadful mystery of death and by the obvious weakness of the corpse of which they had to take care.

This cursory sketch of several meanings assigned by scholars of comparable competence to the funerary rites emphasises the complexity of the problem of their interpretation. It is not our intention to review the whole question once again; we shall confine ourselves to the statement that Israel was not immune from the fear of the dead; this fear has been manifested all over the world, and still exists to-day in the form of more or less superstitious practices, vaguely Christianised, which are prevalent amongst the most unbelieving of our contemporaries; in the last resort, the demonic power of departed spirits does not yield except to the power of the Living God, which, even among His own People, was violently and constantly denied Him.

Old Testament mourning ritual is thus to be explained in terms of the paradoxical attitude that man in general, and the Israelite in particular, adopts in face of death; the dead are endowed with higher knowledge, they possess a quasi-divine power; they must be honoured, and at the same time all contact with them must be shunned and all possibility of return to the land of the living must be forbidden them. Therefore a stringently prescriptive code of taboos regulates funerary ceremonials, in order to prevent the power of the dead, his *mana*, from spreading and contaminating the clan or the whole people; thus whatever has been in contact with the dead must be put away or destroyed. But, from another angle, the perished are poor beings, insubstantial shades, strengthless, and at the mercy of the living; they are especially dependent on their kinsmen; it is these who will provide them with the lodging, food, and clothing they need, which will revive their failing power.

The whole body of funerary ceremony is governed by a detailed code, a firmly established tradition, and not primarily by personal or spontaneous emotions; in face of death the Hebrew knows what it is fitting to do; his gestures, his lamentations, and his tears are prescribed for him by convention rather than inspired by his heart. Most of the mourning practices of Israel are to be found among other peoples and originally have nothing to do with the revelation of Yahweh; some of them, such as cutting the flesh and offering hair, were condemned by the Yahwist legislators, others were tolerated and ultimately accepted as part of the religious usage of Yahweh's People; they were even used, in times of trouble and pestilence, to express the sentiments felt by the Chosen People to its God; thus it is that Israel shows its repentance by "putting on sackcloth and ashes," by fasting as upon a day of mourning (Joel i. 8 ff.)

When he learns of the death of a kinsman, the Israelite rends his garments,[4] puts on a mourning habit, a sack of coarse material which he wears day and night,[5] he puts off his shoes, unbinds his hair, and neglects himself (Mic. i. 8); originally, according to E. Dhorme, he stripped himself of all his clothing.[6] His probable intention was to try to make himself unrecognizable in order to avoid all risk of contamination, or else, as E. Dhorme considers, by his nakedness to identify himself as far as he could with the dead; like Ishtar who, going down to the nether world, has to go naked.[7]

At the same time, the mourning Hebrew rolls on the ground,[8] and covers his head with dust and ashes.[9] This gesture would bring to remembrance the earth whence the human being was taken and whither he must return (Gen. III. 19; Ps. XC. 3), the grave in which his body is buried, and Sheol which, like a shadow, he must henceforth inhabit.

---

[4] Gen. XXXVII. 34; Lev. X. 6; I Sam. IV. 12; II Sam. I. 2; Lev. XXI. 10.
[5] Gen. XXXVII. 34; II Sam. III. 31, XXI. 10; Is. III. 24, XV. 3.
[6] DHORME, *op. cit.*, pp. 123 ff.
[7] Job I. 20; Ecclesiastes V. 15; Is. XX. 3.
[8] Is. III. 26, XLVII. 1; Jer. VI. 26; Lam. II. 10; etc.
[9] I Sam. IV. 12; II Sam. I. 2; Job II. 12; Ezek. XXVII. 30; etc.

He beats his breast and his thighs, and even cuts himself, which is formally interdicted by Israelite law; [10] he plucks out his beard and shaves off his hair, gestures which are also forbidden.[11] As the vital force resides in the hair and the blood (Jg. xvi. 17 ff.), this rite can come to have the significance, not of a gift to the departed to strengthen his vitality, but, as in other religions, of a veritable sacrifice in honour of the dead.

Moreover, the Hebrew does not fail to utter cries, to lament, and to intone a ritual dirge, often chanted by professional wailing-women, accompanied now and then by music; [12] the object is perhaps to intimidate the dead by a terrific hullabaloo, or to propitiate him, as much as to express grief.

Fasting is also included among the funerary customs (1 Sam. xxxi. 13; 11 Sam. iii. 35); the fast may be broken by a ritual meal in which, originally, the dead man was doubtless associated with his kinsmen, and during which sacrifices are offered on behalf of the departed or to him.[13]

All these rites are invested with the utmost importance for the dead; the absence or denial of the traditional funerary ceremonies is a dreadful misfortune for him and an exceedingly severe punishment.[14] The heart of the matter, however, is the treatment of the corpse.

His kinsmen shut the eyes and mouth of the departed, doubtless to prevent the dead man's spirit from escaping through some aperture and going into hiding in some badly-closed vessel (Num. xix. 15); they kiss the dead as though to receive his breath. According to a tradition related by the Mishna,[15] "Moses was not willing to die, his soul did not want to leave his body . . . then the Holy One kissed him and took his soul with a kiss, and He wept. Thus," the account concludes,

---

[10] Is. xxxii. 12; Jer. xvi. 6; xli. 5, xlvii. 5, xlviii. 37; 1 Kings xviii. 28; Deut. xiv. 1; Lev. xix. 28.

[11] Is. iii. 24, xxii. 12; Jer. xlviii. 37; Lev. xxi. 5; Deut. xiv. 1.

[12] 11 Chron. xxxv. 25; Am. v. 16; Jer. ix. 17 f.; Zech. xii. 10; Mk. v. 38 and Jer. xlviii. 36; Mt. ix. 23.

[13] Jer. xvi. 7; Ezek. xxiv. 17; Deut. xxvi. 14; Hos. ix. 4; Ezek. xxiv. 22; Tob. iv. 17; Ecclesiasticus xxx. 18.

[14] 1 Kings xiv. 11; Jer. viii. 1 f.; vii. 33; 1 Kings ii. 31; Ps. lxxix. 2 f.; Ecclesiastes vi. 3; Tob. i. 17 f., ii. 7; etc.

[15] G. QUELL, *Die Auffassung des Todes in Israel*, 1925, pp. 42 f.

"death is a misfortune deserving the tears of God, but its suffering is transfigured by a redeeming kiss."

According to the information provided by the New Testament, the body is then washed, anointed, and wrapped in cloths.[16] Embalming must have been exceptional (Gen. L. 1, 26). The body, laid in a chest or on a litter,[17] is carried to the grave. Burial is the general rule; cremation was sometimes practised, as it was, for example, in the case of Saul and his sons, whose bodies had been mutilated by their enemies (1 Sam. XXXI. 9 ff.) Death by fire is a particularly fearful chastisement (Lev. XX. 14, XXI. 9), and the crime of the King of Moab, who burned the bones of the ruler of Edom to ashes, remains inexpiable (Am. II. 1 ff.; 1 Kings XIII. 2). Exposure of their corpses is a severe punishment which great criminals like Jeroboam (1 Kings XIV. 11) and Jezebel (1 Kings XXI. 23 f., etc.) deserved.

The lot of the departed depends on what happens to his body. It has to have a roof; a dead man without a grave is like a man without a home, he is condemned to perpetual wandering, he haunts the places that he has known and becomes a danger to the living; it is to their interest to settle him somewhere, to shut him up somehow in a sepulchre which will be at once his resting place and his prison. Even the enemy, even the condemned by common law are entitled to burial (Deut. XXI. 22 f.; II Kings IX. 34; II Sam. XXI. 14). Not to be buried is a terrible penalty.[18] The lot of such as have met a violent death, soldiers fallen on the field of battle and murdered men is especially hard.[19] Their condition in Sheol is worse than that of those who have died a natural death; moreover, they are unable to rest as long as they go unavenged or, failing that, as long as their blood has not been covered with earth so that it may cease from calling for help.[20]

The dead is not buried anywhere, he must be interred in

[16] Jn. XII. 7; Mt. XXVII. 59; Jn. XI. 44; etc.

[17] II Sam. III. 31; Lk. VII. 14; II Kings XIII. 21.

[18] II Kings IX. 10; Jer. XVI. 4; Ezek. XXIX. 5; Jer. VIII. 1 ff.; Is. XIV. 19; Ps. LXXIX. 2 f.

[19] O. EISSFELDT, "Schwerterschlagene bei Hesekiel," in *Studies in O.T. Prophecy*, 1950, pp. 73-81.

[20] Gen. XXXVII. 26; Lev. XVII. 13; Ezek. XXIV. 17 and Gen. IV. 10; Ezek. XXIV. 7 f; Is. XXVI. 21; Job XVI. 18; 1 Enoch XLVII. 1.

the family sepulchre.[21]   Originally, doubtless, the corpse was buried in the dead man's own house (1 Sam. xxv. 1; 1 Kings II. 34).   The poor, the condemned, and foreigners are only entitled to the public grave (Jer. xxII. 19; II Kings xxIII. 6; Mt. xxvII. 7); this is notably the case of the Servant of Yahweh (Is. LIII. 9), buried with ungodly men and felons. The expressions שָׁכַב עִם־אֲבֹתָיו, *šākab 'im-'ªbōtāyw*, "to sleep with his fathers," and נֶאֱסַף אֶל־עַמָּיו, *ne'ªsap 'el-'ammāw*, "to be gathered to his people," [22] must originally have been understood in a literal sense.

The choice of a tomb plays a significant part among the preoccupations of the Israelites and especially in the traditions about the Patriarchs (Gen. xxIII); similarly, the Israelite writers are at pains to inform us where not only the forefathers of the Chosen People,[23] but also its leaders, such as the Kings and the Judges were buried.[24]

Some writers, such as F. Schwally and A. Lods, have claimed that, in this interest shown by Israel in the tombs of the fathers, they find proof of the existence of an ancestor cult among the Chosen People.[25]   W. Eichrodt, however, observes that the Priestly Writer, who makes studied reference to the burial of the fathers, is the last to establish this relationship, and, in agreement with other writers, considers that these references, while establishing the antiquity of the bonds between the Chosen People and Canaan, could sometimes have had a political significance.   They might have been made to assert the claims of the Israelites upon their lost territories, such as, for example, Hebron, where Abraham and Sarah were buried, but which, since the sixth century, had been held by the

----

[21] II Sam. II. 32; XVII. 23; Gen. XLVII. 30; L. 25; Josh. XXIV. 30.

[22] Gen. XXV. 8, XXXV. 29, XLIX. 29; Deut. XXXII. 50; Jg. II. 10; 1 Kings II. 10; etc.; EICHRODT, *op. cit.* (above, p. 12, n. 3), VOL. II, p. 113; for the opposite view, cf. B. ALFRINK, "L'expression שָׁכַב עִם־אֲבֹתָיו, *šākab 'im-'ªbōtāyw*, 'to sleep with his fathers',", *Oudtest. St.* II (1943), pp. 106-18, and "L'expression נֶאֱסַף אֶל־עַמָּיו, *ne' ªap 'el-'ammāyw*, 'to be gathered to his people',", *op. cit.*, v (1948), pp. 118 ff.

[23] Gen. XXV. 8 ff., XLVII. 29 ff., I. 25; etc.

[24] Jg. VIII. 32, XII. 7, XVI. 31; 1 Kings II. 10 f., XI. 43, XIV. 31; etc.

[25] Cp., for example, SCHWALLY, *op. cit.* (above, p. 25, n. 2), pp. 53 ff.; QUELL, *op. cit.*, pp. 23 ff., for his part, holds it to be connected with a chthonic cult, tombs being frequently merely caves.

Edomites.[26] It must certainly be borne in mind that, for the Israelite, Canaan is Yahweh's peculiar possession; by being buried in the land that Yahweh gave to his fathers, the departed remains, in some sense, in relationship with the Living God, and by resting in the sacred soil, he shares, in some mysterious but real way, in the blessings promised to Israel.

THE DEAD

When the Israelite dies, his breath or spirit, רוּחַ, *rûaḥ*, is withdrawn. It is not in fact a possession freely and eternally at man's disposal, it has only been lent to him, it belongs to God, and so it is quite natural that, in the hour of death, it should revert to its owner.[1] "The spirit returns to God who gave it," declares Ecclesiastes (XII. 7); contrary to the supposition involved in a certain liturgical use of it, this text affirms absolutely nothing but that, at the moment the creature dies, its spirit or soul goes back to God. Here it is a question, not of the lot of the individual soul, but of the principle of life provisionally granted to man. The breath of which the writer is speaking is in reality that of the Living God, an impersonal life force that always remains His own. Here Ecclesiastes is strictly conforming to the Yahwistic doctrine, his words betray no influence of Hellenistic thought; he does not believe in the immortality of the soul; on the contrary, the tendency of his work is towards its complete denial.[2]

Nowadays anthropological studies lay stress on the psycho-somatic nature of man; for the Old Testament, it is sufficient

---

[26] EICHRODT, *op. cit.*, VOL. II, pp. 115 ff.

[1] Gen. II. 7; Ps. CIV. 29; Job XXXIV. 14 f.

[2] MEHL, *op. cit* (above, p. 17, n. 4), p. 40: "At funeral services this text is freely made use of as a means of consolation: it is nothing of the sort. On the contrary, it emphasises the reality of death, the nothingness that death connotes. It means that God takes that which is His own, life, back to Himself; it reminds us that our tenure of our being is not vested in our-selves, and that consequently our existence is a borrowed existence . . . It is not only our physical frame that perishes, but our whole life." Cp. also the comments of E. PODECHARD, in *Et. bib.*, 1912; G. WILDEBOER, in *K. H.-C. A. T.*, 1898; K. GALLING, in *Hb. A. T.*, 1940; LODS, *La croyance à la vie future dans l'antiquité israélite*, p. 59, n. 4; AUBERT, *op. cit.* (above, p. 17, n. 6), p. 11; and MENOUD, *Le sort des trépassés*, pp. 23 f.

to note the works of A. R. Johnson and G. Pidoux already cited.
To repeat one of A. R. Johnson's expressions,[3] man constitutes
a "psychophysical organism," he is composed of a body and a
soul; his life is inconceivable apart from their coexistence and
unity. Israelite thought is not dualistic, it does not set a
material element, the body, and a purely spiritual entity, the
soul, in irreconcilable antithesis. In the Old Testament the
soul is often regarded as a life force, a sort of substance manifest-
ing itself in manifold forms and experiencing all manner of
passions.[4] In a certain sense, death marks the separation of
soul and body; in the hour of Rachel's death, her soul departs,
leaving her body (Gen. xxxv. 18), but this parting does not
mean a bettering of its condition, it does not signify a blessing
or a liberation; the body is not the prison of the soul, but, on
the contrary, is indispensable to it, and therefore to be deprived
of the body is an evil thing for the soul. Without the body the
soul cannot live; though it survives its lot is a pitiful one; it is
condemned to mere existence. It has no prospect of salvation,
no possibility of life, except in returning to the body in the
resurrection of the latter.

When man dies his soul departs; [5] it can, however, re-enter
his body (1 Kings xvii. 21 f.) Doubtless the Israelites think, as
primitives do, that it also leaves the body at other times, in
particular during sleep, sickness, and suffering; a certain coming and going of the soul does not seem inconceivable to them.[6]

The soul sighs, languishes, faints, and is stricken by evil and
death. We actually find the expression נֶפֶשׁ מֵת, *nepeš mēṯ*,
"the dead soul," or more simply נֶפֶשׁ, *nepeš*, "soul," in the
Old Testament, especially in the Holiness Code (H), and in
the Priestly Code (P).[7] The meaning of the words so oddly

---

[3] JOHNSON, *op. cit.* (above, p. 2, n. 2), p. 39; cp. also G. VAN DER
LEEUW, *op. cit. (ibid.)*, pp. 275 ff.

[4] PIDOUX, *op. cit.* (above, p. 2, n. 2), pp. 10 ff.

[5] Gen. xxxv. 18; Jer. xv. 9; Job xxxi. 39.

[6] Lam. ii. 12, i. 11, 19; Ps. xxiii. 3.

[7] Lev. xix. 28, xxi. 1, xxii. 4 (H); and Num. v. 2, vi. 6 f., 11, ix. 6 f.,
10, xix. 11 (P); Hag. ii. 13. Cp. SCHWALLY, *op cit.* (above, p. 25, n. 2),
p. 7; R. H. CHARLES, *A Critical History of the Doctrine of a Future Life*, 1899,
pp. 42 f.; W. STAERK, "נֶפֶשׁ חַיָּה and נֶפֶשׁ מֵת," *Th. St. Kr.*, 1903,
pp. 156 f.; M. SELIGSON, *The Meaning of* נפש מת *in the O. T.*, 1951,
pp. 78 ff.; JOHNSON, *op. cit.*, pp. 25 f.; and PIDOUX, *op. cit.*, pp. 10 ff.

juxtaposed is uncertain, and the exegetical interpretations of them vary; according to F. Schwally, the reference was to the continued existence of the dead man's soul after death; for R. H. Charles, the Hebrew expression asserts that the soul dies, that is to say, is destroyed, when the spirit withdraws from the body; in a recent study, M. Seligson has maintained that this term recalled the mysterious power resident in the dead, which is especially manifested in the stillness and in the decomposition of the corpse. But with A. R. Johnson and G. Pidoux, the words must rather be taken more simply as meaning, for the minds of those who used them, the corpse; in post-Biblical Hebrew, as in Aramaic and in Syriac, the word "soul" denotes the memorial or tombstone.

Be that as it may, the soul ceases to live when the hour of death is come and then continues in monotonous and precarious existence, either in the near neighbourhood of the tomb or the family home, or in a far-off underworld where all the perished are gathered together. The former conception appears to be the more primitive.[8] Yet it must be particularly noted that both these possibilities were simultaneously entertained. The soul of the departed is bound both to the grave and to Sheol.

The diversity of opinion among the Israelites about their dead is reflected by the variety of names that they give them, denoting their power or their weakness.

The dead are called the "*elohim*," the "gods," or rather "divine spirits" (I Sam. xxviii. 13); in the famous scene in which Saul, at his wit's end, wants to communicate with Samuel and asks the pythoness of En-Dor to call him up, the witch sees an אֱלֹהִים, '*elōhîm*, rise from the earth; by his look and his dress the King is able to recognise the prophet who informs him of his imminent end: "Tomorrow you and your sons shall be with me" (I Sam. xxviii. 19).

Thus the dead, or at least some of them, are endowed with a power denied to the living; they know the future. It is doubtless to this tradition that Isaiah refers, when he ironically invites his faithless contemporaries to call on their gods (that

---

[8] ADDISON, *op. cit.* (above, p. 16, n. 2), p. 55, and C. BARTH, *op. cit.* (above, p. 1, n. 1), p. 84.

is to say, their dead) since they refuse to believe in Yahweh
(Is. VIII. 19).

Israelite law strictly forbade recourse to them; the frequent
renewal of this ban reveals how ineffective it was.[9]   The speech
of the dead is low, it is like a murmur, a whisper (Is. XXIX. 4),
it requires interpretation, and those who call up the dead are
held in high esteem, in spite of all official condemnations.
The dead are also אֹבֹת, *ōḇōṯ*.[10]   The meaning of this term is
obscure, it may signify "ghosts"; at least that is what the
Semitic parallels seem to suggest.[11]   According to Lev. xx. 27
these "spirits" can enter into a man, take possession of him in
some fashion, and speak through him;   here we doubtless
have an echo of the animistic conception, according to which
the spirit of the departed invades inanimate objects or living
beings and thus reappears in the land of the living.

But in the Old Testament the dead are mainly designated
by the word רְפָאִים, *rephā'îm*, "rephaim." It is not easy to
determine the precise signification of this term, which, in the
course of the centuries, appears to have had various and even
contradictory connotations.   Thus it is employed, at one and
the same time, to designate the inhabitants of the nether world
and a race of giants who formerly lived in Canaan; [12]   thus,
simultaneously, the same term seems to call to mind the
strengthlessness of the dead and the might of a prehistoric
people.

Then, from the etymological point of view, the theories of
the specialists bear witness to the ambiguity of the name given
to the inhabitants of Sheol.   Most of them, with F. Schwally,
B. Stade, and K. Budde, connect the *rephaim* with the root
רָפָה, *rāpâ*, which means "to be weak," or more accurately
"to be flabby, soft, limp"; on this hypothesis, they were insubstantial beings, shades similar to the Manes of the Romans.
On the contrary, according to T. K. Cheyne, the *rephaim* were
the "terrible" or the "wise" or for M. J. Lagrange, the

---

[9] Lev. XIX. 31, XX. 6; Deut. XVIII. 11; I Sam. XXVIII. 3, 9.

[10] Lev. XIX. 31, XX. 6, 7; Deut. XVIII. 11.

[11] In Arabic and Sabaean the root אוֹב, *'ōḇ*, means "to return."

[12] In the first sense: Ps. LXXXVIII. 10; Prov. II. 18; Is. XIV. 9, XXVI. 14,
19; etc. And in the second: Gen. XIV. 5 ; XV. 20; Deut. II. 11, 20;
III. 11, 13; Josh. XII. 4, XIII. 12; etc.

"healers," from the verb רְפָא, *rāpā'*, meaning "to mend, to sew," whence "to tend, to heal." [13]

In the same way the texts themselves reveal a great variety of significations. The oldest documents to mention the *rephaim*, those of Ras Shamra, do not represent them as departed, but as divine beings who are companions of Baal and his son, and who, like them, are associated with the agricultural cults. They number seven or eight, and they go down to the nether world with Baal and their primary function is to take care of, that is to say to increase, fertility. [14] Thus, originally the *rephaim*, far from being dead men, appear to be healers, whose mission it is to ensure the renewal of nature. [15]

Their agricultural character seems in point of fact to be the more primitive view taken of them, but as their functions require their descent to the nether world, they will consequently be identified with the inhabitants of Sheol. Chthonic divinities in the Ras Shamra texts, for the Hebrews and the Phoenicians they will at first constitute a sort of aristocracy among the dead. [16] Later, in accordance with the trend of the times, the term *"rephaim"* will be democratically applied to the whole body of the perished, and this will be found in the canonical texts as well as in the later Phoenician documents. [17]

But whether it is a question of an aristocracy invested even in the Beyond with the tokens of its earthly glory, or, more

---

[13] Cf. LAGRANGE, *op. cit.* (above, p. 25, n. 3), pp. 318 f. Are the *rephaim* to be taken as connected with רפה, $\sqrt{rph}$ (*rāpâ*), or with רפא, $\sqrt{rp'}$ (*rāpā'*)? JOHNSON, *op. cit.*, pp. 90 ff., cites the interesting suggestion of R. GORDIS, "Studies in Hebrew Roots of Contrasted Meanings," in *Jewish Quarterly Review*, 1936, pp. 55 f., according to which רפה, $\sqrt{rph}$, and רפא, $\sqrt{rp'}$, have a common origin and serve to express the opposing ideas of strength and weakness.

[14] C. VIROLLEAUD, "Les Rephaïm: fragments de poème de Ras Shamra," *Syria*, 1941, pp. 1-30; T. H. GASTER, *Thespis, Ritual, Myth and Drama in the Ancient Near East*, 1950, p. 205; J. GRAY, "Canaanite Kingship in Theory and Practice," *Vet. test.*, 1952-3.

[15] GRAY, *op. cit.*, p. 207; רפא, $\sqrt{rp'}$, in the sense of "to fertilise," cp. Gen. XX. 17; II Kings II. 21.

[16] This expression is used by LODS, *op. cit.*, p. 213. LAGRANGE, *op. cit.*, p. 319, speaks of the "privileged dead," cp. esp. Is. XIV. 9.

[17] L. DUSSAUD, *Les religions des Hittites, des Phéniciens et des Syriens*, 1945, pp. 386 f.

generally, of the nameless dead, the *rephaim*, in so far as they
inhabit Sheol, appear to be strengthless obliterated beings,
condemned to drag out a gloomy existence in the world of the
dust. The Yahwistic theologians were certainly capable of
laying stress on the pitiful character of their plight, but they
did not invent it, for it must not be forgotten that elsewhere,
in Babylon for example, the state of the departed is scarcely
more enviable than in Israel.

Nevertheless, for primitive man the dead are also to be
dreaded. It is possible to find a trace of the fear of the dead
in the Hebrew traditions that make the *rephaim* giants of
antiquity, and, according to popular belief, megalith-builders.
In reality, as various studies, and particularly that by P. Karge,[18]
have shown, the *rephaim* are nothing other than the spirits
of the dead, bound to their burial places, which serve them as
house and prison alike. They are to be found in association
with other beings such as the *Emim* and the *Zazummim* who,
again according to P. Karge, may be connected with the
departed.[19] The traditions concerning races of giants who
inhabited Palestine in prehistoric ages were not then character-
istically Israelite, but were founded upon aetiological folklore
connected with the megaliths, and, in the final analysis, upon
fear of the dead.[20]

Thus the ambivalent nature of the emotions aroused by the
departed is reflected in the very names given them by the
Israelites, and even in the very term *rephaim* which, was
particularly employed in designating them.

THE WORLD OF THE DEAD

The Israelites, like most of the primitive peoples, believe that
the dead are gathered together in a vast and usually sub-
terranean region that is set apart for them. The world of the

[18] P. KARGE, *Rephaim, der vorgeschichtliche Kultus Palästinas und Phöniziens*,
1917, pp. 619 ff.
[19] The *Emim* (Deut. II. 10 f.; Gen. XIV. 5), might perhaps be the "terrible
ones" and the *Zamzummim* (Deut. II. 20 f.) "the murmuring ones" (KARGE,
op. cit., pp. 626 ff.)
[20] KARGE, *op. cit.*, pp. 645 ff.

dead, the Sheol of the Hebrews, corresponds in every particular
to the Hades of the Greeks and the Arallu of the Assyro-
Babylonians. Certain scholars consider that the Israelites
borrowed this idea of a kingdom of shadows from their neighbours; but if this theory be established, the borrowing is
certainly very early and perhaps dates to before the entrance
of the Hebrews into Palestine.[1]

The place in which the dead are assembled is called שְׁאוֹל
(שְׁאֹל), *šeʾ ôl* (=*šeʾ ōl*), "Sheol"; the etymology of this word
is still in dispute. Old Testament specialists observe that it is
used without the article as a proper name, is feminine in gender,
and appears in Israel after the period of the monarchy.[2]

שְׁאוֹל, *šeʾ ôl*, has been connected with the verb שָׁאַל, *šāʾal*, "to
ask, to demand," in which case it was the place of the trial and
judgment of the departed (Ed. König, O. Schilling). In the
view of Vollers and E. Sellin, it brought the depth of the underworld to mind and came from שָׁעַל, √*šʿl*, "to be deep.'
Without adopting it, W. Eichrodt recalls another theory:
שְׁאוֹל, *šeʾ ôl*, was derived from שׁל, *š-l*, and, like the Babylonian
"*Shil(l)an*," meant the Western Land; for the point where the
sun goes down is often thought to be the gateway of the nether
world. Recently L. Köhler and W. Baumgartner have proposed other etymologies; the former considers that the ל, *l*,
does not belong to the primitive root; the stem שׁאה, *šʾh*
(unpointed as root), means "to be waste" (Is. VI. 11; Nah.
I. 5, etc.); thus Sheol was the lifeless land, the world of chaos,
the non-world. W. Baumgartner, for his part, in agreement
with W. F. Albright, sees in the Hebrew word an equivalent
to the Babylonian term "*šuaru*," which is the abode of Tammuz
and in a more general sense, the realm of the dead.[3]

Although the origin of the word remains obscure, what it

---

[1] This is the opinion of A. JEREMIAS, *Die babylonisch-assyrischen Vorstellungen
vom Leben nach dem Tode*, 1887; *Hölle und Paradies bei den Babyloniern*, 1903,
2nd edn., cp. also G. BEER, *Der biblische Hadès*, 1902, pp. 7 ff.; LODS, *op.
cit.* (above, pp. 16, n. 3), pp. 209 ff.; E. DHORME, "Séjour des morts chez les
Babyloniens et chez les Hébreux," *Rev. bib.*, 1907, pp. 5 ff.

[2] Gen. XXXV. 37, XLII. 38; Num. XVI. 30, 33; etc.

[3] Cp. esp. EICHRODT, *op. cit.* (above, p. 12, n. 3), VOL. II, pp. 112 f.;
L. KÖHLER, in *Th. Z.*, 1946, pp. 71 ff.; W. BAUMGARTNER, in *Th. Z.*, 1946,
pp. 233 ff.

D

represents for the Israelites is clear; to describe Sheol is
comparatively easy. The world of the departed, as it is, is
brought to mind by several terms which, as well as designating
it, serve to describe certain of its features. Thus Sheol is
quite simply קֶבֶר, *qeḇer*, the "grave" (Ps. LXXXVIII. 11);
or בּוֹר, *bôr*, the "pit," originally the "dungeon," which was
sometimes used as a prison, and sometimes as a grave.[4] It is
also אֲבַדּוֹן, *'aḇaddôn*, "perdition or destruction," that is to say,
the place of perdition;[5] and again שַׁחַת, *šaḥaṯ*, also with the
meaning of "grave."[6] The world of the dead is often called
אֶרֶץ, *'ereṣ*, the "earth,"[7] or בַּיִת, *bayiṯ*, the "house" (Job
XVII. 13;   XXX. 23), and, in Ecclesiastes XII. 5, בֵּית עוֹלָם,
bêṯ-'ôlām, the "eternal home."

Like the Assyro-Babylonians, the Hebrews located Sheol
under the earth, the departed have to go down to it;[8] "they
that go down into the pit" is a technical expression describing
the dead.[9] Yahweh has the power to bring down to Sheol and
to bring up from it (1 Sam. II. 6). The world of the dead is at
the opposite extreme to heaven, the nethermost point of the
universe, אֶרֶץ תַּחְתִּיּוֹת, *'ereṣ taḥtiyôṯ*, the "lowest parts of the earth,"
(שְׁאוֹל תַּחְתִּיָּה, *še'ôl taḥtiyyâh*, the "lowest Sheol"). It is located in
the depths of the Abyss,[10] as far as possible from the place where
Yahweh reigns.[11]

Sheol is, in fact, a sort of vast grave of which the individual
tombs are merely particular manifestations. For the Israelite
the question as to whether the departed is dwelling in his
sepulchre or in the realm of the dead does not arise; the former
(*das Grab*) connotes the latter (*das Urgrab*).[12] Moreover, the
nether kingdom rather resembles a colossal cemetery where
each has his place, with the articles required for his existence

[4] Jer. XXXVIII. 6 ff.; Gen. XL. 15 and Ps. XXVIII. 1; Ps. XXX. 3; Is.
XIV. 15; Lam. III. 55; Is. XXXVIII. 18.

[5] Ps. LXXXVIII. 11; Job XXVI. 6, XXVIII. 22, XXXI. 12; Prov. XV. 11.

[6] Ps. IX. 15, XVI. 10, XXX. 9, XLIX. 9, LV. 23, CIII. 4; Is. XXXVIII. 17;
Jon. II. 6; etc.

[7] Pss. XXII. 29, XLIV. 25, LXI. 2, LXIII. 9, LXXI. 20, XCV. 4; etc.

[8] Gen. XXXVII. 35, XLII. 38; 1 Kings II. 6; Num. XVI. 28 ff.

[9] Pss. XXVIII. 1, XXX. 3, LXXXVIII. 4, CXLIII. 7; Is. XIV. 19.

[10] Pss. LXIII. 9, LXXXVI. 13, LXXXVIII. 6, CXXXIX. 15; Lam. III. 55; etc.

[11] Am. IX. 2; Job XI. 8; Ps. CXXXIX. 8; Is. VII. 11.

[12] C. BARTH, *op. cit.*, (above, p. 1, n. 1), p. 84.

beside him. This vast necropolis, in which the departed seem sometimes to be gathered in national groups, is "the house appointed for all living." [13] There dwell the small and the great together, the slave and his master (Job III. 19); all inequality seems done away. But against this conception of a levelling-down, there is opposed a contradictory and apparently more primitive tradition, in which each retains his rank in the Beyond, where social order is perpetuated, and where the common lot of death does not, even in shadowy Sheol, exclude definite distinctions among the perished.[14]

The differentiations prevailing among the departed are by no means contingent on moral considerations, but are essentially dependent, on the one hand, on the social status of the departed, and on the other, on the fate of his corpse. Highest in Sheol are the great of the present world, buried with the honour due to their station, who continue to form a sort of aristocracy, that of the *rephaim*; lowest of all, doomed to dwell in a sort of hole, יַרְכְּתֵי־בוֹר, *yarkᵉtê-bôr*, the "depths of the pit," [15] as A. Lods expresses it, along with the uncircumcised,[16] are those who have died a violent death, suicides, executed criminals, murdered men, children dead before circumcision, and various tyrants, such as the Kings of Tyre and of Egypt, and the arrogant despot mentioned in Is. XIV, who because of their crimes have deserved a particularly pitiless punishment.[17]

Thus, according to some few Old Testament texts, a certain inequality prevails in the world of the dead; this is based on social and ritual considerations; thus the importance attached to funerary ceremony is confirmed. It is on this that in point of fact the future of the departed largely depends. For Sheol is not in fact a place of punishment reserved for the impious, the abode of the perished is not identical with Gehenna; all

[13] Job xxx. 23; Ezek. xxxII. 18 ff.; Is. xIV. 9 ff.; Prov. vII. 27.
[14] Is. xIV. 9, 11, 15 f., 18 ff.; Ezek. xxvIII. 10, xxxI. 18, xxxII. 18 ff. Cp. A. Lods, "De quelques récits de voyages au pays des morts," *C. r. Ac. Inscr.*, 1940, pp. 434 ff.
[15] Is. xIV. 15; Ezek. xxxII. 23.
[16] Ezek. xxvIII. 10, xxxI. 18, xxxII. 32; etc.
[17] A. Lods, "Notes sur deux croyances relatives à la mort et à ce qui la suit: le sort des incirconcis dans l'au-delà," *C. r. Ac. Inscr.*, 1943, pp. 271-297; O. Eissfeldt, "Schwerterschlagene bei Hesekiel," *Studies in O. T. Prophecy*, 1950, pp. 73-81.

the departed are in it, and if in their existence in that place there is nothing of comfort, the evil-doer does not suffer eternal punishment there.

It will not be until the period when the last of the Old Testament documents are appearing that the Jews, or at least some of them, will modify their ideas about the Beyond: Sheol will sometimes become a temporary abode where the dead are waiting for resurrection and judgment; to ensure the separation of the good and the evil, it will even be divided into several sections, of which one will be a place of bliss for the righteous, and another a place of suffering for the sinful.[18]

Generally speaking, Sheol is a place that cannot be quitted,[19] a "land of no return" like the Babylonian Arallu.[20] "I shall go the way whence I shall not return," declares Job (xvi. 22), who is also aware that the realm of shades is like a city or a house with doors [21] and bars,[22] and perhaps even watchers, its Cerberus being, according to A. Lods, Leviathan.[23] The dead is as if imprisoned, he can do nothing (Ecclesiastes ix. 10), he is encompassed by bonds,[24] and sees himself doomed to dwell eternally (id. xii. 5) in this place where gloomy darkness reigns.

Therefore shadows are often synonymous with Sheol. "Are thy wonders known in the darkness?" (that is to say, in the world of the dead), asks the psalmist.[25] In the same way, the dust recalls the dark dwelling of the perished.[26] "To return

---

[18] Cp., for example: 1 Enoch xxII. 1 ff., cIII. 5 ff.; IV Ez. vII. 35, etc., and doubtless Lk. xxIII. 43: the Paradise referred to here would be the place where the faithful are waiting for the Resurrection and it is located in the Hell to which Jesus is going to descend. Cp. P. VOLZ, *Jüdische Eschatologie von Daniel bis Akiba*, 1903, pp. 13 ff.; J. JEREMIAS, *s. vv.* Ἀβαδδών, ἄβυσσος and Ἅιδης, in KITTEL, VOL. I, pp. 4 f., 9 ff., and 146 ff.

[19] II Sam. xII. 23, xIV. 14; Job vII. 8 ff., x. 21; etc.

[20] F. DELITZSCH, *Das Land ohne Heimkehr*, 1911.

[21] Job xxxvIII. 17; Pss. Ix. 13, cvII. 18; Is. xxxvIII. 10.

[22] Job xvII. 16; Jon. II. 6; Mt. xvI. 18; Rev. I. 18, Ix. 1, xx. 1.

[23] A. LODS, "Notes sur deux croyances relatives à la mort et à ce qui la suit: la victoire sur le Léviathan (Is. xxvII. 1)," *C. r. Ac. Inscr.*, 1943, pp. 284 ff.

[24] Pss. xvIII. 5; cxvI. 3; 1 Enoch x. 1 ff.; 1 Pet. III. 19; Rev. xx. 7.

[25] Ps. LxxxvIII. 12; Job x. 21 f., xvIII. 18, xxxvIII. 17; Ps. xLIx. 19.

[26] Pss. xxII. 29, xxx. 9; Job II. 8, xx. 11, xxx. 19; Is. xxvI. 19; Dan. xII. 2.

to dust" means to die,[27] the dead are "dwellers in the dust"
(Is. XXVI. 19; Dan. XII. 2), which is their sole sustenance,[28]
and consequently they suffer a raging thirst (Lk. XVI. 19 ff.)

One of the peculiarities of Sheol is that it is a place where
profound silence reigns,[29] and is, above all, a land of oblivion
(Ps. LXXXVIII. 12). The dead can neither call on Yahweh
nor praise Him. For, as Hezekiah exclaims (Is. XXXVIII. 18):

> Sheol cannot thank thee,
> death cannot praise thee;
> those who go down to the pit cannot hope
> for my faithfulness;

and, as the psalmist laments (Ps. VI. 5):

> . . . in death there is no remembrance of thee;
> in Sheol who can give thee praise? [30]

"The dead know nothing," Ecclesiastes complains, ". . . the
memory of them is lost, . . . they have no more for ever any share
in all that is done under the sun" (Ecclesiastes IX. 5-6; cp. Job
XIV. 21). Here then is expressed a conception of the Beyond
much more pessimistic than the indubitably older one, according
to which the departed, through his offspring and through
funerary rites remains in contact with the land of the living. It
is partly, no doubt, a consequence of the evolution of ideas in
Israel, and particularly of the growing sense of the importance
of the individual that developed among the Chosen People.

Thus the bridges between the perished and the living are
broken down. Between Yahweh and the dead, relationships
are as if they were non-existent. The faithful feels himself
deserted, no longer is he able to pray to his God or to have
communion with Him; the God of Israel Himself sees Himself
deprived of the praises of His worshippers. Any community
is inconceivable in this vast necropolis, where nevertheless
so many shades are gathered together. Hell, to the Israelite

[27] Gen. III. 19; Pss. XC. 3, CIV. 29; Job X. 9, XXXIV. 15; Ecclesiastes
III. 20.

[28] N. H. RIDDERBOS, " עָפָר, ['āpār], als Staub des Totenorts," *Oudtest. St.*,
V (1948), pp. 174-8.

[29] Pss. CXV. 17, XCIV. 17, XXXI. 17.

[30] Pss. XXX. 9, LXXXVIII. 10 ff.

mind, is not "other people," as J. P. Sartre declares it to be, on the contrary it is the absence of others, and, above all, it is separation from Yahweh Himself, and from all those who are walking devoutly under His guidance.[31] The dead man has neither future nor past; his existence is meaningless, it is non-sense; it leads nowhere except to nothingness, where all is lost and forgotten, where all communication is impossible. "Hell is to be alone; solitude is the ultimate horror; the one evil for man is to be alone" (P. Maury). Life always implies fellowship, man is unable to live except in company. "It is not good that the man should be alone," the Creator declares (Gen. II. 18).[32] Now, in Sheol, the departed remains alone. Death is essentially absence, separation, disappearance; the dead man is the absent *par excellence*, the vanished man. The world of the perished is the world where absence rules, where the presence of an absolute absence reigns.[33] This is indubitably the most unendurable characteristic of Sheol, the most mournful consequence of death, that which the believing Israelite contemplates with least equanimity, for then it truly appears as a curse on a People whose life, in community as well as individually, is meaningless apart from the presence of the Living God.[34]

Sheol is no mere remote region passively waiting for mankind to die one by one; it is a power endlessly threatening the living, an insatiable monster opening its jaws to devour Israel.[35] The kingdom of shades is found not only in the depths of the Abyss, at the opposite extreme from Heaven (Is. VII. 11), it is everywhere and surrounds God's creation on every side.

---

[31] Pss. LXXXVIII. 8, 18, XXXVIII. 11; Is. LIII. 3.

[32] VAN DER LEEUW, *op. cit.* (above, p. 2, n. 2), pp. 242-4: "Man cannot be solitary . . . Solitude excites dread in us all: for we possess power and life only in the community . . . Primitive man . . . thinks and acts collectively. Without his fellows the individual is nought; in him acts his family, his stock. . . . Alone, man cannot live . . . To be alone is to die. . . . Whoever is severed from the community cannot live. . . . Ban and interdict, then, are punishments synonymous with death. . . ."

[33] P. L. LANDSBERG, *Essai sur l'expérience de la mort*, 1951, esp. pp. 34 ff.

[34] O. PROCKSCH, *Theologie des A. T.*, 1950, pp. 502 f., and 652: "Death isolates . . . it is an excommunication." Cp. also J. GUILLET, *Thèmes bibliques*, Paris, 1950, pp. 140 ff., etc.

[35] Is. v. 14; Prov. I. 12, XXVII. 20, XXX. 15 f.

In point of fact, Sheol does not denote a mere place; rather, it stands for a state, a condition in which life ceases to be livable for man.[36] The Israelite does not go down to the nether world only in the hour of his death; when adversity or illness lays him low, he has already fallen into death's power. In the time of suffering, defeat, despair, or sin, death means more than a merely potential and more or less distant threat, it enters his existence as an actuality; through one or other of these manifestations, all its destructive reality crushes the creature. The life of the sufferer, the captive, the oppressed or the guilty is passed in the shadow of death, under a negative sign; already he can mourn: "I have passed out of mind like one who is dead; I have become like a broken vessel" (Ps. XXXI. 12). "I am reckoned among those who go down to the Pit; I am a man who has no strength . . ." (Ps. LXXXVIII. 4 ff.; cp. Ps. CXLIII. 3; Lam. III. 6), he has no more part with the living, and when at last he dies, it is not then that he surrenders himself to Sheol, for in a sense he has been a long time there already.[37]

The dynamic nature of Sheol appears again in the fact that it is often identified, in Hebrew thought, with the powers of Chaos which constantly threaten creation. The earth is in fact encompassed by noxious waters seeking to submerge it, and in certain respects, the world of the shades is merely one with the Abyss upon which it rests (Job XXVI. 7; Ezek. XXVI. 19 ff.)

Thus the departed may be likened to a drowned man weltering on the bed of the ocean, the waters have engulfed him (Jon. II. 5 f.; Ps. LXIX. 2, 15, etc.) The prayer of Jonah (II. 2, 6) is a typical portrayal of the condition of the wretched, whatever the cause of his suffering may be.[38]

Many Old Testament texts bear witness to the fact that, for the Hebrew, Sheol is associated with water in its most

---

[36] PIDOUX, *op. cit.* (above, p. 2, n. 2), pp. 68 f.

[37] C. BARTH, *op. cit.* (above, p. 1, n. 1), esp. pp. 114 ff., 145: "The oppressed man is not dead nor is he alive in the strict sense of the word; he is something between the two. But as far as he is concerned the decisive factor is not that he is living but that he is near to the realm of the dead." PEDERSEN, *op. cit.* (above, p. 2, n. 2), VOLS. I-II, pp. 466 f.; A. BENTZEN, *Der Tod des Beters in den Psalmen,* 1947, pp. 57 f.

[38] A. R. JOHNSON, "Jonah ii. 3-10: A Study in Cultic Phantasy," in *Studies in O. T. Prophecy,* 1950, pp. 82-102.

dreadful and destructive aspect, it is in some way present in the Abyss,[39] in the sea,[40] or again in the turbulent waters,[41] in the depths,[42] and even in springs.[43]

Similarly, Sheol is connected with the Wilderness, the country hostile to man, the lifeless land where demons and the spirits of dead men prowl, "a sort of no man's land," [44] where briers and thorns grow,[45] a region of death for whoever ventures there,[46] in contrast with the "good land" flowing with milk and honey promised to Israel.[47]

Sheol, the Abyss, and the Wilderness are revealed as powers inimical to life, places where darkness and disorder reign, they are the manifestations of Chaos, they represent the non-world, the "not-world," as J. Pedersen expresses it; [48] they are the three aspects of one and the same reality, that of the world of confusion and evil, of, in a word, the world of the *Nihil*, that Yahweh did not create and which He rejects from His work, but which is not merely the Void or the Nothing, but a corrosive and destructive power.[49]   In fact Sheol, the Abyss, and the Wilderness correspond with one another and combine in expressing the power of death in its potentiality of assault on the creature and of menace to it.   The life created by God must be continually defended against its attacks, whence the sometimes tense and dramatic character of the Israelite faith as, in particular, it expresses itself in the Psalms: the believer is aware that he is surrounded by hostile forces seeking to deprive

---

[39] Pss. XLII. 7, LXXI. 20, LXXVII. 16; Ex. XV. 5, 8, etc.

[40] Ps. XLVI. 2; Lam. ii. 13; Job XXVI. 5 ff.

[41] Pss. XVIII. 16, XXXII. 6, LXIX. 1 f., CXLIV. 7.

[42] Pss. LXVIII. 22, LXIX. 2, 15, LXXXVIII. 6, CVII. 24.

[43] Pss. LV. 23, LXIX. 15; cp. PEDERSEN, *op. cit.*, VOLS. I-II, pp. 463 ff.; E. DISERENS, s.v. "Eau," in *Voc. bib.*, pp. 77 ff.

[44] PIDOUX, *op. cit.*, p. 67.

[45] Is. XXXIV. 9 ff.; Ezek. VI. 14; Jer. ii. 6; etc.

[46] C. BARTH, *op. cit.*, pp. 86 f.

[47] Ex. III. 8; Num. XIII. 27; Deut. XXVI. 9, 15; Jer. XI. 5; etc.; cp. A. HALDAR, who in "The Notion of the Desert in Sumero-Accadian and West-Semitic Religions," *Upps. U. Årsskr.*, 1950, makes this comparison between journeying through a waste-land and descending to the nether world.

[48] PEDERSEN, *op. cit.*, VOLS. I-II, p. 464.

[49] MEHL, *op. cit.* (above, p. 17, n. 4), p. 17: "For the living man, for the individual, non-being is not nothing."

him of all contact with Him who is his only resource, the Living God; whence his cries, his urgent appeals, and his thanksgivings as well, when Yahweh has answered his prayer. The Old Testament, then, takes a serious view of the power of death over man, it knows what it means for him to fall into its hands.[50]

Thus Sheol is seen as a reality, in some sense autonomous, which is not the work of Yahweh and which, by its dynamic, disputes the authority of the God of Israel over His creation and seeks to bring it back into primeval chaos again. Nevertheless the Old Testament rejects dualism: the destiny of the world is not to be explained as an interminable struggle between two divinities of coequal power; it is not the reflexion of that antagonism which is found in nature in the opposition of night to day or of death to life. For the believer, the supremacy of Yahweh is in no way in question: the Living God is able to intervene in Sheol.[51] At the same time as he assesses all the power of the forces of death, the Israelite learns that Chaos can do nothing against Yahweh Himself. "Sheol is naked before God" (Job XXVI. 6), and nothing can conceal itself there and escape Him (Job XII. 22, XXXIV. 22; Prov. XV. 11). The very demonic powers serve the righteousness of the God of Israel (Am. IX. 3).

In short, Yahweh is neither Vital Force apotheosised nor deified Death, nor is He both of these at once; He is the God who has made the heavens and the earth, but not Sheol, the God of the living and not of the dead (Mk. XII. 27), calling His creatures to life, the God of Abraham and of Isaac and of Jacob, leading history on towards the manifestation of His kingship, the God who rejects the *Nihil* before annihilating it.[52]

---

[50] J. ELLUL, "Le livre de Jonas," *Foi et Vie*, 1952, p. 127: "Every man lives above the Abyss; like Jesus, when He walked on the waves, above the twofold Abyss of damnation and death. And Scripture teaches us that the Abyss is not a bottomless pit, but it is an active power, seeking to take possession of, seeking to destroy what God has created. . . . Death is not a matter of chance, governed by the principle of indeterminancy and expressing itself in the stopping of the heart, but a purposeful force, which confronts each man personally, gradually encroaching upon his life, gnawing and wasting it away, disrupting and rusting it with diabolical dexterity, till the day comes when there is nothing left. . . ."

[51] Am. IX. 2; Is. VII. 11; Pss. CXXXV. 6, CXXXIX. 8 ff.

[52] C. BARTH, *op. cit.*, pp. 73 f.

The Old Testament not only declares that the Creator repels the shadows and keeps Chaos far from His creation, but it also reveals that Yahweh makes use of the forces of disorder for the fulfilment of His purpose; so at first it feels, and then it asserts, that the Living God utterly destroys the reality of death.[53]

The hope of the ultimate overthrow of death, which an anonymous believer expressed in the phrase "He will swallow up death for ever" (Is. xxv. 8), is the precise subject of the second part of our study.

CONCLUSIONS

In conclusion, it is appropriate to observe that in its multitude of testimonies, spanning several centuries, the Old Testament represents death to us essentially in two aspects which may appear to be contradictory. Firstly, death seems primarily to consist in a loss of power, a diminution of vital energy, in which case it is connected with other conditions such as sleep, fatigue, or illness. From this point of view, which is perhaps the more primitive, it is easy to envisage a return to life; the resurrection will be a reawakening of the energies of life, "a simple reanimation of dormant forces." [54] Viewed thus, it is seen as a possible, almost a natural, phenomenon.

But, secondly, death is also an absolute separation from the Living God, an apparently total breach with the world of the living, and moreover a terrible and constant threat to human existence; it intrudes upon man everywhere; life finds itself continually disturbed, reduced to inexistence, and emptied of all meaning by death; the creature then becomes the prey of Sheol, and falls into a sort of nothingness, over which Yahweh is certainly sovereign, but in which He seems, in the last resort, to be disinterested.

According to this conception, in certain respects more recent, the resurrection becomes an extraordinary, almost inconceivable

---

[53] On God and the *Nihil*, cp. K. BARTH, *Kirchliche Dogmatik*, VOL. III. 3, Zürich 1950, pp. 327-425; and A. WEBER, *Karl Barth's Church Dogmatics, an Introductory Report on Vols. I.1 to III.4*, (tr. A. C. Cochrane, London 1953, pp. 187-94).

[54] PIDOUX, *op. cit.*, p. 55.

event; it means a veritable rescue from the power of Chaos; while the believer may sometimes have experience of it, although only in a partial and temporary way, it ultimately remains all the more improbable, inasmuch as Yahweh, far from showing Himself inclined to effect it on behalf of the departed, has, in a general manner and once and for all, hermetically sealed the gates of Sheol upon them.[55]

[55] EICHRODT, *op. cit.* (above, p. 12, n. 3), VOL. II, pp. 118 f.

PART II

VICTORY OVER DEATH

IN the first part of this study, death ultimately emerged as the adversary of man, the supreme enemy which St Paul declares will be the last to be overcome (1 Cor. xv. 26).

Originally, however, death seems to be part of the natural order of creation: the creature is born mortal, the dust must return to the earth from which it was taken (Gen. III. 19); immortality is the prerogative of the Living God and, at best, the reward of the man who has lived in perfect communion with Him.

By the sin of Adam and his descendants, death is transformed into an unnatural event, and is then the sign of a breach between the Creator and mankind, and betrays, by its manifestations, the existence of a disorder that brings the very reality of human life into question. It ought not to be, and, behold, it is, and its presence constitutes a fundamental and permanent threat to the creature, it is the impossible become possible, the result of human rebellion.

The nature of death, too, is changed; at every instant, the eye of the believer sees it, not as a natural fact, but as a scandalous irregularity; it becomes something other than a biological phenomenon and concerns the human being in his totality, assailing him body and soul. It is not, in point of fact, in so far as he belongs, with the plant and the beast, to the realm of creation, and is therefore a transient being, that death concerns him, but because he is a person, determined by his relationships with God and his neighbour. Death attacks man at the deepest level of his being, it sets a question-mark over against his enterprises and his sentiments alike, its reality tends to destroy the reality of his own existence; in this sense, for the Old Testament, as for the Apostle Paul, "the wages of sin is death" (Rom. vi. 23).[1]

---

[1] MEHL, *op. cit.* (above, p. 17, n. 4), pp. 11 ff.; H. THIELICKE, *Tod und Leben, Studien zur christlichen Anthropologie*, 1946.

Death, the common lot of creatures, still remains a particular event for the human being; there is nothing automatic about it, but rather, it presents itself as a personal and direct "No" spoken by God to the man whom He has called to life. Death bears witness to a refusal on the part of the Creator, to His withdrawal, to His absence; if, in fact, Yahweh kills, He is not really present in death, for all of Him is in life; He is the God of the living and not of the dead, and the latter know themselves to be bereft of Him (Ps. vi. 5; Ps. lxxxviii. 5).

But abandonment by the Living God cannot be absolute; His indifference towards those who are no more cannot be His final word; one day He will cease to suffer the existence of Sheol along with Himself. Slowly, under the pressure of manifold circumstances, the Old Covenant believers progress towards the conviction that the Living God can and will make all things new; Israel's vision of the future in store for the dead little by little grows distinct, until at last, almost at the very moment of the coming of Him, who by His destiny was going to give them incomparable succour, it culminates in belief in the resurrection.

In the following pages our object is to gather together the various testimonies in favour of renewal of life after death by listening to those who grope for a breach in the wall of the prison where the departed are doomed to dwell for ever.

In Chapter I are grouped the passages that lay stress on Yahweh's power over death; the various manifestations of that power, although still exceptional, are the pledge of a more general and decisive activity.

A certain number of passages more clearly proclaim the resurrection of Israel, and even ultimately that of the Israelites; they will be studied in Chapter II. We have to deal with some fragments, few in number but of capital importance, which clearly indicate the different ways in which the Chosen People, in the course of its history, envisaged the possibility of a new life and of an annihilation of death.

Finally, Chapter III, the last of this second part, will be devoted to a study of the texts in which the believer expresses, more or less confusedly, his hope of remaining in everlasting communion with the Living God.

The exegetical study which we propose to undertake here

will enable us to show, in the third part of this work, how the Old Testament, after having asserted the quasi-decisive power of death over those who, seemingly forgotten by Yahweh, dwell in Sheol, proclaims, at first hesitantly and then with more assurance, the resurrection of the dead.

Chapter I

Yahweh kills and makes Alive

The texts studied in this chapter stress Yahweh's power over death and indicate a certain number of facts that confirm it. Most of these passages are difficult to place chronologically; some of them are incorporated in psalms which were seemingly composed either at the close of the period of the Monarchy, or during the first decades following the Return from Babylon, and thus date from between the seventh and fifth centuries; others come from the collections of stories about the prophets Elijah and Elisha, and are indubitably anterior to the Exile; others again (and this is particularly the case of the account of Enoch), although more recent, refer to very ancient traditions.

It is therefore impossible to make any precise use of these passages to illustrate the development of thought in Israel; this, however, involves no great disadvantage, since, as we shall see, these texts introduce scarcely any entirely new matter bearing on the manner in which the possibility of life after death was conceived.

SONGS IN PRAISE OF YAHWEH

Yahweh kills and makes alive, He wounds and He heals. This power of the Living God over both life and death is celebrated in two songs, that of Moses (Deut. xxxii) and that of Hannah (i Sam. ii).

> Deut. xxxii. 39: "I kill and make alive."
>
> "'See now that I, even I, am he[*sc.* God],
>   and there is no god beside me;
> I kill and make alive;
>   I wound and I heal
>   and there is none that can deliver
>   out of my hand. . . .' "

The Song of Moses is dedicated to the glory of the God of
Israel, upon whose power a direct assault is being made by the
sins of the Israelites. They have become corrupt; yet Yahweh
is responsible neither for their mistakes nor for their misfortunes. To repeat an expression of Cornill's, cited by S. R.
Driver,[1] this song is a sort of compendium of the Prophetic theology;
it does, in point of fact, bring to mind the great historical
evocations of a Hosea (Hos. II), a Jeremiah (Jer. II), and an
Ezekiel (Ezek. XVI, XXIII) and the historical theology of the
school of Deuteronomy. Critics consider this song to be of
recent date, and to have been composed after the period of the
Monarchy, or even at the end of the Exile.[2]

The heavens and the earth are summoned to give heed to
the pleasure of Yahweh (vss. I ff.); the God of Israel is
righteous and faithful; if His People is in trouble, it has only
itself to blame (vss. 4-6). This theme will be developed
extensively: Yahweh's care (vss. 7-14) has been requited by
the ingratitude of the Israelites. They have forsaken their
benefactor to worship false gods (vss. 15-18); so Yahweh is
resolved to smite them (vss. 19-25), but not, however, to blot
Israel out, for the world, beholding the destruction of the Chosen
People, would be able to deride Him (vss. 26-34); therefore
mercy finally moves Him; the God of Israel smites His
servants' enemies so that all may know that none is able to
deliver out of His hand (vss. 35-43).

The Living God contrasts His unlimited power with the
impotence of the idols to which, nevertheless, Israel has
offered so many sacrifices and libations (vs. 38). He insists
on the fact that He alone is able to deliver His People. "I,
even I . . ." In content and in form alike, vs. 39 calls to mind
the message and the style of Deutero-Isaiah. The prophet of
the Exile, like the writer of this song, passionately pleads the
cause of a God whose People is vanquished and given over to
the will of the heathen; yet Yahweh is God alone and none

---

[1] S. R. DRIVER, *I. C. C.*, 1896; C. STEUERNAGEL, *Hk. A. T.*, 1898;
A. BERTHOLET, *K. H.-C. A. T.*, 1899; T. ANDRÉ, *B. Cent.*, 1941.

[2] PEDERSEN, *op. cit.* (above, p. 00, n. 2), VOLS. III-IV, pp. 637 f., favours
the first solution; STEUERNAGEL, DRIVER, and BERTHOLET, *comm. ad loc.*,
favour the second.

E

but He is able to foretell, act, and save.[3] The Israelites have
to be convinced of His absolute power. Yahweh, in point of
fact, has the ability, the prerogative of the divine, "to kill and
to make alive" (II Kings v. 7). Therefore Israel must understand that its destiny is dependent on Him who is able to
wound or to heal, to destroy or to save, and whom none can
escape.

The expression "to kill and to make alive" perhaps does not
primarily refer to the truly extraordinary possibility of restoring
life to the dead, but may more simply connote the whole of
Yahweh's power. That the God of Israel kills and makes alive,
that He wounds and heals, that He thus accomplishes antithetical and complementary works, is a way of stating that
He is able to do all things and that His power is unlimited.[4]
Nevertheless it is not without interest to note that the divinity
of Yahweh is manifested expressly in this capability of His of
withdrawing and granting life. Moreover, the terms "dying,
living, wounding," and "healing" are appropriate to describe
the miserable or the happy condition into which the Chosen
People comes, by reason of its sins or through the forgiveness of
Yahweh.

The significance of vs. 39 is emphasised by its context;
this lays stress on Yahweh's absolute power and on His un-
bounded activity, which is in striking contrast with the witless
inertia of the idols. Yahweh asserts Himself as the Living
God whom none is able to resist, truly there is no other God
than He.

Here there is no question of the resurrection of the Israelites;
this has to do with the People of Israel as a whole, which
Yahweh has smitten with death in His anger, but which nevertheless He is able to heal by His sovereign power. The Song
of Moses speaks to us about the destiny of a nation and not
about the future of the individual, it tells the Israelites, in
subjection for their sins, of a deliverance that they will owe

---

[3] Is. XLIII. 10, 13, and also XLI. 4, XLVIII. 12, LI. 13.
[4] On the use of antitheses to express totality, cp. G. LAMBERT, "Lier-
Délier," in *Vivre et Penser*, 1945, pp. 91-105; P. BOCCACIOLI, "I termini
contrari come espressione della totalità in ebraico," in *Biblica*, 1952,
pp. 173-90; A. M. HONEYMAN, "Merismus," in *J. Bib. Lit.*, 1952, pp. 11-18;
PIDOUX, "Encore les deux arbres," in *Z. alttest. W.*, 1954, pp. 38 f.

to Yahweh alone, but in no way tells of the God of Israel's intention to restore life to the perished. Yahweh is here revealing Himself as the God of supreme and unique power, the weight of which the Chosen People and its enemies alike must feel.

In conclusion, the terms "death" and "life," "wounding" and "healing," seem to express, at one and the same time, both the blessing and cursing of Israel, and the extent of the power of its God who is able to accomplish anything; they do not imply expectation of the resurrection of the dead.

1 Sam. II. 6: "The Lord kills and brings to life. . . ."

The same observations may be made regarding the second song, attributed to Hannah, in which we read (1 Sam. II. 6):

> "The Lord kills and brings to life;
>   he brings down to Sheol and
>   raises up. . . ." [5]

Here, in fact, we find again, couched in more definite terms, the same assertions as in the Song of Moses. This psalm composed in praise of the God of Israel celebrates His succour in the past (vs. 1), sings of His limitless power in the present (vss. 3-8), and finishes by proclaiming the victory of His Anointed (vss. 9 f.) This hymn has the appearance of a confession of faith, in which the believer acknowledges the wisdom and might of his God; a sequence of antitheses, of present participial construction, stresses the fact that Yahweh's sovereignty extends over all ages and realms: life and death, barrenness and fruitfulness, riches and poverty, triumph and disaster, strength and weakness are in His hands. The Living God is able to strike down or save whom He will.

[5] H. P. Smith, *I. C. C.*, 1899; K. Budde, *K. H.-C. A. T.*, 1902; P. Dhorme, *Et. bib.*, 1910; W. Staerk, *Schr. A. T.*, 1911; W. von Baudissin, *Adonis und Esmun*, 1911, p. 417; E. Sellin, "Die alttestamentliche Hoffnung auf Auferstehung und ewiges Leben," in *N. k. Z.*, 1919, pp. 238 f.; W. Caspari, *K. H.-C. A. T.*, 1926; F. Nötscher, *Altorientalischer und alttestamentlicher Auferstehungsglaubens*, 1926, pp. 133 f.; Pedersen, *op. cit.*, vols. III-IV, 1940, pp. 628 f.; J. A. Maynard, *B. Cent.*, 1947; Eichrodt, *op. cit.* (above, p. 12, n. 3), vol. II, p. 7; A. Heidel, *op. cit.* (above, p. 1, n. 1), pp. 208 f.

The Song of Hannah has been interpreted in many ways; [6] contradictory explanations of vs. 6 have likewise been put forward. K. Budde asserts that it deals with the question of the resurrection of the dead, in which the Jewish people took only a belated interest. E. Sellin believes that the writer has some extraordinary eventuality in mind; Yahweh has the power to bring back the dead from the nether world. On the contrary, for other exegetes, such as E. Reuss, W. Eichrodt, and F. Nötscher, the expressions employed in this verse are not to be taken literally; the psalmist is pointing out that the God of Israel is always able to intervene and save the most desperate situations. When all seems lost, Yahweh is able to effect miraculous deliverances.

P. Dhorme connects vs. 6 with a hymn addressed to an Assyrian divinity to whom it is said: "Thou raisest up the body of him who descends into the nether world." [7] Following him, A. Heidel points out the expression *"muballiṭ miti,"* meaning "the giver of life to the dead," which is applied to various Babylonian gods, generally solar divinities, including Marduk, Napu, and Shamash. Thus, according to a citation by P. Dhorme, Marduk is "he who loves to restore the dead," and again "the lord of the holy incantation who gives life to the dead"—that is to say, he has power to heal and to save. In reality, then, for the Israelites as for the Babylonians, the expression "to raise up from Sheol" means no more than "to deliver from some serious sickness" or "from some sore distress." "To give life" again is synonymous with "to keep alive." [8]

In the final analysis, the writer of the hymn attributed to Hannah is saying nothing but what whoever composed the Song of Moses said: he is exalting the power of Yahweh, who is able to save His People in sorest straits, and, generally

---

[6] Père Lagrange (according to P. Dhorme) holds it to be a typical Messianic psalm. R. Smend and W. Nowack (also cited by P. Dhorme) consider that the writer is speaking in the name of the whole community and is telling the story of the Chosen People. According to B. Duhm, 1 Sam. II. referred to the struggles between conservatives and modernists in Maccabean times; J. Pedersen, on the other hand, thinks that this hymn presupposes the existence of the Monarchy and must have had its place in the Temple worship at Jerusalem.

[7] Cp. also *Rev. bib.*, 1907, p. 63.

[8] Cp. also p. 64.

speaking, to occasion upheavals as absolute as they are sudden in the fortune of peoples and individuals alike.

I Sam. II. 6 does not speak of a renewal of life for the departed and has no eschatological *nuance*, it simply acknowledges that the power of the God of Israel is limitless, and clearly divine, since it is the prerogative of the gods to bestow and withdraw life. Yahweh is seen as the master of human destiny, and it is this supremacy of the Living God that the psalm of Hannah sings.

Conclusion

In conclusion, the songs in praise of the God of Israel stress His extraordinary power. Yahweh freely disposes of life, He bestows it, withdraws it, and gives it again. The history of the Chosen People and the existence of the Israelite alike abundantly testify to this sovereign power that Yahweh exercises at the expense of His enemies and for the sake of His own. The writers of these hymns did not envisage the resurrection of the dead, they are simply asserting that the Living God is able to intervene, effectively, everywhere, and at all times, even in the darkest hour; His liberating interventions are particular evidence of His tremendous power.

RESURRECTIONS WROUGHT BY YAHWEH'S PROPHETS

The Books of the Kings mention resurrections wrought by Elijah and Elisha: I Kings XVII. 17-24; II Kings IV. 31-7, XIII. 21.[1]

In these three cases we are concerned with exceptional actions from which we learn nothing about the possibility of a general resurrection. Moreover, there is no question at all here of a victory permanently gained over the grave; some day the "resurrected" will have to die. As in the case of the miracles performed by Jesus Christ, the resurrections reported in the Books of the Kings primarily testify to the power of

---

[1] I. BENZINGER, *K. H.-C. A. T.*, 1899; R. KITTEL, *Hk. A. T.*, 1902; H. GRESSMANN, *Schr. A. T.*, 1910; HEIDEL, *op. cit.* (above, p. 1, n. 1), p. 210.

Yahweh who manifests Himself by the agency of His servants. "Now I know that you are a man of God, and that the word of the LORD in your mouth is truth," declares the widow of Zarephath to Elijah after the resurrection of her son (1 Kings XVII. 24). The Shunammite prostrates herself before Elisha, who has just restored her child to her, as if he were a divine being (II Kings IV. 37). These mighty acts are thus signs given to the contemporaries of the prophets, and, after them, to the readers of the Books of the Kings, in confirmation of the authentic character of the ministries of Elijah and Elisha.

In the first two narratives, those who are brought back to life by the men of God are children (1 Kings XVII. 17 ff.; II Kings IV. 31 ff.), and thus their death is an unnatural event, a cause of disquiet. Elijah himself is aware of this (1 Kings XVII. 20) and the Shunammite, for her part, vehemently upbraids Elisha for having deceived her (II Kings IV. 28). Order cannot be restored in Israel unless these young beings recover their lives.

Elijah is revealed to the eyes of the widow of Zarephath as a veritable messenger of Yahweh (1 Kings XVII. 17 ff.) The woman, who feels that she is being punished for her sin, imagines that the prophet has come to remind her of her transgressions, but Elijah intervenes on her behalf. Humbly but firmly he prays to God to cause the soul to enter into the child again (vss. 20 ff.) The widow's son had lost his "breath," נְשָׁמָה, nešāmâ; [2] in contact with the man of God, he will recover it (vs. 22). Here the prophet seems to possess the power of bringing the soul back into the body of the departed.

Elisha makes even more use of thaumaturgy (II Kings IV. 17 ff.) The raising of the child at Shunem recalls the previous case, but the narrative magnifies its miraculous character. At first Elisha thinks of intervening by proxy, by means of his servant or even his staff (vs. 29), but nothing but his personal presence will do (vs. 31). He shuts himself in with the departed and no one is allowed to see him at work. He paces to and fro about the room and stretches himself seven times upon the child's body as if to re-warm it. [3] Like

---

[2] Gen. II. 7 ff.; cp. PIDOUX, *op. cit.* (above, p. 2, n. 2), pp. 50 ff.

[3] With B. DUHM, *Israels Propheten*, 1922, p. 85, vs. 35 may be so understood.

a witch-doctor compelling the spirit of the dead to withdraw
from the corpse or the soul of the living to resume its place,
Elisha performs the miracle. H. Gressmann justly observes
that this story primarily furthers the glory of the prophet, who
behaves more like a witch-doctor than like a witness of Yahweh.
This same characteristic of the marvellous devoid of religious
content reappears in the third resurrection narrative, in which,
through mere contact, the bones of Elisha restore a dead man
to life (II Kings XIII. 21).

With H. Gressmann and A. Heidel, we think the following
point should be noted: the miracle takes place before the body
is laid in the grave. It seems that this question of time plays
an important part; the Shunammite, for instance, has only
one thought in her mind: to reach the man of God as quickly
as possible (vss. 22 ff.), to urge his immediate intervention,
before the soul of the child has gone down to Sheol, whence
nothing could bring it up.

In point of fact, the soul, according to a fairly widespread
belief, would remain near the corpse for some time; thus,
West African natives believe that it wanders in the vicinity of
its birthplace before departing for the nether world,[4] and
according to the Persians it does not leave the neighbourhood
of the body until three days after death.[5] For a space of time
the soul would in some way be within reach of the hand of a
being able to hold it and bring it back into the corpse.

In conclusion, the resurrections wrought by Elijah and
Elisha remain special cases and enable us to make no assertion
whatever about a resurrection granted to all the dead. They
are signs attesting the power of Yahweh and His messengers;
they re-establish an order overturned by premature death:
but they have no eschatological significance. Further, the
miracles wrought by the prophets seem to have been facilitated
by the fact that they were performed shortly after the death
and before any burial; thus they appear to be almost natural
phenomena, at least no more extraordinary than the miracles
of healing sung by the psalmists or the eleventh-hour deliverances remembered in the hymns composed to the glory of
Yahweh.

[4] ADDISON, *op. cit.* (above, p. 16. n. 2), p. 12.
[5] W. VON BAUDISSIN, *op. cit.* (above, p. 55, n. 5), p. 409.

Thus on the ground that we do not actually have any reason for supposing that the son of the widow of Zarephath was really dead, and that the lad's mother may have thought that he had died, while he was still dying, R. Kittel holds that this resurrection was merely a miracle of healing. This interpretation is doubtless untenable; it should always be borne in mind that the Hebrews made no absolute distinction between disease and death. Both are evidence of an enfeeblement of life, of the soul wilting and withering and needing to be awakened and aroused. In this particular instance, resurrection, like healing, does no more than "revive sleeping powers." [6]

Returned thus to the framework of Hebrew thought, the mighty acts of the men of God are only a special instance of the whole body of the liberating interventions of Yahweh on behalf of His own.

PSALMS OF SICKNESS AND SUFFERING

Many psalms are devoted to the theme of deliverance from some deadly peril; some voice the lamentations of sufferers who, crushed by adversity, broken by disease, surrounded by hostile powers, call with strong crying for the speedy intervention of their God; others relate the infinite gratitude of creatures who have brushed against death, and whom Yahweh has rescued from their troubles to bring them into the experience of a new kind of life.

H. Gunkel who made a systematic type-classification of the lamentations and songs of thanksgiving in the Old Testament,[1] says of them: "It is here that the religion of the Psalms finds itself at grips with death." [2] The psalmist is here taking account of the seriousness of his situation; he is faced by the question of life and death, or rather he cannot in fact escape destruction apart from the immediate action of Yahweh on

---

[6] PIDOUX, *op. cit.*, p. 55.

[1] H. GUNKEL, J. BEGRICH, "Einleitung in die Psalmen," *Hk. A. T.*, 1933, esp. paras. 6-7.

[2] GUNKEL, *op. cit.*, p. 185.

his behalf. C. Barth, following the work of H. Gunkel and J. Pedersen in particular, has recently written an important book on this problem; [3] we need not go over the ground of his study again, it will suffice if we recapitulate certain of his points here, especially as we have already touched on several aspects of this subject in dealing with the extent of the power of death.

As in the Babylonian and Egyptian parallels, sickness is often, but not always, the occasion of these psalms.[4] The believer may have lost not only his health but his freedom and reputation as well; he sees himself surrounded by foes; he feels himself deserted by his friends and even by God; he suddenly finds himself in the presence of death, already he sees its signs, and he takes count of the havoc that, even now, it is working in his existence; he knows that he is being attacked body and soul, all his being is threatened. His life is life no longer; for it has neither prop nor prospect, and it is passed in the shadow of death. In his trouble the faithful continually cries to God, in whom he sees his sole resource; importunately he implores for help, he pleads for healing, deliverance, pardon, and peace; in his suffering he may again pray asking to live; he wants to see the light and to dwell in the presence of Yahweh in the land of the living.

The Israelite is inventing nothing, he is stating a fact; he is not giving way to unbridled imagination; he is aware that death has come into his life, and that it puts an end to the life that God gives him; he is not reconciled to it, he will not believe that the die is cast; his hour has not come yet, death comes too soon, he rejects it beseeching the help of his God (Ps. LXXXVIII):

> O LORD, my God, I call for help by day;
>   I cry out in the night before thee.
> Let my prayer come before thee,
>   incline thy ear to my cry!

---

[3] C. BARTH, *Die Errettung vom Tode in den individuellen Klage- und Dankliedern*, 1947; cp. the warnings against making everything conform to a pattern, given by A. BENTZEN, "Der Tod des Beters in den Psalmen," in *Festschrift O. Eissfeldt*, 1947, pp. 57-60.

[4] Pss. VI, XXXI, XXXVIII, CII, etc.; Is. XXXVIII.

For my soul is full of troubles,
and my life draws near to Sheol.

I am reckoned among those who go down
to the Pit;
I am a man who has no strength
like one forsaken among the dead,
like the slain that lie in the grave,
like those whom thou dost remember
no more,
for they are cut off from thy hand.
Thou hast put me in the depths of
the Pit;
in the regions dark and deep.
Thy wrath lies heavy upon me,
and thou dost overwhelm me with
all thy waves.
Thou hast caused my companions to
shun me;
thou hast made me a thing of
horror to them.
I am shut in so that I cannot
escape;
my eye grows dim through sorrow. . . .

Afflicted and close to death from
my youth up,
I suffer thy terrors; I am helpless,
Thy wrath has swept over me;
thy dread assaults destroy me.
They surround me like a flood all
day long;
they close in upon me together. . . .

The writer of Ps. LXXXVIII perfectly portrays the sorry plight
of the sick or suffering man who finds himself alone, without
friends, without God, at grips with a terrifying reality hemming
him in on every side. His power is spent; he is no longer
counted among the living; God has put him out of His
remembrance. He is like one tossed about on the billows of
the divine wrath, thrust into the shadows whence he is not able
to emerge.

Conversely, the faithful saved by Yahweh sings of his deliverance in these terms:

> O LORD my God, I cried to thee for help,
>   and thou hast healed me.
> O LORD, thou hast brought up my soul
>   from Sheol,
>   restored me to life from among
>   those gone down to the Pit. . . .
>
> Thou hast turned for me my mourning
>   into dancing;
>   thou hast loosed my sackcloth,
>   and girded me with gladness. . . .[5]
>
> I give thanks to thee, O LORD my God, with
>   my whole heart,
>   and I will glorify thy name for ever.
> For great is thy steadfast love toward me;
>   thou hast delivered my soul from the
>   depths of Sheol. . . .[6]
>
> Bless the LORD, O my soul;
>   and all that is in me, bless his holy
>   name . . .
> who forgives all your iniquity,
>   who heals all your diseases,
> who redeems your life from the Pit,
>   who crowns you with steadfast love
>   and mercy,
> who satisfies you with good as long as
>   you live
>   so that your youth is renewed like
>   the eagle's. . . . [7]
>
> . . . thou hast held back my life
>   from the pit of destruction,
> for thou hast cast all my sins
>   behind thy back. . . .[8]

[5] Ps. XXX. 2-3, 11.
[6] Ps. LXXXVI. 12-13
[7] Ps. CIII. 1, 3-5.
[8] Is. XXXVIII. 17.

These passages have been taken to be hyperbole (by H. Gressmann), poetry (by J. J. Stamm), and fantasy (by H. Gunkel); certain exegetes have laid stress on the particularly imaginative nature of the Semites (A. Bertholet), or on the passionate temperament of the Orientals (H. Gunkel); [9] but, as against these interpretations, C. Barth has shown that, for Israel, this is not a matter of symbolism, nor of imagination, but of reality; the sick and the suffering are at grips with a malignant power which, taking possession of them, wrests them from their people and from their God. Death, in the thought of the psalmists, is not merely the reflexion of a troubled existence, for them it is a fact and an event, since it intrudes its presence upon them and shatters the harmony and unity of their life; the deliverance that they are waiting for is a veritable liberation from its fatal power.[10]

The Israelite knows that his life is constantly threatened, the obstacles of every sort that he encounters on his way are so many manifestations of the power of death lying in wait for him; but he also discovers that Yahweh is able to break the bonds that constrict him, to shatter the servitudes that oppress him, in a word, to make death retreat. He is, of course, at every moment, in danger of falling into the hands of Sheol, but he never ceases to set his hope in the redemptive intervention of his God. It happens that he is numbered among those who "go down to the pit," but he also knows the experience of salvation; thus power is exerted upon him from two directions; death seeks to make him its prey, the Living God rescues him from its bonds and changes his mourning into gladness. In some sense, and doubtless more than once in his life, he enters the realm of the dead while yet in the land of the living; turn and turn about he repeats Pss. LXXXVIII and XXX, the complaint of the suffering and the song of the saved.

In these psalms there cannot be any question of the resurrection in the precise sense in which it came to be understood in the Maccabean period. There is no eschatological nuance in the prayers of the psalmists. Here death is merely repulsed, warded off for a while, it is neither avoided nor

---

[9] C. BARTH, *op. cit.*, p. 14.

[10] Cp. also H. J. FRANKEN, *The Mystical Communion with JHWH in the Book of Psalms*, 1954, pp. 63 ff.

abolished. The expressions employed by the believers in Israel describe a concrete situation, a lived experience; they bear witness to their faith in the delivering power of Yahweh, but they do not proclaim the destruction of Sheol.

In conclusion, these lamentations and hymns of thanksgiving confirm what we have learnt from the Songs of Moses and Hannah and from the miracles wrought by Elijah and Elisha. The power of the Living God is exerted not against death in itself, but against what C. Barth calls " evil " death, that is to say, premature death, death that disrupts the natural order. This conception will be held for centuries by the whole body of the Israelites; the Old Testament believers will only belatedly concern themselves with actually raising the question of the very existence of death and with proclaiming that Yahweh has power to destroy it, not only for a time, but for ever.

THE TRANSLATIONS OF ENOCH AND ELIJAH

The descendants of Adam must return to the earth from which they were taken (Gen. III. 19); the law is the same for all: Sheol is the "house appointed for all living" (Job xxx. 23). Nevertheless the Old Testament knows of two men who escaped the common lot and entered the world of God alive: they are Enoch (Gen. v. 21-4) and Elijah (II Kings II. 1-15).

Gen. v. 24: The Translation of Enoch

Enoch appears in the list of the Antediluvian Patriarchs in Gen. v; the author usually called the Priestly Writer (P), enumerates the ancestors who succeeded Adam to Noah; there are ten of them, fabulous in longevity, the name of each is given, together with that of his eldest son, and the length of his life. Except in the case of the first and the last, and especially in that of Enoch, the schema is always invariable:

> When A had lived x years, he became the father of B. A lived after the birth of B y years, and had other sons and daughters. Thus all the days of A were $(x+y)$ years; *and he died.*

As generation succeeds generation, so more and more length of life diminishes, as though, in growing older, mankind was becoming more and more alienated from its Creator. But "in Enoch's case the sinister refrain is, as it were, momentarily interrupted. The verb 'to die' is set aside. . . . The death of Enoch is a disappearance from the sight of men, but an entrance into the life and purpose and world of God." So one commentator declares.[1] The account devoted to Enoch in fact differs appreciably from the information supplied about the other Patriarchs:

> When Enoch had lived sixty-five years, he became the father of Methuselah. *Enoch walked with God* after the birth of Methuselah three hundred years, and had other sons and daughters. Thus all the days of Enoch were three hundred and sixty-five years. *Enoch walked with God; and he was not, for God took him.*[2]

Doubtless P has only made use of part of his material on Enoch; Ecclesiasticus (XLIV. 16, XLIX. 14 ff.) already knows of a tradition according to which the Patriarch had been initiated into the heavenly mysteries. It was on this point that later Jewish tradition laid stress; in the Pseudepigrapha especially, Enoch is represented as a hero who visited the heavenly places and the abode of the dead, where the secrets of God were revealed to him, and, in particular, the events that are to mark the end of human history. It is sufficient to note here the First Book of Enoch (the Ethiopic Enoch), and particularly the Similitudes of Enoch,[3] the Book of Jubilees,[4] which makes the Patriarch not only the custodian of the

[1] C. GENEQUAND, *Vers l'invisible*, Geneva 1940, p. 87.
[2] Gen. v. 21-4. H. HOLZINGER, *K. H.-C. A. T.*, 1898; H. ZIMMERN, *Komm. A. T.*, 1903; H. GUNKEL, (1) *Schr. A. T.*, 1911, (2) *Hk. A. T.*, 1922, (3) *Rel. G. G.*, 1928, VOL. II, cols. 1800 f.; A. BERTHOLET, *Rel. G. G.*, 1928, VOL. II, cols. 170 f., 1898 f.; H. ODEBERG, 'Ενώχ, in KITTEL, VOL. II, 1935, pp. 553 ff.; M. FREY, *Die Botschaft des A. T.*, VOL. I, 1940; W. ZIMMERLI, *Prophezei*, VOL. I, 1943; J. CHAINE, *Lectio divina*, 1948; G. VON RAD, *A. T. D.*, 1949; E. STAUFFER, *Theologie des N. T.*, 1945, pp. 329 f.; EICHRODT, *op. cit.* (above, p. 12, n. 3), VOL. III, p. 89; F. NÖTSCHER, *op. cit.* (above, p. 55, n. 5), pp. 12 ff.
[3] I Enoch XXXVII-LXXI: FR. MARTIN, *Le livre d'Hénoch*, Paris 1906.
[4] Jub. IV. 17-25, VII. 38, X. 17, 19, 24-27, XXI. 10.

mysteries of the things to come, but also the heavenly High Priest, and even the New Testament, which refers to him three times—Lk. III. 37; Heb. XI. 5; Jude 14.[5]

It is long since exegetes first observed the remarkable resemblances that exist between the list of the Patriarchs in Gen. v and that of the Antediluvian kings of Mesopotamia, as given by Berosus and the cuneiform texts;[6] Babylonian tradition tells of ten kings, and similarly P speaks of ten forefathers; moreover, some of the Patriarchs have the same names or the same characteristics as their Babylonian counterparts; thus the third, Enos (= "man") is equivalent to *En-men-lu* (= "man"); Enoch, like the seventh ruler, Enmeduranki, is in particular relationship with the divinity; and, according to Berosus, the last monarch is, like Noah, the hero of the Flood.

Thus it appears to be a reasonable inference that the Israelites borrowed their ideas about the Antediluvian generations from their neighbours, afterwards to reset them within the framework of the revelation of Yahweh. The Priestly Writer made a selection from the Enoch traditions. Of those that he rejected some survived in Israel for several centuries, in a greater or lesser degree, and attained to an extraordinary popularity near the dawn of the Christian era.

P gives three important items of information about the seventh Patriarch: (*a*) he lived for 365 years, (*b*) he walked with God, and (*c*) God took him.

The number 365 has a significance that leaps to the eye, corresponding as it does with the length of the solar year. Now, the connexion between Enoch and the sun is confirmed by the fact that the seventh Antediluvian king, Enmeduranki ("En-me-duran-ma," in a cuneiform text, "Enedorachus," according to Berosus), lord of the oracles, custodian of the divine secrets, renowned astrologer and authentic prophet, is King of Sippar, city of the sun.

Thus Enoch was originally an astral divinity, a sun-god, but his presence in the list compiled by P gives him another significance. As W. Zimmerli observes, the number 365 stands

---

[5] The whole of the passage Jude 4-15 might in fact be an imitation of the Ethiopic Enoch; cp. H. ODEBERG, s.v. ʾΕνώχ, in KITTEL, VOL. II, 1935, pp. 553 ff.
[6] Cp. especially H. Gunkel, W. Zimmerli and J. Chaine.

for a whole and so indicates that the Patriarch accomplished a complete cycle, his life being fulfilled when God takes him; the divine decision is not a sign of reprobation but, on the contrary, sanctifies a life lived with God. Enoch, who is perhaps no more than a sort of representative of "primordial man" (*Urmensch*),[7] was then the example of a human life which was able to achieve entire fulfilment, and which is therefore full of hope for mankind.

The Priestly Writer also states that Enoch "walked with God." This expression may suggest that the Patriarch, like Enmeduranki, was initiated by God into the divine mysteries. The King of Sippar, ancestor of an order of priests, is in fact renowned for his learning and for his skill in the art of divination; Ecclesiasticus (XLIV. 16) also is aware that Enoch was "an example of knowledge to all generations."

Although later Judaism laid stress on this element in the tradition, P does not seem to have attached any importance to it. For him, Enoch is primarily the pattern of the devout man, the righteous, in the Biblical sense of the word; according to W. Eichrodt, "to walk with God," to the mind of the Priestly Writer, means nothing other than "to live in total righteousness."[8] Enoch, according to Gen. v. 21 ff., is revealed as an example of perfect devoutness, he lived in communion with his God and the bonds that bind him to his Creator cannot be broken by death.

Enoch, in fact, escapes the lot laid upon all men. The text (Gen. v. 24) tells us succinctly: "Enoch was not, for God took him"; it gives no details about the Patriarch's ultimate lot; the apocalyptic writers were by no means so reticent. P makes the relationship between Enoch's righteousness and his translation abundantly clear, the latter being the reward of the former. The Patriarch who always walked with God is still living with Him.

As for antiquity, it, too, is acquainted with translations: those of Ganymede, Menelaus, and Apollonius of Tyana, in Greece, for example, and especially that of the hero of the Babylonian Flood, Uta-napishtim (called Xisuthrus by

---

[7] H. ODEBERG, *op. cit.*, p. 553.
[8] EICHRODT, *op. cit.*, VOL. III, p. 89.

Berosus) who was granted immortality after the cataclysm by the god Ea.[9]

It may be noted that the verb לָקַח, *lāqaḥ*, "to take," with "God" as subject and "man" as object, which is employed here by P, occurs again in connexion with the translation of Elijah (II Kings II. 3, 5, 9-10, etc.), and with that of Uta-na-pishtim (*liqû*, Epic of Gilgamesh, TAB. x, l. 205), and probably in other Old Testament passages;[10] it seems to be used as a technical expression to denote the assumption of a human being to God.

The lot of Enoch remains exceptional, his personal destiny is determined by the special bonds that bind him to God, and it marks a break in the order imposed upon the descendants of Adam. If it is possible to discern, behind the Biblical figure of Enoch, an ancient solar divinity, or else a high priest of God initiated into the mysteries of things to come, it is important to emphasise that the believers in Israel, as P witnesses, primarily exalted the Patriarch's piety and the uncommon lot it procured him; the personal destiny of Enoch perhaps had the effect of inspiring some of the faithful to hope that the life of a man absolutely dedicated to God would not necessarily end in Sheol, but would find its reward and fulfilment in Yahweh.[11]

II Kings II. 1-15: The Translation of Elijah[12]

This story belongs to the Elisha cycle, and tell show Elijah

[9] With reference to Egypt, let us note the following text, as it is given by G. LEFÈBRE in *Romans et contes égyptiens*, 1949, p. 5. We read in the Story of Sinuhe, in connexion with the death of Amenemhet I: "The King of Upper and Lower Egypt, Seḥetepibrē, was translated to heaven and united himself with the sun-disk, and the body of the god was merged with him who had begotten him." [Cp. also *The Cambridge Ancient History*, VOL. I, 2nd edn., 1923, p. 304; H. FRANKFORT, *Kingship and the Gods*, 1948, p. 101; —TR.] Here the reference is rather to a god being reunited with his father than to a mortal man being called to dwell with the gods.

[10] Pss. XLIX. 15, LXXIII. 24; cp. also Ecclesiasticus XLIV. 16, XLVIII. 9, XLIX. 14 f.

[11] Cp. pp. 156, 163.

[12] II Kings II. 1-15: I. BENZINGER, *K. H.-C. A. T.*, 1899; R. KITTEL, *Hk. A. T.*, 1900; H. GRESSMANN, *Schr. A. T.*, 1910; H. GUNKEL, *Rel. G. G.*, VOL. II, 1928, col. 107; J. JEREMIAS, s.v. 'Ηλ(ε)ίας, in KITTEL, VOL. II, 1935, pp. 930-43; W. VISCHER, *L'Ancien Testament, témoin du Christ*, VOL. II (*Les premiers prophètes*) Fr. edn., 1951, pp. 462 ff.

F

bequeathed his powers to his successor. Elisha asks and receives a double share of Elijah's spirit, that being the right of the first born, according to the Law of Moses (Deut. xxi. 17).

Elijah, who knows that his hour has come, tries to dissuade Elisha from following him, but he follows him step by step, retracing with him the road which, according to tradition, the Chosen People travelled when first it entered into Palestine.

The hour of their parting draws near. Through the action of Yahweh, Elijah vanishes in the midst of a whirlwind (II Kings II. 11; cp. Job xxxviii. 1); this scene recalls the earliest theophanies of the God of Israel, since He first appeared to the Israelite tribes as the lord of war and of storm.[13] Elisha, who seems more sorrowful than afraid, cries to his master, "My father, my father!" and in a striking phrase, which perhaps was first of all applied to himself,[14] he characterises Elijah's work for the Chosen People as having been "the chariots of Israel and its horsemen" (II Kings II. 12). The expression describes the ministry of the two prophets of the God of Israel who waged a veritable Jihad against Baal and his acolytes.

It is in a flaming chariot, drawn by horses of fire, that (vs. 11) Elijah is suddenly taken from his disciple. These details are significant, they recall the myth of the sun travelling through space to give light to the world, of which Israel does not appear to have been altogether unaware, since the Kings of Judah dedicated chariots and horses to this luminary in the very Temple at Jerusalem (II Kings xxiii. 11); thus the setting of the translation of Elijah helps to show that the prophet is making a triumphal entrance into the heavenly places, there to continue the battles he fought on earth for the God of hosts; he achieves an exaltation commensurable with his earthly course.

According to certain traditions, Elijah is the prophet *par*

---

[13] H. FREDRIKSSON, *Jahve als Krieger*, 1945, pp. 47 ff.

[14] II Kings xiii. 14; cp. E. JACOB, "La tradition historique en Israël," *Et. th. r.*, 1946, p. 126: "This title is obviously an allusion to the fact that the King of Syria allowed Israel to maintain a defensive force of only 50 horsemen, 10 war chariots, and 10,000 infantry (II Kings xiii. 7). In virtue of the divine power which possessed him, the prophet was ample compensation for this military inferiority (Ps. xx. 7). In another passage the same title is bestowed upon Elijah, but there it is clearly borrowed from the Elisha cycle (II Kings II. 12)."

excellence, it is he with whom Jesus converses on the Mount of Transfiguration (Mk. ix. 4 ff.) By his zeal, his struggles, his sufferings, and ultimately by his translation in reward of his ardour in defending the Law of the God of Israel (1 Macc. ii. 58), Elijah played a prominent part among the People of God. The Old Testament foretells his return (Mal. iii. 23-4); the New Testament sees him as the precursor of Christ; [15] for post-Biblical Judaism, he is above all the predecessor of the Messiah or of Yahweh Himself, whose mission it is to restore and judge Israel, the High Priest who is to purify his people.[16]

It must therefore be observed that the prophet's return at the end of the age seems to have been more significant, for the primitive Church and for post-Biblical Judaism alike, than his translation: in their eyes, Elijah is primarily an actor in the apocalyptic drama, he is not first and foremost the one who teaches the faithful the way to everlasting life.

Conclusion

The Old Testament knows no other translations than those of Enoch and Elijah, but according to certain traditions, particularly in Hellenistic Judaism, Moses himself escaped death also. It is true that according to the Book of Deuteronomy (xxxiv. 5) Moses died, but no man knows where he is buried, since God buried him Himself. Basing their belief on Deuteronomy (xviii. 15, 18), the Alexandrian Jews expect him to return, and so they think that he was translated like Elijah, or at least his soul was raised to heaven.[17]

---

[15] His name is mentioned twenty-eight times in the N.T., e.g. in Mt. xi. 14, xvi. 14; Lk. i. 17; Jn. i. 21; etc.

[16] Certain traditions, which are admittedly of a later date, assign him a part in the resurrection of the dead. Both the Jews and the Christians know of a suffering Elijah, contending with Antichrist (Rev. xi. 3 ff.); Tertullian refers to a Jewish tradition about the martyrdom of Elijah and Enoch, who, according to the Christian theologian's interpretation, "destroyed Antichrist by their blood" (*De anima,* l; cp. J. JEREMIAS, *op. cit.* (above, n. 12). pp. 930 ff.)

[17] Ass. Mos. x. 12 ff.; ps.-Philo xix. 12, 16, etc. Cp. also J. JEREMIAS, s.v. Μωυσῆς, in KITTEL, VOL. IV, 1942, pp. 852, 878.

The Pseudepigrapha, again, speak of the translations of the Son of Man (I Enoch LXXI. 1, 14, XC. 31; IV Ezra XIII. 3, etc.), of Ezra (IV Ezra XIV. 9, 13 ff.), of Baruch (II Baruch XIII. 3), and of Melchizedek (Melchiz. 4).[18]

If, in the background of all these Biblical Jewish or other stories, there lies an animistic conception according to which the soul is able to escape from the body, especially in sleep or in ecstasy (I Enoch LXXI. 1; cp. II Cor. XII. 2 ff.), and roam and be raised to the heavenly places, the authentic Biblical traditions insist on the fact that it is the totality of the human being that is brought to the presence of God; but under these conditions translation is in some sense synonymous with resurrection; the elect who gains heaven directly, body and soul, has no need of resurrection; moreover, his case remains too exceptional to afford much comfort to those who must conform to the general law. Enoch and Elijah seem to be merely the exceptions that prove the rule.

Thus translation remains an "aristocratic" privilege as E. Sellin expresses it; [19] it involves, of course, a breach of the natural order of human destiny and introduces a new possibility into the creature's ultimate lot; it is not, however, available for the ordinary Israelite, being the prerogative of certain favoured individuals, such as Enoch or Elijah; even Moses, in spite of the later traditions, did not escape Sheol.

Nevertheless it is possible that, afterwards, some of the faithful, meditating on the examples of Enoch and Elijah, found in the end of these men reason for hoping that the believer would not be cut off from the presence of his God by death; in a way known to Yahweh alone, those who had lived in this world solely for Him would remain in communion with Him after their earthly life.[20] Yet this expectation, aroused by the extraordinary adventure of the patriarch and the prophet was doubtless shared only by some groups of believers; for the Chosen People as a whole, Enoch and Elijah remained witnesses of the last hours of human history, because God had initiated them into the mysteries of His wisdom.

---

[18] E. STAUFFER, *Theologie des N. T.*, 1945, pp. 329 f.
[19] E. SELLIN, *op. cit.* (above, p. 55, n. 5), p. 263.
[20] Cp. Pss. XLIX. 15, LXXIII. 24; and above, p. 69, n. 11.

GENERAL CONCLUSIONS

In the course of this chapter, we have studied two songs that extol Yahweh's power over death; this power is confirmed in a striking fashion by the accounts of the resurrections wrought by His servants, and by the psalms that are sung by the faithful, miraculously healed and redeemed; the might of the Living God is again made manifest when He calls to Himself Enoch and Elijah, who thus escape Sheol.

But though the God of Israel is able to rescue His own from the clutches of death, though the history of the Chosen People is an eloquent testimony to His supremacy over the forces of destruction, and though the faithful can count on the intervention of his God in his direst need, still we do not find in these texts any allusion to a final victory that Yahweh will win over death, nor to a resurrection that will be tantamount to a definite deliverance from the powers of Sheol.

Such a possibility may of course be implied in the stories and songs we have studied; but the theory of it appears to be alien to the thought of those who wrote them. For these, death retains its reality and its power, although it cannot contend on equal terms with Yahweh; He tolerates it, because He is more concerned with His will being done in the land of the living than with intervening in Sheol. Thus though we may speak of these passages as signs pointing to the possibility of a life after death, we must not overestimate their importance. The deficiencies they reveal in the dominion of death over the departed, and which are the presupposition of the resurrection of the perished, will not assume their full significance until, by force of new circumstances, the Chosen People comes to believe not only that Yahweh is able to restore life to His own but that He wills to do it. Generally speaking, at the time when these passages were composed, the interest of believers is mainly focussed on the future of the nation of Israel as a whole, and their first concern is to dwell as long as possible in their land, in communion with their God and their brethren. Yahweh is their hope and their joy, because He delivers them from premature, "evil" death, and enables them to live their life to its appointed end.

CHAPTER II

THE PROCLAMATION OF THE RESURRECTION AND OF THE DESTRUCTION OF DEATH

Several rare Old Testament passages proclaim that Yahweh will put a definite end to the power of death and that the shades reduced to dwelling in Sheol will live again. In the following pages we shall study these; they fit easily enough into the framework of the history of the People of Israel and allow of exact definition of the reasons that led the Old Covenant believers first to hope for, and then to assert, the possibility of a resurrection. These important texts are so many signposts on the way followed by the Chosen People until they reached the revelation of a truth which became a fundamental dogma of Judaism and was subsequently adopted by the disciples of Christ, as it was by those of Mohammed. A veritable reversal of the conception of man's destiny took place when Israel discovered that its God would break through the bonds of death and seek out His own there; this chapter shows us how that revolution was prepared for and accomplished.

IN HOSEA

Hos. VI. 1-3: The Restoration of Israel

The Book of Hosea, an eighth-century prophet, contains one of the earliest witnesses in favour of the resurrection.[1]

---

[1] K. MARTI, *K. H.-C. A. T.*, 1904; W. R. HARPER, *I. C. C.*, 1905; A. VAN HOONACKER, *Et. bib.*, 1908; H. GRESSMANN, *Schr. A. T.*, 1919; A. ALT, "Hos. v. 8-vi. 6," *N. k. Z.*, 1919, pp. 537-68, or *Kleine Schriften zur Geschichte des Volkes Israel*, VOL. II, 1953; E. SELLIN, *Komm. A. T.*, 1929; H. S. NYBERG, "Studien z. Hoseabuche," in *Upps. U. Årssk.*, 1935-6, pp. 38 ff.; T. H. ROBINSON, *Hb. A. T.*, 1938; J. J. STAMM, "Eine Erwägung zu Hos. VI. 1-2," *Z. alttest. W.*, 1939, pp. 26 ff.; A. BAUMGARTNER, *B. Cent.*, 1947, A. WEISER, *A. T. D.*, 1949; F. NÖTSCHER, "Zur Auferstehung nach drei Tagen," *Biblica*, XXXV (1954), 3, pp. 313 ff.; VON BAUDISSIN, *op. cit.* (above p. 55, n. 5), pp. 403 ff.; EICHRODT, *op. cit.* (above, p. 12, n. 3), pp. 153 ff.; F. NÖTSCHER, *op. cit.* (above, p. 55, n. 5), pp. 138 ff.

a. Text

1 "Come, let us return to the LORD;
for he has torn, that he may heal us;
he has stricken, and he will bind us up.

2 After two days he will revive us;
on the third day he will raise us up,
that we may live before him.

3 Let us know, let us press on to know
the LORD;
his going forth is sure as the dawn;
<5c> ⟨his judgment *will arise* as the light;⟩
he will come to us as the showers,
as the spring rains that water the earth. . . ."

In vs. 1, the term טָרַף, *ṭārap*, "to tear," makes reference to Hos. v. 14; read וַיַּךְ, *wayyak*, "he has stricken," instead of יָךְ, *yak*, "he will strike."

In vs. 2, "to live before (someone)" signifies to live under his protection, in his presence, and is here the antithesis of "to go away, to withdraw, to hide the face" (cp. vs. 15), which is equivalent to "to abandon, to reject."

In vs. 3, with T. H. Robinson, we hold that vs. 5c may be read here in parallel with vs. 3b. Moreover, it must be emended, in agreement with the LXX, the Syriac, and the Targum, to read thus: וּמִשְׁפָּטוֹ כָאוֹר יֵצֵא, *ûmišpāṭô kā'ôr yāṣā'*, "his judgment will arise as the light."

Israel would then be expecting a prompt intervention on its behalf, the Chosen People would be sure of deliverance. H. S. Nyberg takes יָצָא, *yāṣā'*, "to go out," in the sense of "to be extinguished," and following the Masoretic Text, interprets vs. 5c as follows: "Thus thy judgments are as a light going out," that is to say, "disappearing." This would refer to the judgments of the false prophets, and not to those of Yahweh.

The LXX reads for vs. 3c, εὑρήσομεν αὐτόν, corresponding to כְּשַׁחֲרֵנוּ כֵן נִמְצָאֶנּוּ, *kešaḥarēnû kēn nimṣā'ennû*, in Hebrew, meaning: "When we seek, we shall find Him."

The autumn rains, גֶּשֶׁם, *gešem*, and the spring rains, מַלְקוֹשׁ, *malqôš*, are indispensable to cultivation. In Palestine, water is the sign and guarantee of life. יַרְוֶה, *yarweh*, must be read in place of יוֹרֶה, *yôreh*, i.e. with R.S.V. "that water" instead of A.V. "the former (autumn) rain."

b. *Historical Background*

With A. Alt, followed especially by E. Sellin and A. Weiser, this text must be read in the light of its historical and literary background.[2] Hos. VI. 1-3 is in point of fact one of a series of oracles pronounced on the occasion of the Syro-Ephraimitish War (735-4). We know that, from the second half of the eighth century onwards, and in particular under the leadership of Tiglath-Pileser, Assyria invaded Palestine several times. In 738, the King of Israel, Menahem, has to pay a heavy tribute to induce the Assyrian sovereign to withdraw his troops from the country (II Kings xv. 19 ff.) In 735, his successor, at the instigation of the King of Damascus, seeks to shake off the yoke of Assyria, and tries to draw the little kingdom of Judah into a great coalition against Tiglath-Pileser. Jerusalem refuses to become involved in this foolhardy enterprise; then the Syrian and Israelite troops march against the southern capital while King Ahaz, in spite of the clear counsel of Isaiah (Is. VII, VIII), appeals to the Assyrian ruler for aid.

Tiglath-Pileser needs no coaxing, he intervenes with savage speed. By 732, Damascus has fallen. A great part of its northern and eastern territories (Galilee, the land of Naphtali, and Gilead) is taken from the Kingdom of Israel; by favour of the conquerors, Hoshea is set on the throne of Samaria (II Kings xv. 28-30). The Assyrians are practically masters of all the land; dark days are ahead for the states of Judah and Israel; the latter will be destroyed in 722, and, about 701, the

---

[2] K. Marti holds the passage v. 15-VI. 3 to be post-Exilic and inspired by Ezek. XXXVII; according to P. Humbert, these verses are a later addition, though perhaps by Hosea's own hand, and are designed to modify the over-harsh assertion of v. 14; T. H. Robinson would detach VI. 4-6 from the preceding passage (v. 15-VI. 3), while recognising the intimate connexion that subsists between the two of them, but in the final analysis there is no reason for doubting the authenticity of this text, which is perfectly compatible with its context, as the majority of the commentators, and especially A. Alt, allow.

former will only just escape from falling into complete sub-servience (II Kings XVIII. 18 ff.)

In Hos. v. 8-VI. 6, the prophet recalls the events of the Syro-Ephraimitish War and its melancholy consequences. He speaks to Judah and Israel turn and turn about, he sounds the alarm for the southern cities of the Kingdom of Israel, against which, while Tiglath-Pileser is invading the north of the land, a Judean column is doubtless advancing (v. 8 ff.), and he likewise reproaches the army captains of Judah, who in their counterattack, have probably crossed the frontier fixed by Yahweh (v. 10).[3]

Hosea recalls, perhaps a little later, that Israel is reaping the reward of its sins; the Northern Kingdom, now become an Assyrian province, is lamenting its lost cities and lands (v. 11); but the prophet has a more definite message to proclaim to his brethren: it is not enough that Israel should count its wounds, still less that it should expect some sort of assistance from Assyria: Tiglath-Pileser is unable to do anything for Israel, for in reality he who has torn the Northern Kingdom asunder is not the Assyrian ruler, but Israel's own God (v. 12 ff.)

The Israelites have to learn that the root of their troubles is spiritual and not political. The remedy is not to be found outwith Yahweh Himself. It is in fact with Him that Ephraim has to do, it is He whom the Israelites are encountering in their military set-backs. In order that none may misunderstand the meaning of recent events, Hosea declares in the name of his God: "I am like a moth to Ephraim, and like dry rot to Judah. . . . I, even I, will send and go away, I will carry off, and none shall rescue" (v. 12, 14). The Living God, God Himself, and no mere earthly power, is holding Himself ready to carry Israel off as a prey; already Yahweh is disposed to withdraw from His People, which means that He is abandoning it to its sorry lot (v. 15).

One choice remains to the Israelites, one single possibility of salvation: repentance—that is to say, unconditional and absolute return to Yahweh.

So, by his successive prophecies, Hosea seeks to reveal the true reason of their failures to his contemporaries; in pointing

---

[3] In Is. x, Isaiah also condemns Assyria, the rod of the divine anger, for having abused its conquests.

out to them the real purpose of the disasters that have befallen them, he sets before them a final choice whereby all may yet be saved, but wherein all may be definitely lost. History, as interpreted by the prophet, becomes an urgent appeal to them to return to God.

c. A Penitential Psalm and its Meaning

Israel listens to the spokesman of Yahweh, agrees with his message and hastens to respond to his call. The people chants a confession of sin, doubtless on a day of national mourning, accompanied by impressive religious ceremonies,[4] among which sacrifices would have a prominent place (Hos. vi. 6).

The consensus of opinion is that vss. 1-3 contain a penitential psalm voiced by the Israelites in manifestation of their repentance; in vss. 4-6 the reply of Hosea to his brethren is heard. This prayer of the inhabitants of the Northern Kingdom expresses their desire to return to God; it implies their acknowledgment of their misdeeds, and, above all, their certainty that they will be heard by Yahweh; it appears that Hosea has not spoken in vain; his assurance of forgiveness seems to have brought a great penitential movement into being (vi. 1-3).

Yet God adjudges their confession to be incompetent! Israel's repentance leaves Him sceptical; He calls the people itself to witness to the superficiality of its conversion. Over against the impulse that urges the Israelites to turn to Him, Yahweh sets the melancholy fact that their piety has no future at all, their repentance no foundation.

"Your love is like a morning cloud, like the dew that goes early away" (vi. 4). Israel's prayer is fine, its actual state less so. The penitence of Ephraim is still superficial, it will not last. Israel is too sure of salvation, its confidence borders on sacrilege, and it is under a misapprehension about Yahweh as it is about itself. The Living God is not obliged to forgive, pardoning is not His business, His mercy is never automatic; a prayer and some sacrifices are not enough to ensure healing. The point is that the confession of the Israelites testifies against them by disclosing that they do not really know the God upon

---

[4] I Kings viii. 33-53; Joel ii. 12 ff.; Jer. iii. 21 ff.; Ps. lxxxv.

whom they are calling.   Yet Yahweh has already taught them,
and that severely, by means of His messengers.[5]

Yahweh reminds Israel once again of His demands, He
requires love rather than sacrifices, the offering of the heart
rather than religious ritual. חֶסֶד, *hesed*, is not mere piety, it
implies the love, the goodwill, the selflessness, that should distinguish the relationships of the Israelites with their God, and
with one another too; this term is a favourite one of Hosea's.[6]
Moreover, the knowledge that Yahweh expects from His
People is, for the Israelite, more than intellectual apprehension;
it is devotion of heart and will, self-surrender, and sharing the
life of others.

In its own way, this sixth verse sets forth the whole meaning
of the Law; Jesus reminds the Pharisees of it (Mt. ix. 13,
xii. 7).   Here Hosea is not making, as has sometimes been
asserted, an absolute distinction between cultus and ethic;
he does not exclude ritual altogether, but he makes it sub-
ordinate to the practice of חֶסֶד, *hesed*, "piety." [7]   In once again
confronting Israel with the will of Yahweh, Hosea is offering
another chance of salvation to his contemporaries; God's
People now knows exactly what its God expects of it; Yahweh
has condemned a false penitence only to summon His own to
genuine repentance, He has rejected their false worship only
to call them to true service, which alone is the pledge of
salvation.   The God of Israel cares too much for the nation
that He chose for Himself to give it over to its illusions.

---

[5] Vs. 5 perhaps referred to past events, to the chastisements with which
God visited Israel for its timeous enlightenment.   According to H. SCHMIDT,
Sellinfestschrift, 1927, p. 120, and S. SPIEGEL, both cited by T. H. Robinson,
this verse might contain an allusion to the Decalogue, and be translated
thus: "Therefore I engraved it [the Decalogue], I instructed them by the
words of My mouth."

[6] Hos. ii. 1, iv. 1, vi. 6, x. 2; and also Jer. ii. 2, xxxi. 30 ff.; Is. lv. 3,
lxiii. 7; cp. H. J. STOEBE, "Die Bedeutung des Wortes Hesed im A. T.,"
Vet. test., 1952, pp. 244-54.

[7] Van Hoonacker justly points out that vs. 6*a* must be understood in the
light of 6*b*; A. GUILLAUME, *Prophétie et Divination*, Paris 1944, p. 439, cited
by E. JACOB in "Le prophétisme israélite d'après les recherches récentes,"
in *R. h. p. r.*, 1952, p. 64, similarly considers that וְלֹא, *welô*, usually
translated "and not," should be rendered as "rather than" and not as an
absolute negative.

d. Healing or Resurrection?

In its prayer Israel expresses its hope or indeed its certainty of being saved; it declares (VI. 1-2):

> 1 "Come, let us return to the LORD;
> for he has torn, that he may heal us;
> he has stricken, and he will bind us up.
>
> 2 After two days he will revive us
> on the third day he will raise us up,
> that we may live before him. . . ."

The terms employed bring to mind first a healing, and then a resurrection. Are the two ideas synonymous? Are they complementary or mutually exclusive? The question has recently been raised by J. J. Stamm, who points out that the commentators are far from being agreed on this matter. According to W. von Baudissin, E. Sellin, W. Baumgartner, and T. H. Robinson, to cite no more than these, here the Israelites are referring to resurrection; for J. Wellhausen, W. Nowack, and K. Budde, on the other hand, Israel is an invalid, relying on the help of God for relief. This is also the opinion of J. J. Stamm, who, in an ingenious study, upholds the view that Hos. VI. 1 ff. tells the story of a sufferer who, thanks to the care of Yahweh, recovers his health and resumes a normal life.[8]

For J. J. Stamm there is absolutely no question of death and resurrection in this passage; but in our judgment that does not necessarily follow. The verbs employed here by Hosea's interlocutors definitely have the strongest sense in other texts (Is. XXVI. 14, 19; Dan. XII. 2), and clearly assert the resurrection. Thus it is not only feasible but even inevitable that the same conception should be involved here. Moreover, J. J. Stamm reads a standard Hebrew poetical parallelism [9] as a

---

[8] According to J. J. Stamm, חָיָה, *ḥiyyâ*, the *piel* of חָיָה, *ḥāyâ*, does not mean "to live again" but "to recover health," and הֵקִים *hēqîm*, the *hiphil* of קוּם, *qûm*, ought to be translated as "to rise" (from bed) and not as "to be raised."

[9] In vs. 1*b*: "torn" is parallel to "stricken," "that he may heal us" to "that he will bind us up"; and, in vs. 2*a*, "He will revive us" is parallel to "He will raise us up," and "after two days" to "on the third day."

particularised description of the lot of the invalid,[10] which seems over-subtle to us. It appears to be simpler to take vs. 2*a* as repeating, in a somewhat emphasised form, the information already given in 1*b*; Israel is expecting salvation, which is conceived in terms of healing, or rather of resurrection. J. J. Stamm wrongly overlooks an essential element in the Israelites' prayer, the hope that, by the grace of Yahweh, they will pass from death to life.

We must therefore ask ourselves whether the antithesis between "healing" and "resurrection" which exercises Old Testament specialists, may not be the artificial creation of scholars who find difficulty in entering into the Semitic mentality. As we have already said, the Hebrews make no clear-cut distinction between sickness and death or between healing and resurrection.[11] Hence, in our opinion, Stamm's question is fallacious. Here the Israelites are expressing their expectation of a saving intervention by their God in distinct and complementary terms.

In our view, Hos. vi. 1-3 does in fact refer to resurrection, but we must immediately make it clear that it is not concerned with the resurrection of the Israelites personally, but with that of the People as a whole, or, in other words, with a national restoration, which is to take place primarily on the political plane. The resurrection of Ephraim is first and foremost a revival of its power; the Northern Kingdom is confidently expecting the day of reckoning: "*Post tenebras lux!*"

e. *The Provenance of the Idea of Resurrection used in Hos. vi. 2*

If it be correct that here we must translate חִיָּה, *ḥiyyâ*, as "restore to life," and הֵקִים, *hēqîm*, as "raise up" (from the earth and not from a bed), and conclude that vi. 2 refers to the resurrection of the Chosen People, then, it may well be asked, whence does this idea come? We believe that the answer to this question is to be found in a curiously precise definition

---

[10] First of all he is cared for, then his wounds are bound up, thereafter he recovers his health, rises from bed, and at last resumes his former way of life.

[11] Cp. above, p. 60.

contained in this same verse: namely, in the words "in two
days," מִיָּמִים, *miyyōmāim*, and "on the third day,' הַשְּׁלִישִׁי, *haššᵉlîšî*.
It is true that, as some writers such as J. Wellhausen,
K. Budde, A. Bertholet, and J. J. Stamm think, the expression
might have a certain proverbial sense and merely mean a short
interval, being equivalent to "soon." In that case the Israelites
were counting on a swift intervention by Yahweh, they thought
that salvation was near.

We find, occasionally in a slightly different form, similar
references in the Old Testament, especially in the story of
Jonah (Jon. I. 17), and in connexion with Hezekiah's illness,
when, in the name of Yahweh, the prophet says to the King:
"Behold, I will heal you; on the third day you shall go up into
the house of the LORD" (II Kings xx. 5; cp. also I Sam. xxx. 12);
and also in the New Testament, where Jesus, when He is
foretelling His Passion, declares that He will rise again on the
third day.[12]

Nevertheless, curiously enough, the numbers given by
Hosea are to be found in other documents relating to the
agricultural cults practised in the countries round about
Palestine, which were fairly similar to those that must have led
Hosea's contemporaries astray.

W. von Baudissin mentions a certain number of facts whose
correspondence is disquieting: Lucian, *De Syria dea* (VI),
states that "at Byblos, the faithful expect the resurrection of
Adonis 'on another day'." The expression is vague enough;
nevertheless it suggests that the interval observed between
the ceremonies celebrating the death and the resurrection of
the god is fairly short. According to Plutarch, *De Iside et
Osiride*, the death of Osiris was celebrated on the 17th of Athyr,
and his "discovery," that is to say, his resurrection, on the 19th,
two days later. In the Roman cult of Attis, who is the counterpart of Adonis, the death of the god was bewailed on the 22nd
of March, and his renewed life was celebrated on the 25th.

---

[12] Cp. Mt. XII. 40; Mk. VIII. 31; Lk. XIII. 32, XVIII. 31, etc. Here
Christ does not necessarily have a precise date in mind, but is stating a
fact that must have appeared to be quite extraordinary to His contemporaries; for they, in point of fact, conceived of the resurrection of
the dead as taking place at the end of the age; but Jesus dares to proclaim
that His Father will restore Him to life shortly after His Passion.

Recently, F. Nötscher has called attention to the publication of a Sumerian fragment on the descent of Inanna into Hell, in which it is said that the goddess remained in the nether world for three days and three nights.[13]

Thus, according to these various testimonies, the agricultural divinity must reappear on the third day after he has vanished into the underworld. It is perfectly credible that the prophet's interlocutors were aware of some such tradition and, whether consciously or not, adopted it. With W. von Baudissin and W. Baumgartner, among others, and in spite of the reservations of F. Nötscher, we think that the numbers given in Hos. VI. 2 are cultic in origin, even if, later on, they assumed a purely proverbial significance.

Whence is this exact figure derived? Various theories have been put forward. The moon, in its monthly cycle, remains invisible for three days, and it is possible that we have here the vestige of a lunar cult; moreover, this luminary is often associated with the idea of fertility.[14] It must be mentioned, with W. von Baudissin, that certain peoples, and even the Jews after the Christian era, consider that the soul remains near the corpse for three days;[15] not until then does it leave for the world of the departed, unless, re-entering the body, it re-animates it.

Be that as it may, we believe that the people of the Northern Kingdom borrowed the idea of the resurrection from the agricultural cults. Since it is based mainly on texts that are definitely later than the eighth century, or whose interpretation is still a subject of debate, this, it is true, may seem to be a bold

[13] F. Nötscher, "Zur Auferstehung nach drei Tagen," *Biblica*, 1954, p. 314.

[14] Eliade, *op. cit.* (above, p. 2, n. 2), pp. 155 ff.: "The lot of man is 'corroborated' by the course of the moon. . . . Just as the moon is born again on the fourth evening, even so the dead comes into possession of a refashioned life. . . . The moon reveals his personal human situation to man."

[15] For this reason the Talmud categorically forbids burial before the third day after death; cp. Von Baudissin, *op. cit.* (above, p. 55, n. 5), pp. 412 ff., who cites Gen. R., para. 100; Lev. R. para. 18, the Testament of Abraham, and the Apocalypse of Elijah; Addison, *op. cit.* (above, p. 16, n. 2), p. 12, mentions that in certain parts of China, the spirit of the dead man is supposed to appear at his home on the third day after his burial.

conclusion. Quite recently, F. Nötscher has again categorically rejected it.[16] On the evidence of this one passage, in which the hope of the Israelites is specifically stated by Hosea, it could scarcely be argued that a rigid relationship subsisted between that hope and those systems of faith that were inspired by the phenomena of nature, and were widely current for centuries throughout the Middle East. But it is a matter of fact that the People of Yahweh had scarcely entered Canaan when it came under the influence of Canaanite practices, particularly in the times of Elijah and Hosea. Even the latter, while protesting vehemently against the Baal cults, was himself profoundly steeped in the mentality he opposed, as his prophecies show. Thus, in the text that we are studying, many connexions with the agricultural religions may be found: the lion to which Yahweh likens Himself (Hos. v. 14) is often used as a symbol of death, or of a divinity dwelling in the nether world; [17] the dawn, שַׁחַר, *šaḥar*, "dawn," called to mind by Hosea's interlocutors (vi. 3), plays a significant part in the Ras Shamra texts as well as in the Old Testament; [18] associated with Shalem, Shaḥar is one of the benevolent gods begotten by El, who intervene at the time of the rainy season; [19] according to H. G. May,[20] Shaḥar is not so much the dawn as the sun at the winter solstice, his presence brings the rains that will make the earth fruitful. From Yahweh's "coming forth," מוֹצָאוֹ, *môṣā'ô*, the Israelites are hoping for similar beneficent results. The dew, טַל, *ṭal*, disappearing in the morning, which the prophet compares with his contemporaries' fleeting piety, likewise appears in the Ras Shamra texts as the daughter of Baal, himself the god of rain. Baal descends into the nether world with all his retinue, clouds, winds, and rains, his servants and his daughters; when he appears again with his attendants, the rain must needs

---

[16] NÖTSCHER, *op. cit.* (above, n. 13), pp. 313 ff.

[17] Cp. W. MICHAELIS, s. v. λεών, KITTEL, VOL. IV, pp. 258 ff.

[18] Cp. especially Is. XIV. 12; Pss. CX. 3, CXXXIX. 9; Song of Sol. VI. 10.

[19] C. VIROLLEAUD, "La naissance des dieux gracieux et beaux," in *Syria*, 1933, pp. 128-51; R. DUSSAUD, in *R. h. r.*, 1933, pp. 5-12; T. H. GASTER, *Thespis, Ritual, Myth and Drama in the Ancient Near East*, 1950, pp. 225-37; etc.

[20] *Z. alttest. W.*, 1937, p. 269.

follow.[21] Thus the dew, in the Ugaritic documents as well as in the Old Testament, is linked up with the idea of the renewal of life (Hos. xiv. 5; Is. xxvi. 19; Ps. cx. 3).

These facts appear conclusive to us. The Israelites are living in a world that deifies the forces of nature and considers that these play a decisive part in the destiny of men and the universe alike. The Chosen People, in its turn, imagines that Yahweh is merely one among these powers, and His activity is confused with that of divinities like Baal, Adonis, Tammuz, and yet others, who are constrained by a higher law continually to pass from life to death. If the expressions "in two days" and "on the third day," if the terms "dawn" and "dew" betray the cultic and heathen origin of Hosea's contemporaries' hope of national revival, the reluctance of Yahweh, or rather the clear-cut refusal with which He meets them, is the more easily understood.

For it is not Yahweh's will that, in the eyes of the Ephraimites, He should be merely a power, albeit deified; He is not Life, hypostatised indeed, but constrained from time to time to descend to the nether world; there is nothing automatic or periodic about either His mercy or His wrath; He is the Living God who freely disposes of life without identifying Himself with any of its manifestations, the God of the Covenant whose existence is entirely independent of that of His People, and who is able, at any point in its history, to tear it or heal it, destroy or create it anew, according to His absolute sovereign power. But the free will of Yahweh, more or less explicitly denied by Hosea's interlocutors, and recalled by the prophet, is in no sense arbitrary; it is settled in His Word, it is true to His Covenant, which is a work of love. Yahweh loves His People in all circumstances, and expects it to love Him in return; His compassion cannot bear the sight of His own straying far away from Him; His mercy consists in continually leading Israel back into the true way of life.

Hosea has to give his contemporaries a renewed vision of the true face of their God. Yahweh is not some sort of Baal, a blind and brutal natural force, an impersonal power ultimately limited by the operation of other powers; His destiny, like

---

[21] Cp. GASTER, *op. cit.*, p. 128; C. H. GORDON, *Ugaritic Literature*, Rome 1949, p. 34.

G

that of His People, is not identical with the cycle of the seasons, the regular succession of the day and the night, the growth and decay of the vegetation; Yahweh is the Lord of history, whose Word alone creates and preserves Israel in life.

f. Conclusion

Basing ourselves on Hos. vi. 1-3, we believe we can legitimately hold that the idea of the resurrection was known in Israel before the exile, and as evidence we have this text from Hosea, an eighth-century prophet.

The Israelites took the conception from the Canaanites who, in deifying the forces of nature, primarily explain the appearance and disappearance of the vegetation as the death and resurrection of gods; thus originally, the resurrection has nothing to do with Yahweh-worship; it comes from the agricultural cults.

The expectation of a new life, expressed by Hosea's contemporaries, which the prophet rebuffs, is concerned here not with the personal resurrection of the Israelites, but with the restoration of the nation; it is political and has no eschatological character.[22]

Hos. xiii. 14: "O Death, where are your plagues . . .?"

This text is cited by the Apostle Paul as proclaiming the end of the power of death over mankind, and, in virtue of that, is relevant to our study.

The Christians at Corinth, steeped in the Greek way of thought, are unable to admit the resurrection of the body (Acts xvii. 32). Paul is obliged to go over the whole question. He bases his argument on the formal testimony of those who saw Jesus alive after His crucifixion (1 Cor. xv. 1 ff.), and shows the Corinthians that the Christian faith is rooted and grounded in the bodily resurrection of Christ and that His resurrection

[22] The Targum interpreted Hos. vi. 2 in an eschatological sense: "He will cause us to live again on the Day of Consolation appointed for the dead, on the Day of the Resurrection He will make us stand up."

implies that the bodies of believers also will escape from the bondage of death (1 Cor. xv. 12-19). Then the Apostle recalls what the transformation that the living and the dead will undergo at the end of the age will be: "For this perishable nature must put on the imperishable, and this mortal nature must put on immortality" (1 Cor. xv. 53). Moreover this event—and this is of primary evidential importance—is foretold in the Scriptures. Therefore Paul cites two Old Testament passages, one of which (1 Cor. xv. 54 f.) is Hos. xiii. 14*b* itself:

> O death, where is thy victory?
> O death, where is thy sting?

The Apostle's plea then concludes with a prayer of thanksgiving to God, who thus grants us to share in the victory of Christ (1 Cor. xv. 57).

a. Text

a *From the power of Sheol I will/would*
    ransom them,
    from Death I will/would deliver them.
b *Where are thy plagues, O Death?*
    Where is thy sting, O Sheol?
c *Repentance is hidden from my eyes.* . . . [1]

Thus for St Paul, this passage from Hosea is telling Death of the end of its dominion; its power is impotent against Christ, its triumph is turned to defeat, its weapons are contemptible in face of Him who won the Easter victory; ironically questioned by the prophet, Death has to acknowledge its defeat. The text of 1 Cor. xv. 55 does not exactly correspond to Hos. xiii. 14*b*; it may be that the Apostle is citing it from

---

[1] K. Marti, *K. H.-C. A. T.*, 1904; W. R. Harper, *I. C. C.*, 1905; A. van Hoonacker, *Et. bib.*, 1908; E. Sellin, *Komm. A. T.*, 1929; T. Brandt, *Hosea*, 1931, pp. 68 f., 77; H. S. Nyberg, "Studien z. Hoseabuche," *Upps. U. Årssk.*, 1935-6; T. H. Robinson, *Hb. A. T.*, 1938; A. Baumgartner, *Bib. Cent.*, 1947; A. Weiser, *A. T. D.*, 1949; W. von Baudissin, *op. cit.* (above, p. 55, n. 5), p. 406; H. M. Féret, *op. cit.* (above, p. 16, n. 1), p. 48, etc.

memory, but it is also possible that he may have read a version slightly different from that which comes to us from the Masoretes.[2]

[2] This translation is based on the supposition that אֶהִי, *'ehî*, "I will be," should be read אַיֵּה, *'ayyēh*, "where," in accordance with the versions. דֶּבֶר, *deber*, denotes pestilence and appears in the account of the plagues of Egypt (Ex. v. 3, ix. 3, 15; Lev. xxvi. 25, etc.) According to L. KÖHLER, דֶּבֶר, *deber*, in Ps. xci. 3, 6 is a homonym meaning "thorn, sting" (Ps. xci. 3, 6). קֶטֶב, *qeteb*, also means thorn, sting, and is synonymous with "a disease" in Deut. xxxii. 24, Ps. xci. 6 ; in the course of time, the Jews identified קֶטֶב, *qeteb*, with "a demon." These two terms connote all the destructive power of death.

נֹחַם, *nōḥam*, may be interpreted in various ways. Although A. WEISER takes נֹחַם, *nōḥam*, as meaning "vengeance," W. GESENIUS, like L. KÖHLER, translates it as "pity, mercy," deriving from the root נחם, *n-ḥ-m*, √*nḥm*, which, in the *niphal*, signifies "to repent," and in the *piel*, "to console." It may also be rendered as "repentance"; in the first case, vs. 14c indicates that Yahweh is weary of forgiving Ephraim, in the second, that the People of God is persistently impenitent, and, at all events, this passage implies condemnation of the Israelites.

Basing himself on the versions, and esp. on the LXX, H. S. NYBERG, has attempted, *op. cit.* (above, n. 1), pp. 103 ff., to reconstruct the text that the Apostle must have read:

M. T.: אֱהִי דְבָרֶיךָ מָוֶת אֱהִי קָטָבְךָ שְׁאוֹל, *'ehî debāreykā māwet, 'ehî qāṭābekā še'ôl*, "I will be thy plagues, O death, I will be thy destruction, O Sheol."

LXX: ποῦ ἡ δίκη σου, θάνατε; ποῦ τὸ κέντρον σου, ᾅδη;

Paul: ποῦ σου, θάνατε, τὸ νῖκος; ποῦ σου, θάνατε (ᾅδη), τὸ κέντρον;

Thus the LXX, the Syriac, and Paul read אַיֵּה, *'ayyēh*, "where," instead of אֱהִי, *'ehî*, "I will be"; δίκη is doubtless an emendation for νίκη and would correspond to the Hebrew גברך, *gbrk*, "thy victory" (cp. גָּבַר, *gābar*, "he prevailed," (Ex. xvii. 11)) suggested by the Pauline text and the Syriac version. κέντρον, "sting", would be derived not from קֶטֶב, *qeteb*, "thorn," "corruption," "pestilence": but from דָּרְבָן, *dorbon*, "goad," βούκεντρον, which is found (in the plural) in Ecclesiastes xii. 11. Thus the Apostle had the following text before him: איה נברך מות איה דרבנך שאול, *'yh gbrk mwt 'yh drbnk š'ôl*.

In H. S. Nyberg's view, this version is not original; it dates from a period when, under Persian influence, the Jews conceived of death as a malign power, utterly inimical to good. The Masoretic text is to be considered as the more primitive—אֱהִי, *'ehî*, meaning "alas," "woe " (Hos. xiii. 10), and דֶּבֶר, *deber*, and קֶטֶב, *qeteb*, characterising the conduct of the Israelites.

Basing himself primarily on the Massoretic text, which he considers to be more primitive, H. S. Nyberg proposes to translate verse 14*b* thus: "Alas, thy pestilential deeds ⟨are as evil as⟩ death, alas, thy evil works ⟨are as malignant as⟩ Sheol. Pity is hidden, that is to say, disappears from my sight."

This is an interesting hypothesis, even although some of its details are questionable; in any case it is sensibly divergent from the Pauline interpretation of the passage in Hosea, and gives it a negative sense; According to H. S. Nyberg the situation is that Israel in its trouble remembers its God, and cries to Yahweh for deliverance from death. But the God of Israel refuses mercy, are not the ways of His People leading it to Sheol? ". . . even now the Assyrians are at the gate of Samaria." [3]

Without agreeing with the entire position of the Scandinavian scholar, many exegetes hold with him that there is a clear-cut difference between Hosea's thought and the Apostle's assertion; the latter read a promise of life in the prophet's book, while the former had to proclaim an absolute condemnation to his contemporaries. In any case, whatever text Paul may have read—and it is difficult to reconstruct it exactly—we have to consider whether I Cor. xv. 55 is a correct exegesis of Hos. xiii. 14*b*.

b. Context

It is impossible to interpret this verse in Hosea in isolation from its context. Throughout the whole of CH. XIII the prophet is proclaiming dire punishment for his people, because of the ingratitude and consequent idolatry of Ephraim.

Israel has turned to Baal (XIII. 1), has forgotten Him who had known it, that is to say chosen and loved it, in the wilderness (vs. 5); now Yahweh, like a famished leopard or raging bear, is risen against it to devour it (vs. 7). Israel cannot be saved, having rejected Him who alone is able to preserve it (vss. 9-11).

The Israelites' crimes are being stored up against the day of judgment (vs. 12); already pangs wrack the guilty, but with no effect (vs. 13). There is perhaps a reference here to the

[3] NYBERG, *op. cit.*, p. 106.

first punishments that have smitten Israel, and which ought to have moved it to return to Yahweh, but these sufferings are not producing what the Living God expects of His own: Ephraim stupidly procrastinates and puts off the hour of conversion, like a child reluctant to leave its mother's womb (vs. 13).

The prophet goes on to describe the plagues that are about to fall on a rebellious land: a country, fertile above all others, famed for its orchards and fruitfulness, will be dried up by a wind from the wilderness (vs. 15); in fact, the Assyrian hosts from the east, sent by the God of Israel, will mount an attack on Samaria, they will come to cut off its men of war, to dash its children asunder, and to rip up its pregnant women (XIII. 16; cp. X. 14 f.)

It seems that, with this dreadful vision haunting his imagination, Hosea could not refrain from making one final appeal to his brethren: "O Israel, return to the LORD your God . . ." (Hos. XIV. 1 ff.)

The words of the prophet appear to be spoken towards the close of his career, at a moment when the die seems to be cast. Can it be that the army of Shalmaneser is already before the walls of Samaria?   In any event, throughout all this chapter Yahweh is seen as quite resolved to smite His rebellious People, Ephraim has lost its last chance, the hour of death has come for a nation that refuses to be reborn in repentance (vs. 13*b*).

c. Interpretation

The Apostle Paul, then, read the prophet's words as foretelling the downfall of Death before the Risen Christ; Luther followed his interpretation; Calvin made more reservations; and today the majority of commentators are inclined to regard this passage as a threat to Israel; the whole context confirms this point of view.

It certainly seems strange that Hosea should have informed the Israelites that their God would rescue them from destruction at the very moment when he was foretelling the fall of Samaria. We must not claim, with T. Brandt, that here we have a gleam of light in the darkness. The dialectic of death and life, judgment and grace, which ultimately may amount to no more than a sort of theological game, is not relevant here. Hosea himself, in spite of all his sensitiveness, is not playing with paradox at this point, he is speaking about salvation to his adulterous people (Hos. ii. 16 ff., xi. 8 f., xiv. 4 ff.), but not superficially. In our opinion, Hos. xiii. 14 does no more than ratify the irrevocable sentence pronounced upon Ephraim. The prophet has to announce not an extraordinary deliverance, but an unprecedented calamity: night will definitely fall on Samaria.

Thus, with W. R. Harper, K. Marti, E. Reuss, A. Baumgartner, W. von Baudissin, and others, we are adopting this exegesis; but if the general sense of Hos. xiii. 14 is thus to be found, its detailed exposition still presents difficulties.

According to the Jewish exegete Kimhi, followed by J. G. Eichhorn, who are cited by W. R. Harper, the imperfect does not denote continuous action, but is conditional: "I would deliver you if . . ." This is also the opinion of E. Reuss, who considers the condition cannot have been fulfilled, as the prophet continues: "My eyes know compassion no more." [4]

Modern commentators, such as K. Marti, W. Nowack, A. Baumgartner, and W. von Baudissin, understand vs. 14*b* as a question: "Can I deliver you . . .?" The answer can be no other than: "No, since repentance is hidden from my eyes," that is to say "you refuse to return to Me." Yahweh is then summoning Death to unleash itself upon Ephraim, He is urging it to immediate action: "O Death, where are thy weapons . . .? Make haste against Israel, for pity is disappearing from My eyes,"; that is to say, "I have done with forgiving" (vs. 14*b*).

Nevertheless, certain specialists still uphold Luther's exegesis; according to T. H. Robinson vss. 12-14*b* constitute a section in themselves: Israel must be born to a better life but is too weak. Ephraim is like a stillborn child. Yet Hosea is looking to Yahweh to intervene on its behalf, and, in its catastrophic condition, call His People to life. A. Weiser considers that vs. 14*c* should be rendered as follows: "For vengeance is

---

[4] For another Jewish commentator, Rashi, who also is cited by W. R. Harper, vs. 14 referred to past events: Hosea, in his view, is recalling the many deliverances wrought by Yahweh in former days. "Several times, I set you free. . . ."

hidden from My eyes"; that is to say, "I am resolved to pardon." He thinks that vss. 12-14 contain a promise of salvation; Israel has chosen death, but Yahweh is able to seek out His own even in the Nether Kingdom. The God of Israel has the right to avenge Himself, but the love in His heart prevails. In our opinion, these interpretations do not take sufficient account of the context.

More ingenious is the theory of E. Sellin, who excises XIII. 14, vs. 15 then follows vs. 13 as its natural sequel, and as for vs. 14, its proper position is, he holds, in CH. XIV, after vss. 4 ff.; in this passage, Yahweh confirms His love for His People (vs. 4), along with life He will restore to it its former glory (vss. 5 ff.), He will satisfy it with His blessings . . . and at need He would go to the depths of the Abyss to bring it thence (vss. 13-14).

But we do not think that it is necessary to take XIII. 14 out of its actual context; the passage is perfectly clear as it stands, it declares that Yahweh has refused to save Ephraim, that the end of Samaria is approaching, and that, summoned by God Himself, the powers of darkness are at work against a rebellious and obstinate nation.

d. Conclusion

Obviously the interpretation that we are upholding is not in accordance with the mind of the Apostle Paul when he quoted Hosea's words. Where he saw an incomparable promise, we are reading irrevocable doom. Nevertheless our explanation tallies with the Pauline assertion in this respect: it evidences the extraordinary power of the God of Israel; Yahweh treats Death as a lord treats one of his subjects, He commands it as a vassal, and, in spite of all, Sheol is at His disposal. In face of the Living God, even the dominion of death has to yield.

Thus, according to one theory, Yahweh commands Death to hasten to accomplish His purpose; or, on the other interpretation, the God of Israel claims that even should His People fall into the clutches of Sheol, He would be able to deliver it thence—if Ephraim would really repent!

This fragment of Hosea's message shows, even more than

other Old Testament texts,[5] Yahweh's crushing superiority over the infernal powers; thus in the words of the eighth-century prophet the premises of the Pauline assurance are found: Yahweh appears as He who is able to master the forces of evil and make them subserve the ends of His will, and even, at need, uses the fearful power of Sheol. Several centuries later, the herald of the Risen Christ, re-reading the declarations of the prophet of Israel in the light of Easter, discovers in them the proclamation of the Living God's decisive victory over the powers of death; the words of Hosea that once sounded like a death-knell in his contemporaries' ears, then become the prelude to a hymn of thanksgiving sung to the glory of God.

IN EZEKIEL

Ezek. xxxvii. 1-14: The Resurrection of Israel

a. Ezekiel xxxvii in Jewish and Christian tradition

From the anonymous Dura-Europos paintings down to the most recent works such as Claudel and Honegger's "Danse des Morts" the scene described in this chapter has been a favourite theme of art.[1]

The Jews, and afterwards the Christians, read an announcement of the resurrection of the dead in the last days into this passage from the prophet of the Exile; at that time, according to Ezekiel, the dead will come forth from their graves, and their bodies and souls will be reunited. For the Targum, this chapter more particularly foretells the resurrection of the Ten Northern Tribes and their reunion with the Kingdom of Judah.

The Fathers made frequent use of this vision of Ezekiel as evidence of the resurrection of the body, especially Justin Martyr (*Apol.* II. 87); Irenaeus (*Adv. haer.* v. 1); and Tertullian

---

[5] Am. IX. 2; Is. VII. 11; Ps. CXXXIX. 8, 12; cp. also pp. 52 ff. above.

[1] W. NEUSS, *Das Buch Ezechiel in Theologie und Kunst bis zu Ende des 12. Jhdts.*, Münster im W. 1912; for the Dura-Europos Paintings: DU MESNIL DU BUISSON, "Les peintures de Dura-Europe," in *Rev. bib.*, 1914, esp. p. 117; A. GRABAR, *R. h. r.*, 1941, pp. 148 ff. and *C. r. Ac. Inscr.*, 1941, p. 78; H. RIESENFELD, *The Resurrection in Ezekiel xxxvii and in the Dura-Europos Paintings*, Uppsala 1948.

(*De resurrectione carnis*, XXX), who had to refute the Gnostic opinion according to which Ezek. XXXVII referred only to the restoration of Israel, "*de terrestri restitutione Israelitum*," and not to personal resurrection.[2] Jewish and Christian faith alike found a message of hope in this passage of Scripture, and it was often put to liturgical use as well; the Jews read it at the Passover, and even as early as the time of Jerome it was used in all Christian churches on Holy Saturday, the Paschal eve or Vigil, when the catechumens were baptised, and sometimes, although more rarely, at offices for the dead.[3]

Thus tradition saw a prophecy of personal resurrection in this chapter, and found in it a proclamation of the ultimate victory of the Living God over death; yet a re-reading of the prophet's words would appear to show that Ezekiel had other interests; so to-day exegetes wonder whether the heretics with whom Tertullian contended did not understand his meaning better than their fiery antagonist.

b. *Vss. 1-10: Ezekiel's Vision* [4]

The Spirit of Yahweh takes possession of Ezekiel once again (XXXVII. 1) and brings him to a valley or plain, also mentioned in Ezek. III. 22 ff., and doubtless well known to the prophet. It is impossible to tell whether Ezekiel is actually there or is only experiencing an extraordinary vision; in any case, there,

---

[2] A. BERTHOLET, *comm. ad loc.*
[3] G. A. COOKE, *comm. ad loc.*
[4] L. GAUTIER, *La mission du prophète Ezéchiel*, Lausanne 1891, pp. 319-27; A. BERTHOLET, *K. H.-C. A. T.*, 1897; H. SCHMIDT, *Schr. A. T.*, 1915; A. BERTHOLET, *Andreas-Festschrift*, 1916, p. 35; J. HERRMANN, *Komm. A. T.*, 1924; O. PROCKSCH, *Rel. G. G.*, I (1927), col. 627; A. BERTHOLET, *Hb. A. T.*, 1936; G. A. COOKE, *I. C. C.*, 1936; H. BARDKTE, *Hesekiel*, Leipzig 1941; R. BRUNNER, *Ezechiel, Prophezei*, Zürich 1944; E. BRUSTON, *B. Cent.*, 1947; P. AUVRAY, "Ezéchiel," in *Témoins de Dieu*, Paris 1947; H. RIESENFELD, *The Resurrection in Ezekiel xxxvii and in the Dura-Europos Paintings*, Uppsala 1948; O. SCHILLING, *Der Jenseitsgedanke im A. T.*, Mainz 1951, pp. 90 ff., etc.; G. FOHRER, *Die Hauptprobleme des Buches Ezechiel*, Berlin 1952; J. STEINMANN, "Le prophète Ezéchiel et les débuts de l'exil," *Lectio divina*, Paris 1953; VON BAUDISSIN, *op. cit.* (above, p. 55, n. 5), pp. 416 ff.; NÖTSCHER, *Altorientalischer und Alttestamentlicher Auferstehungsglauben*, 1926, pp. 146 ff.; EICHRODT, *Theol. des A. T.*, VOL. III, pp. 154 f.

probably in the very place where the glory of the Living God was revealed to him, thousands of bones are scattered on the ground. The scene is thus entirely changed, and the believer who has gazed on the glory of the God of Israel and felt His ineffable power now finds the remains of his people, bleached under the scorching sun. Thus Ezek. I and XXXVII are complementary; "the two visions are articulated to each other . . .: the blazing of the supernatural beings is succeeded by the utter listlessness of the dead, reduced to their earthy elements." [5]

The "plain" is full of bones (XXXVII. 2). What follows shows that here we have not a burial-ground but a battle-field. It is to be noted that the bones are utterly dry. All life has long since disappeared, so that any return to existence seems impossible. But this is only going to make the miracle that is about to follow all the more marvellous. There is no question here, as there was in the case of the interventions of Elijah and Elisha,[6] of somehow warming corpses up again and recalling souls that are hovering beside them.

All hope of life seems gone, but (in vs. 3) Yahweh begins to speak: "Can these bones live?" It seems to be an idle question, because the answer is obviously "No": no-one in Israel has ever thought that absolutely dry bones can be restored to life. Yet the prophet is aware that he is in the presence of the Living God. His reply—"O Lord GOD, thou knowest"— voices his discomfiture in presence of the scene before his eyes, but at the same time his conviction that nothing is impossible to the God of Israel.[7] Yahweh alone knows what can become of these bones, for He alone can grant them life. Ezekiel should have said "No," but "he is dealing with God, and this qualifies his feelings. Here it is not a case of man and death face to face, but God and death. And God is not halted by death." [8]

At the same time the prophet's words bear witness to the

---

[5] STEINMANN, *op. cit.*, pp. 185 f., who adopts Bertholet's theory connecting III. 22 ff. with XXXVII. I.

[6] I Kings XVII. 17 ff.; II Kings IV. 34; cp. above, pp. 57 ff.; cp. also Acts XX. 9 ff., and, for the contrary position, Jn. XI.

[7] NÖTSCHER, *op. cit.* (above n. 4), p. 149, considers that Ezekiel knows that God is able to raise the dead but that he does not know whether God is willing to raise these particular dead men.

[8] H. BARDKTE, *comm. ad loc.*

fact that in the age of Ezekiel the possibility of a resurrection of the dead was not entertained in Israel; several centuries later, the attitude of Martha, the sister of Lazarus, will be very different (Jn. XI. 23 ff.)

The prophet's faith is soon put to the test (vss. 4 ff.) He has to speak to these lifeless bones, rebuke them, and command them to hear Yahweh's word. God explains nothing to His servant, He issues His order; the miracle will not be performed except through human mediation. "Without God we cannot, without us God will not" (St. Augustine). For Ezekiel obedience must precede understanding; like Abraham, he must believe in Him "who gives life to the dead and calls into existence the things that do not exist" (Rom. IV. 17).

"With the command to prophesy, the prophet receives the power of the Word of God." [9] Ezekiel is not merely the witness of the resurrection, he becomes its instrument. For this reason, later Judaism sometimes endows him with the power of raising the dead and likewise represents him as wielding a rod in the act of bringing the departed to life.[10] In one sense, this is a true tradition, for it is an historical fact that Ezekiel, by his message, aroused the exiles who were sunk in sin and despair, and by his ministry, prepared the way for the emergence of a new People of God.

Ezekiel prophesies and, while he is speaking, the power of the God of Israel is put forth (vss. 7 ff.); the process of revivification is effected in two stages: the bones begin to come together with a mighty noise, the earth trembles; the skeletons are clothed with sinews, flesh, and skin; the corpses thus refashioned still lack what is essential: the breath of God that alone makes a living man out of a dead (vs. 8), the Spirit of Yahweh, bestowed long before upon Adam (Gen. II. 7), is required by all living beings (Ps. CIV. 29-30).

Then (XXXVII. 9) Ezekiel receives the command to call upon the Spirit of God to hasten from the four points of the compass, and enter the corpses. The miracle is complete, the dead arise, and a great army stands up as in battle array before the prophet, who is now going to tell us the meaning of his vision himself.

[9] H. BARDKTE, *comm. ad loc.*
[10] Bab. Sanh. 92*b*; Eccl. R. III. 15, cp. RIESENFELD, *op. cit.*, pp. 28 ff.

c. Vss. 11-14: Meaning of Ezekiel's Vision

Ezekiel gives us the key to the scene that he has witnessed. The event that he has just described is the prediction or even the pledge of what Yahweh intends to do for His People; he is giving a firm assurance of the restoration of Israel, of its return to its land, and of the complete rebuilding of the Holy Nation.

Fundamental to the vision of the prophet is this word that is being repeated (XXXVII. 11) among the exiles: "Our bones are dried up, and our hope is lost; we are clean cut up." Now, "bone" is a metaphor for "strength", as J. Steinmann recalls.[11] Following upon the fall of Jerusalem in 586 B.C., the prophet's contemporaries have lost all heart, they feel themselves strengthless, like dry bones, they abandon themselves to despair. In CH. XXXVII, Ezekiel answers them by means of this vision, which is "built on a play on words" (J. Steinmann). Yahweh will restore life to His exhausted People; He who can perform a greater miracle can accomplish a smaller one; He who has power to revive bones that are as dry as dead wood will be able to bring about the renewal of Israel.

Thus the prophet's vision is a parable of the restoration of the Chosen People. The dead here are the living, Ezekiel's interlocutors themselves; they refuse to believe the prophet's prediction of salvation; overwhelmed by their misfortunes and sins, they see no end to their troubles, no prospect at all for their nation. The fall of the City of God has shattered their foolish hopes, the capture of the Temple by Nebuchadrezzar's troops has dispelled their illusions, and they fall all the deeper into despair because they have dreamed for so long of some miraculous deliverance. Just as, before the capture of the Holy City, Ezekiel contended with his contemporaries who would not believe in the judgment of Yahweh, so now he has to struggle against a resignation that is the reverse of real repentance. The exiles are repeating, "Our sins are upon us . . . how then can we live?" so constantly because they do not want to hear the call of their God: "I have no pleasure

---

[11] STEINMANN, *op. cit.*, p. 183, who bases himself on P. DHORME, *L'emploi métaphorique des noms de parties du corps en hébreu et en accadien*, Paris 1923, pp. 9 f.

in the death of the wicked, but that the wicked turn from his way and live; turn back, turn back from your evil ways . . ." (Ezek. xxxiii. 10 ff.)

If we grant that the Book of Ezekiel as we have it follows the chronological sequence of the utterance of his oracles, then it appears that, in spite of the prophecy of the "good shepherd" (Ezek. xxxiv), in spite of his proclamation of an entirely new life for the people of Israel (Ezek. xxxvi), Ezekiel's interlocutors continue to bewail themselves, they misdoubt Yahweh's intentions and do not think of turning to Him; the vision in Ezek. xxxvii is to put an end to their depression once and for all, and to enable them truly to set their faith in a God who calls men to life and not to death (Ezek. xxxiii. 10; cp. xviii. 23, 32 ff.) By persisting in their attitude of despair, the Israelites are forfeiting all chance of salvation, they are condemning themselves to exile and perdition.

Vss. 12 ff. may possibly be a later gloss by the prophet himself or by one of his disciples.[12] The picture is, in point of fact, somewhat different; the exiles are no longer likened to bones scattered about a battle-field but are represented as dead men buried in a graveyard. Yahweh promises to open their tombs, that is to say, to put an end to their exile; has not he who no longer lives in the Holy Land already come under the power of death? [13] These verses, as J. Steinmann observes, may have prepared the way for the literal interpretation of Ezek. xxxvii as a whole.

The prophet's gloss ends with the assertion that Yahweh can and will give new life to His People (vs. 14),[14] and is concluded by a solemn formula: "Then you shall know that I, the LORD, have spoken, and I have done it," [15] which confirms the will of the Living God to intervene on behalf of the exiles and gives them the assurance that the future depends on a divine word that is certainly going to be fulfilled. The lot of Israel is

[12] BERTHOLET, STEINMANN, *comm. ad loc.*

[13] Cp. above, p. 7.

[14] CH. xxxvi has given a detailed description of the nature of the new life offered to Israel by Yahweh.

[15] On the manifestation of Yahweh as the purpose of His interventions in history, cp. W. ZIMMERLI, *Erkenntnis Gottes nach dem Buche Ezechiel*, Zürich 1954.

bound up with Yahweh's purpose, which is to reveal His glory in creating a Holy Nation again; the honour of the God of Israel is the surest pledge of the resurrection of the Chosen People. Ezekiel's interlocutors must take fresh heart; the end pursued by their God is clear and His power is manifest: "You shall know that I am the LORD, when I open your graves, and raise you from my graves, O my people. And I will put my Spirit within you, and you shall live . . ." (vss. 13-14).

d. *Is the Resurrection of the Dry Bones a reality or a metaphor?*

The answer to this question seems hardly doubtful. The consensus of exegetical opinion is that this chapter is symbolical in character. Thus J. Hermann writes that "death and the grave are metaphors. . . . Ezekiel is fighting against the defeatism of the exiles, he believes in the impossible, and here the impossible is the restoration of his people." For A. Bertholet,[16] the vision is an allegory of the political renaissance of the nation. O. Procksch, however, considers that Ezek. XXXVII proclaims not only the return from the Exile, but also the resurrection of all Israel, including that of the Israelites who have died in exile. F. Nötscher supposes that the question of the resurrection of the dead must already have been a subject of controversy in the time of the prophet Ezekiel.[17]

With A. Bertholet,[18] we must above all bear in mind that the line of demarcation between reality and image is much less definite for an Israelite than for us. The latter is not opposed to the former; the transition from the one to the other is easy. Ezekiel's hearers doubtless understood that the prophet was predicting the end of the Exile to them, but the gripping description of the bleached bones standing erect again, through the operation of the Spirit of Yahweh, and forming once more a mighty army did not fail to strike their imagination. The question of a general resurrection was doubtless not raised before Ezek. XXXVII, but emerged after this passage was written,

[16] A. BERTHOLET, "Pre-Christian Belief in the Resurrection," *Am. J. Th.*, 1916, p. 27; cp. also VON BAUDISSIN, *op. cit.* (p. 55, n. 5), pp. 416 f.; GAUTIER, *op. cit.*, pp. 319 f., etc.

[17] O. PROCKSCH, *s.v.* "Auferstehung," in *Rel. G. G.*, VOL. I, col. 627; NÖTSCHER, *op. cit.*, pp. 148 f.

[18] BERTHOLET, in *Andreas-Festschrift*, 1916, p. 55.

O. Schilling observes:[19] and H. Schmidt justly concludes that with Ezek. xxxvii we are on the eve of the awakening of faith in the resurrection—on the eve, but no more; for this belief to become a reality in Judaism, many other influences will have to be exerted upon it.

Thus Ezekiel's motive in describing the vision he had had to his contemporaries is clear, but the vision itself, in virtue of its unusual nature, did not fail to have profound repercussions among the Chosen People.

e. *Provenance of Ezekiel's Vision*

Like, for example, A. Bertholet,[20] most critics connect the vision of the prophet of the Exile with the text of Hos. vi. i ff. In each of them we do, in point of fact, find themes common to both; in both, resurrection means the national revival of the People of Yahweh, is to be the work of the God of Israel, and concerns the nation as a whole and not individuals. Ezekiel found the idea of a possible renewal of life after death in the message of his eighth-century predecessor; in this respect, as in others, (cp. especially Ezek. xvi, xxiii, with Hos. i-iii) he was inspired by Hosea.

H. Riesenfeld shares the same opinion and goes even further; he thinks that the vision of Ezekiel, as well as the passage from the prophet Hosea, can be shown to be based on the myth of the god who dies and rises again annually, and on its concomitant ritual. According to the Scandinavian scholar, the symbolism employed by Ezekiel was in use considerably earlier than the sixth century; the belief in the resurrection dated from before the Exile and was derived from the New Year festival, whose central idea is the continuation or periodic regeneration of life.[21] Thus the idea of a new life had its origin in the ritual of the annual festival in which the king plays a principal part, symbolically representing the god of nature or of the nation. In particular, H. Riesenfeld thinks he finds certain traces of these sacral ceremonies in Ezek. xxxvii, especially in the reference to the battle-field on which the

---

[19] O. Schilling, *op. cit.* (above, n. 4), pp. 47 ff.

[20] In *Andreas-Festschrift*, p. 55.

[21] Riesenfeld, *op. cit.* (above, n. 1), pp. 5 ff.

bones are scattered. In his opinion, the source of this reference was not historical reminiscences but cultic traditions; in point of fact, one of the acts in the drama performed at the New Year festival is the combat which the king has to engage in with his enemies which represents the struggle of the creative forces with the powers of chaos.[22]

This thesis seems doubtful to us and its argument weak. Ezekiel does not seem to be inspired by the agricultural cults and the vision in CH. XXXVII has other sources. Though H. Riesenfeld lays stress on the allusion to the combat which used to take place during the New Year festival, a festival whose significance is still obscure, in spite of all the studies that have been devoted to it, especially by the Scandinavian theologians,[23] we think that it is beyond doubt that here the prophet is primarily remembering the countless corpses left on the field of battle by the Babylonian armies in their march on Jerusalem; perhaps he had looked with his own eyes upon the great piles of bodies at the approaches to the Holy City or by the sides of the roads taken by the fugitives and exiles. His imagination could not but have been struck by sights like these, for again and again he refers to these "unburied dead." [24]

Thus historical fact affords a perfect explanation of certain details in the prophet's vision and it is not at all necessary to have recourse to the oriental myth of the god who dies and rises again annually for their interpretation. H. Riesenfeld lays far too much stress on the cultic element in Ezek. XXXVII, and it seems to us that he has gone astray. Indeed it is advisable not to over-emphasise the resemblances that are postulated between this chapter and Hos. VI; it is by no means certain that Ezekiel is strictly dependent, here, on his predecessor; on the contrary his starting-point appears to be totally different. Hosea's contemporaries reveal that they conceive of the resurrection in the light of practices of heathen provenance, based on the phenomena of nature; Ezekiel, on the other hand,

---

[22] RIESENFELD, *op. cit.*, p. 20.
[23] Cp. also the reservations recently made by J. J. STAMM, in *Vet. test.*, 1954/1, pp. 29 ff.; and cp. below pp. 199 ff.
[24] Cp. esp. Ezek. XXVIII. 10, XXXI. 18, XXXII. 28, 32, etc.; cp. O. EISSFELDT, "Schwertserschlagene bei Hesekiel," *Studies in O.T. Prophecy*, 1950, pp. 73-81.

founds on the Yahwistic conception of the creation of man, as it
is set forth in Gen. II. 7. The prophet of the Exile, as he is
taught by the tradition of his people, considers that the creature
lives by the breath of Yahweh.[25] The foundation of the Vision
of the Dry Bones is ultimately in Ezekiel's faith in the creative
power of the Living God; what Yahweh has done before, He
is able to do again. He who brought men out of nothingness
can also restore life to their bones. Yahweh alone is the master
of life, and nothing can hinder Him from conferring it upon
whomsoever He will.

The ground of Ezekiel's proclamation of the resurrection of
the bodies, even after they have been utterly decomposed under
the sun, is the revelation of Yahweh in Israel.

f. Conclusion

Ezekiel is informing the captives of their return to their land
and the rebirth of Israel, of which the Vision of the Dry Bones
is the pledge; for the prophet, as for the contemporaries of
Hosea, resurrection is the symbol of national restoration.

The prophet is not concerned with the resurrection of the
dead as such, but there is no doubt that the symbolism that
he employs raised among the Jews the question of renewal of
life for the departed, and it is in this sense that both Jewish and
Christian tradition re-read this chapter.

Ezekiel's confidence is founded on the sovereign power of
the God of Israel, a power that was made especially manifest
when He created man. He dares to expect the renewal of his
people because he believes in Yahweh as He has revealed Himself to him and to Israel. The tradition of his people and his
own personal experience alike enable him to assert that the
Living God is capable of repeating the miracle of creation on
behalf of His own.

Though Ezek. XXXVII and Hos. VI bear witness to one and
the same expectation of the restoration of Israel, the starting-
point of the Prophet of the Exile is very different from that of
Hosea's interlocutors; he founds his hope on the revelation of
Yahweh to His People, they found theirs on the feelings that
the phenomena of nature awaken within them.

[25] Gen. II. 7; Ps. CIV. 29 f.; Job XXXIV. 14 f.; Ecclesiastes XII. 9.

IN ISAIAH

Is. LIII. 10*b* ff.: The Vindication of the Servant of Yahweh

a. General Observations

Here we do not intend nor do we pretend to be able to answer all the questions that are raised by the Servant Songs,[1] to which B. Duhm particularly drew the attention of the critics in 1892. We are not even going to embark on the study of the whole body of problems that is raised by the last of these songs: Is. LII. 13-LIII. 12, beyond a doubt one of the finest and most moving passages in the Old Testament, but also one of the most difficult, which was to have so great a significance for the New Testament writers.[2]

There may be something providential in the fact that not-withstanding the innumerable studies of the Servant of Yahweh that have been published in the last fifty years, as witness the works of A. Lods, C. R. North, H. H. Rowley, and W. Zimmerli,[3] the question put long ago to Philip by the Ethiopian eunuch: "About whom, pray, does the prophet say this, about himself or about someone else?" (Acts VIII. 34) has never received an absolutely satisfactory answer from the Old Testament specialists. The words spoken by the anonymous prophet of the Exile were not, in fact, to assume their full significance until almost five centuries later, after the death and resurrection of Jesus of Nazareth; thus, in some sense, the key to the mystery of the Servant of Yahweh is to be found outwith the Old Covenant message in the Gospel of Jesus Christ.

But for the very sake of understanding the work of Christ, it is profitable to enter as far as is possible into the mind of the man who foretold His extraordinary destiny; the incessant research of the Old Testament exegetes is therefore amply justified, even although, in making the role of the Servant

---

[1] Is. XLII. 1 ff., XLIX. 1 ff., L. 4 ff., LII. 13 ff.

[2] J. JEREMIAS, s.v. παῖς θεοῦ, in KITTEL, VOL. V (1952), pp. 676-713.

[3] A. LODS, *Histoire de la littérature hébraïque et juive*, Paris 1950; C. R. NORTH, *The Suffering Servant in Deutero-Isaiah, an Historical and Critical Study*, Oxford 1950; H. H. ROWLEY, "The Servant of the Lord in the Light of Three Decades of Criticism," and "The Suffering Servant and the Davidic Messiah," in *The Servant of the Lord, and other Essays on the O.T.*, London 1952; W. ZIMMERLI, s.v. παῖς θεοῦ in KITTEL, VOL. V, 1952, pp. 653-76.

entirely His own, Jesus fulfilled a mission of even greater scope than Deutero-Isaiah had imagined.

Our own immediate concern is to find out whether and in what sense a part of the fourth Song (Is. LIII. 10*b*-12) bears witness to a victory over death and, in particular, proclaims the resurrection of the Servant. But, to be in a position to estimate the scope of this text, we have to elucidate another problem, namely, whether the Servant represents a group or an individual.

Deutero-Isaiah usually calls the People of Israel "the Servant of Yahweh" [4] (Is. XLI. 8*b*, XLIII. 10, XLIV. 1, etc.), but it is not certain whether, in the four Songs, this title necessarily corresponds to the Israelite nation as such; exegetical opinion is distinctly divided on this matter; a survey of the works of C. R. North or H. H. Rowley is sufficient to carry conviction of this. Some consider that the Servant can only be the Chosen People itself, or a group of the faithful, a holy or even ideal community; others, with equally cogent arguments, hold the opinion that by this term Deutero-Isaiah is designating an individual person belonging either to the past (*e.g.*, Moses, Jeremiah, Josiah, or still others), or to the present (*e.g.*, Deutero-Isaiah himself), or to the future (*e.g.*, the Messiah). It is not precluded that the prophet's thought may have developed, and that his understanding of the Servant's personality, which plays such an important part in his message, may have continued to become more clearly defined, as A. Causse puts it: "At the outset, the Servant represents the exiled nation, then the Yahwistic community, the minority of the '*anavim*'. In the end he is in fact a personal hero, the mysterious saviour, a hero comparable with the Messiah." [5] H. H. Rowley, for his part, considers that the prophet doubtless was hard put to it to define with precision just what he intended by the title he was employing, for he "was carried by the dynamic of a thought which possessed him to the implications of his initial thought, which was more pregnant than he had realised." [6]

The question appears to have been carried a stage further

---

[4] On the theme of the Servant in the Old Testament, cp. C. LINDHAGEN, *The Servant Motif in the O. T.*, Uppsala 1950.

[5] A. CAUSSE, *Israël et la vision de l'humanité*, Strasbourg 1924, p. 54.

[6] H. H. ROWLEY, *op. cit.*, p. 52.

by the works of Wheeler Robinson and O. Eissfeldt.[7] Both of them, following independent lines, based themselves on the writings of Lévy-Bruhl and Durkheim on primitive psychology. It must in fact be realised that the Hebrews, like primitive peoples in general, make no antithesis between the individual and the group, for them the one does not exist apart from the other; where we distinguish and would note distinctions and emphasise differences, the Semites associate, mark resemblances, and tend to confuse.[8]

Thus the Israelite and Israel are intimately bound together, they participate in the same life; the former gives expression to the latter, the second is manifested by means of the first.[9] Thus the Servant of Yahweh is neither an individual nor a group; to postulate such an antithesis is to be foreign to the Old Testament mode of thought; he is what Wheeler Robinson calls a "corporate personality," that is to say, a being incorporating a whole group, embodying and expressing it. The Servant represents and actualises the totality of the servants of Yahweh, in time and in space, as W. Vischer suggests.[10] It must be admitted that there is a certain "oscillation" [11] in Hebrew speech between the individualistic sense and the collective, but this "does not rest on an antithesis between the individual and the group, but on an identification of the individual with the group which he represents. . . . In the light of this conception [of corporate personality] the Servant can be both the prophet himself as representative of the nation, and the nation, whose proper mission is actually being fulfilled only by the

---

[7] H. WHEELER ROBINSON, "The Hebrew Conception of Corporate Personality," in *Wesen und Werden des A. T.*, ed. J. Hempel, 1936, pp. 49-62 ; O. EISSFELDT, *Der Gottesknecht bei Deuterojesaja*, 1933.

[8] C. TRESMONTANT, *Essai sur la pensée hebraïque*, Paris 1953; T. BOMANN, *Das hebräische Denken im Vergleich mit dem Griechischen*, Göttingen 1952; R. MARTIN-ACHARD, "La mentalité hébraïque " in "Pour comprendre l'A. T.," *Le Semeur*, Paris 1954.

[9] Cp. the example given by PEDERSEN, *op. cit.* (above p. 2, n. 2), VOL. I-II, 1926, pp. 109 f., of the Moabitess and the people of Moab.

[10] W. VISCHER, "Der Gottesknecht, ein Beitrag zur Auslegung von Jesaja, XL-LV," in *Jahrbuch der theologischen Schule Bethel*, Bethel 1930.

[11] Similarly, ROWLEY, *op. cit.*, pp. 36 f., speaks about "fluidity" and exemplifies what he means by taking as an illustration the word "church," which we use in speaking of different realities. Its "meanings are all clearly distinguished, yet they are all connected with one another."

prophet and that group of followers who may share his views." [12]

It therefore seems to us that in the matter of the Songs of Deutero-Isaiah it is erroneous to make an absolute antithesis between the individualistic and the collective interpretation: the Servant of Yahweh has reality only because he is performing the task entrusted by the Living God to Israel, His Servant, and, on the other hand, the People of the Living God is only His Servant in the measure that one or several of its members is realising the work that Yahweh expects of it. Behind the figure of the Servant, Deutero-Isaiah seems to see *both* an individual and a community; from time to time the one or the other appears in the foreground, but they are never mutually exclusive.

It seems to us that, in the particular case of Is. LIII, the Servant stricken for the sins of the People of Yahweh (vs. 8), whose body is wrongfully laid with the wicked (vs. 9), and who suffers, not for his own transgressions, but for those of his fellows (vss. 4 ff.), must be, in the eyes of the prophet, not Israel itself, but an Israelite who surrenders himself to death for the salvation of his brethren (vss. 10 ff.) The last Servant Song thus contemplated an individual, whose strange destiny, determined by his people, reacts in its turn on the whole of Israel, and, through it, on all the world.[13]

b. *Is. lii. 13-liii. 12: Fourth Song of the Servant of Yahweh*

Before entering upon the particular question of the ultimate lot of the Servant in a special study of Is. LIII. 10*b*-12, let us briefly recall the content and meaning of this fourth and final Song which, according to P. Auvray and J. Steinmann, comes to us in the form of a dialogue, although it is not always possible "to ascertain where the interlocutory alternations occur." [14] Nevertheless we recognise two main elements in

---

[12] WHEELER ROBINSON, *op. cit.*, pp. 58 ff.

[13] ROWLEY, *op. cit.*, pp. 51 ff.; "We may therefore reasonably ask whether there is not some development in his thought of the mission of the Servant, and whether what began as a personification did not become a person . . . the fourth song is, in my opinion, unmistakably individual."

[14] AUVRAY, STEINMANN *comm. ad loc.*

the Song, which is a prophecy concerning the Servant's ultimate lot, and includes a description of his past sufferings. The greater part consists of a sort of lamentation, penitential psalm or even dirge (W. Rudolph, H. Gressmann),[15] and this is answered by two oracles of Yahweh in approval of His Servant.

The object of this last Song, as S. Mowinckel has observed, is to explain what happened to the Servant; primarily, it provides a revelation, a *"kerygma,"* the purpose of which is the complete elucidation of his strange lot; the Song tells at length of the troubles of the man whom Yahweh, to show that he is doing His work, solemnly and tenderly calls "my Servant" (Is. LII. 13, LIII. 11); above all, it lays stress on the meaning of his dreadful destiny.

Thus the Chosen of Yahweh, through universal enmity and derision, in the midst of blows and clamour, silently takes his way towards martyrdom. Even his death, in spite of its disgrace, does not make an end to his humiliation; his dead body—crowning dishonour—is numbered with the ungodly and the rich; thus the sin of men follows him even to the grave. In striking fashion, the Servant's own contemporaries set forth his many sufferings, of which it is neither possible nor advisable to give a detailed account. All the grief of men seems to have fallen upon him, all physical and spiritual distress is concentrated here.[16]

Upon this Servant with (LIII. 2-3) the pitiful or even repulsive countenance fate fastens in fury; he is sick (vss. 3, 10), perhaps leprous, afflicted with that disease which excites revulsion and is a token of the divine reprobation; [17] he is arrested, beaten, and cast into prison (vss. 5, 7-8); he is judged and

---

[15] I. ENGNELL, "The 'Ebed Yahweh Songs and the Suffering Messiah,"' *B. J. R. L.* XXXI (1948).

[16] A more detailed study would bring out the whole wealth of the expression and imagery used here by Deutero-Isaiah; the motif of the Wilderness and that of the Tree of Life, the themes of the Lost Sheep and the Shorn Lamb, etc., are particularly noticeable; the most characteristic of the older traditions of the Chosen People reappear in the message of the prophet of the Exile.

[17] Vs. 4, נָגוּעַ, *nāgûaʻ*, in the sense of "struck a blow" dealt by the hand of God; this is sometimes used as an expression for leprosy (Lev. XIII. 22, 45; Num. XII. 9 f.; II Kings XV. 5; Job XIX. 17 ff., XXX. 10; etc.

condemned to death (vss. 8-9); all men despise and forsake him (vs. 3).

The Servant, stricken in body and soul, put to shame, misunderstood and betrayed, is seen as typical of the "poor" in the scriptural and especially post-Exilic sense of the word.[18]

But these sufferings have a meaning, they are "vicarious," that is to say, the Servant makes payment for other men, his death atones for the transgressions others have committed; those who sing the lament are acknowledging, in so doing, their own responsibility; they come to realise their solidarity with him whom they have scorned and put to death and understand at last that he was stricken in their stead and for their sakes. "Surely he has borne our griefs and carried our sorrows . . . he was wounded for our transgressions, he was bruised for our iniquities; upon him was the chastisement that made us whole" (LIII. 4, 5). The Servant of the Living God dies that a multitude of men may have life; this condemned man gives his righteousness to the guilty (LIII. 10, 11, 12).

Here we are confronted by that "legal mysticism" which plays a capital part in the Old Testament, and which lies at the heart of the Gospel; [19] "its roots are deeply entwined in the bygone splendours of the ancient Temple liturgy, and, beyond these, in the most primitive reflexes of the religious soul." [20]   The sin-offering, in which a beast is sacrificed instead of the guilty (cp. especially Lev. v. 5-26, VII. 1 ff., etc.) is replaced by the free gift of him who "poured out his soul to death, and was numbered with the transgressors; yet he bore the sin of many, and made intercession for the transgressors" (Is. LIII. 12).

But it was only belatedly that the Servant's contemporaries discovered the meaning of his death. Yahweh Himself had to intervene on his behalf and clothe him with glory. Because the Living God has exalted the victim, his executioners intone their penitential psalm, kings bow the knee, and the humble

---

[18] Cp. among other recent studies, that by A. GELIN, *Les pauvres de Jahve*, Paris 1953.

[19] Cp. among other works: P. VOLZ, "Jesaja LIII" in *Budde Festschrift*, Beihefte z. *Z. alttest. W.*, 1930; T. PREISS, "Le mystère du Fils de l'Homme," *La vie en Christ*, Neuchâtel-Paris 1952, pp. 74 ff.

[20] DOM CHARLIER, "Le Serviteur glorifié," in *B. v. c.*, 1 (1953), p. 68.

rejoice before him; the wondering world is taught to see the work of the God of Israel in the humiliation and glory of His Chosen (LII. 14b-LIII. 1). Thus the vindication of the Servant reveals the plan that Yahweh has formed and performed for the salvation of men.

c. Is.lii. 13 ff. and liii. 10b-12:
Vindication of the Servant of Yahweh

The last of the Servant Songs begins with an assertion, in oracular form, of the heart of the matter: the coming triumph and glory of Yahweh's Chosen, to the confusion of those who saw him humiliated and oppressed (LIII. 13 ff.) It opens with a solemn declaration by Yahweh Himself, "Behold, my servant shall prosper," and explains this term, which has given rise to much discussion, by means of the verbs that follow, which foretell the exaltation and greatness of him whom the God of Israel has chosen.[21] Thereafter vss. 13-15 develop the contrast between the Servant's present miserable but passing plight and his final state, which will be kingly.

The Song ends with another oracle recapitulating what is essential in the assertions of the first verses. Deutero-Isaiah tells of the Servant's exaltation and explains the reasons for his extraordinary destiny; he unveils the principal actor in the

---

[21] In point of fact, the LXX translated the expression יַשְׂכִּיל, yaśkîl, as συνήσει, i.e. "He will become prudent," which is a fairly literal rendering of a verb whose primary meaning is "to behave wisely," "to understand". The connexion between wisdom in all its aspects—cleverness, acumen, understanding (practical rather than intellectual), not excluding the fear of God—and prosperity is one of the favourite themes of Wisdom thought in Israel; but here the stress must be laid on the success which is the consequence of wisdom, and the glory which is its outcome. ENGNELL, op. cit., pp. 24 f., connects this word with מַשְׂכִּיל, maśkîl, which is the title of several psalms which can be nothing else than Enthronement Psalms. Thus he translates יַשְׂכִּיל, yaśkîl, as "he will be exalted" or "he will reign," the term bringing the Servant's triumph to mind. With E. Kissane, it must be observed that this verb is also employed in the sense of "to gain a success " "to prosper," with reference to David (1 Sam. XVIII. 5) and to the Messiah (Jer. XXIII. 5); thus it proclaims the glorious prospects of him who at the first was an offence to men. For L. KÖHLER, K.-B., p. 922, the Servant is going to behave intelligently, that is to say, devoutly.

drama that has just been enacted; this can be none other than
Yahweh Himself, whom it pleased to bruise His Servant to set
him thereafter above every monarch on earth (LIII. 10-12):

> 10 Yet it was the will of the LORD to bruise him
>   *and wound him;*
>   When he makes himself an offering for sin,
>   he shall see his offspring, he shall
>   prolong his days;
>   the will of the LORD shall prosper in his hand;
> 11 *after the trials of his life he shall see the light*
>   and be satisfied;
>   by his knowledge shall [the righteous one] my
>   servant
>   make many to be accounted righteous;
>   and he shall bear their iniquities.
>
> 12 *Therefore I will give him many as his portion,*
>   *and he shall take the multitudes as his spoil,*
>   because he poured out his soul to death,
>   and was numbered with the transgressors;
>   yet he bore the *sins* of many,
>   and made intercession for the transgressors.[22]

[22] In addition to the above-mentioned works by A. LODS, H. H. ROWLEY,
and esp. C. R. NORTH, *The Suffering Servant in Deutero-Isaiah*, London 1948,
and W. ZIMMERLI, s.v. παῖς θεοῦ, in KITTEL, VOL. V, 1952, pp. 653-76,
which give an almost exhaustive bibliography on the question of the
Servant songs, we may note: K. MARTI, *K. H.-C. A. T.*, 1900; A. HALLER
Schr. A. T., 1914; W. RUDOLPH, "Der exilische Messias," in *Z. alttest. W.*,
1925, pp. 90-114; R. KITTEL, *Geschichte des Volkes Israel*, Stuttgart 1927,
VOL. III, pp. 248 ff.; H. GRESSMANN, *Der Messias*, Göttingen 1929, pp. 287-
339; W. VISCHER, "Der Gottesknecht, ein Beitrag zur Auslegung von
Jesaja xl-lv," *Jahrbuch der theologischen Schule Bethel*, Bethel 1930; P. VOLZ,
Jesaja II, übersetzt und erklärt, Leipzig 1932; J. BEGRICH, *Studien z. Deutero-
jesaja*, Beitr. z. Wiss. vom A. N. T., 1938; E. KISSANE, *The Book of Isaiah*, VOL. II,
Dublin 1943; P. HUMBERT, *B. Cent.*, 1947; A. BENTZEN, *Messias, Moses
redivivus, Menschensohn*, Basle 1948 (Eng. trans., *King and Messiah*, London
1955); I. ENGNELL, "The 'Ebed Yahweh Songs and the Suffering Messiah,"
B. J. R. L., XXXI (1948); O. EISSFELDT, *Variae lectiones rotulorum manu scrip-
torum anno 1947*, Supplement to *B. Heb.*, Stuttgart 1951; P. AUVRAY,
J. STEINMANN, "Isaïe," *B. Jerus.*, 1951; C. R. NORTH, *Isaiah XL-LV* (The
Torch Bible Commentaries), 1952; DOM CHARLIER, "Isaïe lii. 13-liii. 12,"
B. v. c., 1 (1953); L. G. RIGNELL, "Isaiah liii. 13-liii. 12," in *Vet. test.*,
1953/3, pp. 89-92; F. NÖTSCHER, *Altorientalischer und alttestamentlicher Aufer-
stehungsglauben*, pp. 150 ff.; EICHRODT, *Theol. des A. T.*, VOL. III, pp. 155 f., etc.

The general sense of this passage is clear, it foretells the complete vindication of the Servant; but in seeking to define Deutero-Isaiah's thought with precision exegetes encounter many difficulties in its details, and the corrupt state of the text makes their task no easier.[23]

[23] In vs. 10, וַיְחַלְּלֵהוּ, *wyḥllhu,* "and to wound him," should be read with D.S. (Is.), and not הֶחֱלִי, *heḥelî* (M.T.), which, on the basis of the versions, is generally interpreted as "sickness," בְּחֳלִי, *boḥᵒlî,* "with sickness." Thus P. Humbert, following the Vulgate, translates: "But it pleased Yahweh to crush him with sickness." The LXX has καθαρίσαι, which gives: "It pleased the Lord to cleanse him of his sickness." The *posuerit* in the Latin version suggests reading יָשִׂים, *yāśîm,* "he shall make," instead of תָּשִׂים, *tāśîm,* "thou shalt make."

אָשָׁם, *'āšām,* a technical term of the Levitical ritual, means either "transgression" or "sin-offering" (Lev. v. 14-vi. 7). חָפֵץ, *ḥāpēṣ,* means "plan," "purpose" (cp. Is. XLIV. 28, XLVI. 10, etc.). With other commentators, P. Volz, E. Kissane, and C. R. North interpret vs. 10*b* as follows: "He will see a posterity that will lengthen its days." Dom Charlier translates the phrase as: "He will see a seed giving length to his days."

In vs. 11, מֵעֲמַל, *mē'ᵃmal,* "because [or 'after'] the trials of . . .," is generally rendered as: "because of his toil, because of his trouble. . . ." The preposition מִן, *min,* "from out of," here "because" or "after," may also have a temporal sense. C. R. North and P. Humbert translate "after the troubles endured by his soul." The text of the LXX is supported by the Qumrân manuscripts, and therefore אוֹר, *'ôr,* "light," must be read after יִרְאֶה, *yir'eh,* "he shall see," and וְ, *wᵉ,* "and," added to יִשְׂבָּע, *yiśbā',* "he shall be satisfied." Seeing the light is equivalent to living. The Servant is going to enjoy fulness of life, salvation, and blessing. P. Humbert proposes: "He will enjoy (this sight) in its fruition." With the LXX, C. R. North connects בְּדַעְתּוֹ, *bᵉda'tô,* "by his knowledge," with what precedes it and translates "He will be satisfied with his knowledge"; but בְּדַעְתּוֹ, *bᵉda'tô,* that is to say, "by his knowledge," is confirmed by D.S. (Is.) and is preferably to be read along with what follows it. P. Humbert proposes to replace בְּדַעְתּוֹ, *bᵉda'tô,* by בְּרָעָתוּ, *bᵉrā'ātû,* that is to say, by "his sufferings." The word צַדִּיק, *ṣaddîq,* "righteous," seems to serve no useful purpose.

In vs. 12, עֲצוּמִים, *ᵃṣûmîm,* generally "powerful," is here used as a synonym for רַבִּים, *rabbîm,* "many" (cp. Prov. VII. 26). With C. R. North, it must be understood that the multitudes are the trophies of the Servant. In general, commentators hold that the Servant is going to share his conquests with the great. D.S. (Is.) reads the plural חֲטָאֵי־רַבִּים, *ḥᵃṭā'ê-rabbîm,* "sins of many," for M.T. singular חֵטְא־רַבִּים, *ḥēṭ'-rabbîm,* "sin of many."

These verses emphasise Yahweh's capital part in the peculiar destiny of the Servant. In his abasement and in his exaltation alike God is always at work, His good pleasure is manifest, and His purpose is being fulfilled. The experiences of the Chosen of Yahweh are not to be explained as either fate or chance; his heroism and his stoicism are irrelevant here; the Servant has been the faithful executor of an interest that concerns the God of Israel. The purpose of God comprehends two moments, a time of suffering and a time of glory, and His Chosen is intimately connected with both (vs. 10). The action of the God of Israel does not end with His Servant's atoning death; it is fulfilled in his triumph; moreover, these verses lay stress on the Servant's paradoxical position: he dies prematurely, yet prolongs his days; he is forsaken by all men and still has his offspring; everything in his pitiful life is a failure and nevertheless the work of Yahweh is established in his hands.

Vs. 10 shows God's intention of answering the Servant's detractors; the blessings with which He satisfies him correspond to his sorrows. The marks of the divine reprobation are, as we have seen, premature death, entire absence of offspring, a meaningless existence which leads nowhere; now Yahweh bestows a posterity on His Chosen, He promises to prolong his days and makes him a partner in his plan. In some sense these gifts are a finding of *nolle prosequi* in favour of the Servant, they attest his innocence and justify him in the eyes of his contemporaries who have considered him guilty and accursed of his God.

Vs. 11 contemplates the new life, radiant and full, with which, in recompense for his former sufferings, the Servant is going to to be satisfied. It indicates the consequence of his martyrdom. Yahweh's Chosen has taken the penalty of others upon himself; because he has known the Living God, that is to say, because he has loved and served Him, he has thereby justified many men, or, to state it in other words, he has reconciled them to God, he has restored the fellowship that ought to unite them to Yahweh.[24] It is for this reason that Deutero-Isaiah mentions, along with the Servant, the group of the רַבִּים, *rabbîm*, the

---

[24] On Justification, cp. especially G. QUELL, G. SCHRENK, s.vv. δίκη, δίκαιος, etc., KITTEL, VOL. II, pp. 176 ff.

"many,"—keyword in the concept of substitution—[25] now united to him from whom formerly all fled, henceforth one body with him.

Finally, vs. 12 recapitulates and develops the same ideas. The Servant's reward will be to share the spoil with the great, or, better still, to receive as his portion the multitude of those for whom he has sacrificed himself. The metaphor of the division of the fruits of victory recalls a Messianic text (Is. ix. 3); here the glory of the Chosen of the Living God consists in keeping for and with himself the sinners with whom he has made himself one.

Thus the Song ends by recalling the work of the Servant; it clearly defines the meaning of his death and enumerates the blessings with which Yahweh will satisfy him and the shining prospects opened up to him by his obedience. The God of Israel, having accomplished His purpose through the humiliation of His Chosen, now raises him to supreme honour.

Thus the meaning of the conclusion of the fourth Servant Song is clear; the martyr will be vindicated, his reward will be great, and his glory commensurate with the shame that he has borne.

The difficulties arise as soon as we ask how Deutero-Isaiah conceived of this vindication and in what sense we are to understand such expressions as "he shall see his offspring, he shall prolong his days, . . . he shall see the light, he shall divide the spoil with the strong . . ." (vss. 10, 11, 12).

The question is relatively simple if, with many exegetes, including A. Lods, P. Humbert, and still others, mentioned by H. H. Rowley,[26] we consider that the Servant represents the actual Israel or at least a spiritual group within the Chosen People. Is. liii then proclaims that the nation chosen by Yahweh, which is now oppressed and despised, and apparently rejected by its own God, is in reality suffering for the heathen or for the unfaithful Israelites; the day is coming when it will be restored and rewarded by Yahweh. The powers of the earth have wrongly supposed that Israel is fading away; the work of

---

[25] P. Volz, *comm. ad loc.*, observes that it occurs several times in this chapter (lii. 15, liii. 11, 12a, b; and also in Mk. x. 45; Rom. v. 19).

[26] Rowley, *op. cit.* (above, p. 103, n. 3), pp. 33 ff.

the Living God is being accomplished through it, its very decline is working out the salvation of the nations; Israel is proceeding through humiliation to glory, and its final triumph will confound all the world.

Thus, on this interpretation, the last Servant Song informs the martyr People of the positive meaning of its sufferings, the redemptive value of its troubles and the certainty of vindication; there is, properly speaking, no question of death in this passage, nor of victory over it; like the contemporaries of Hosea and the prophet Ezekiel, Deutero-Isaiah is only thinking about the abasement of his people and its future restoration. Thus Is. LIII. 10 ff. gives us no definite information about belief in the resurrection in Exilic times.

The problem becomes complicated if we hold, with other exegetes,[27] that the Servant is an individual. A whole section of the poem in fact speaks of his death; it is erroneous to claim that only his suffering is described here.[28]

The person about whom Deutero-Isaiah is speaking to us here is not only humiliated and persecuted, his death is beyond doubt (vss. 8, 10, 12), and his burial is no mere metaphor (vs. 9). Deutero-Isaiah can only be speaking about an actual sacrifice; the information in vs. 10 is utterly meaningless if it is merely symbolical.

But at the beginning of the Song and especially at its end, the writer envisages a totally different situation. The Servant is not in the grave, he is alive; no longer is he condemned to lead a sort of "infra-human" existence, as Dom Charlier expresses it,[29] but rather his "super-human" dignity makes itself manifest to the wondering world.

This reversal implies a special event, which, it is thought, cannot be anything but the resurrection of the Servant. Yahweh restores life to the martyr, so that he may see the light and know abundance and glory. "God Himself brings him out of Sheol," writes Dom Charlier.[30] But it must be realised that there is no explicit reference to the resurrection in these verses: "the resurrection of the Servant of Yahweh is nowhere

---

[27] ROWLEY, *op. cit.*, pp. 3 ff.
[28] E. KÖNIG, *comm. ad loc.*
[29] CHARLIER, *op. cit.*, p. 74.
[30] CHARLIER, *op. cit.*, p. 73.

proclaimed *verbis expressis*," W. Eichrodt justly declares,[31] and for this reason P. Humbert considers "it would be strange if a viewpoint so novel at the time had been expressed in such an inexplicit fashion." [32]

Moreover, some exegetes hold that we must not speak of the resurrection of the Servant; according to E. Kissane,[33] Yahweh was only telling him about his offspring; this was to prolong its days and finally make its name prevail. The glory of a descendant of the Servant was to be tantamount to a sort of requital for him. Deutero-Isaiah was predicting the post-humous victory of the Chosen of Yahweh in the ultimate success of the cause he had vainly maintained.

Among the commentators who consider that the Servant will actually return to life, some think that he is going to come back to earth and, like Job, grow old, blessed with much possession and many children (Job XLII. 16*b*) and make his presence felt in this world, like some David, among the great of the earth; others understand the expressions in vss. 10*b*-12 figuratively and speak of his spiritual exaltation, of his trans-lation into the Beyond, into a richer and fuller reality than earthly life. B. Duhm thinks he is able to find grounds for asserting that the Servant's spirit, if not his body, would be translated to Heaven,[34] and Dom Charlier, for his part, observes that the verb לָקַח, *lāqaḥ*, "to receive, take," (לֻקַּח, *luqqēḥ*, "to be received, taken"), particularly employed in connexion with the "assumptions" of Enoch and Elijah, may here have the sense of "transport" with the twofold implication of "to cause to die" and "to glorify in God." [35]

[31] EICHRODT, *Theol. des A. T.*, VOL. III, p. 156; according to W. RUDOLPH, *op. cit.* (above, n. 22), p. 930, הֶחֱלִי, *heḥᵉlî*, "sickness," should be emended to a *piel* or *hiphil* form of חָיָה, *ḥāyâ*, "to live," which would then give something like כְּדַכְּאוֹ כְחַיֹּתוֹ, *kᵉdakkᵉ'ô kᵉḥayyôtô*, meaning "since it pleased Yahweh to bruise him, it will please Him to restore him to life." In any case, W. Rudolph's view is that the resurrection is implied in vss. 10 ff. We do not think that such a dogmatic position is tenable.

[32] P. HUMBERT, *B. Cent., comm. ad loc.*

[33] E. KISSANE, *comm. ad loc.*; P. VOLZ, *comm. ad loc.*, asks whether it may not be a question simply of spiritual posterity. [34] B. DUHM, *comm. ad loc.*

[35] CHARLIER, *op. cit.*, p. 70, adduces in support of his position the evident ambiguity of the verb ὑψόω "I lift up from the earth," in John III. 14, VIII. 28, XII. 32 ff.

In the final analysis, all these hypotheses are weak enough, they testify to the specialists' difficulties; doubtless it must be admitted, with C. R. North,[36] that in Deutero-Isaiah's time the idea of resurrection was far too vague to be employed by the prophet. It was only later that it was to be defined with precision and ultimately accepted by part of the People of God. If the prophet's contemporaries had been in the habit of speaking about life after death, it is probable that Deutero-Isaiah would have made explicit reference to the resurrection in this passage; but on the contrary we have the impression that he is feeling his way; he senses that the Servant ought to escape death; so he asserts it without being able to explain the modality of an event that is beyond his understanding. Deutero-Isaiah is sure of Yahweh's miraculous intervention on behalf of His Chosen; he cannot say more; he is unaware of how and in what form the Living God is going to rescue him from the dominion of death.

It is important to emphasise that the writer of the Servant Songs is not primarily concerned with relating the Servant's triumph over death; he is foretelling his vindication. His principal interest is not the problem of life after death, but that of the fulfilment of the divine plan in the unique destiny of Yahweh's Chosen who by his voluntary self-sacrifice brings into being new relationships between God, His People, and the world. The final triumph of the Servant is to reveal the meaning of his martyrdom, and therefore, quite as much as his death, it serves the purposes of Yahweh. At the core of Deutero-Isaiah's thought we find, not the question of pro-longation of life, but that of the righteousness which must determine Yahweh's relationships with His own; it is only incidentally, and in connexion with the latter question, that Deutero-Isaiah is led to enter upon the former. In the eyes of the men of the Old Testament, the quest for righteousness is more fundamental than the need of overcoming death; they are concerned not merely with living, but with living before God, that is to say, in relationship with Him. The question of everlasting life is secondary in comparison with that of the situation of the creature in face of the Creator.

---

[36] NORTH, *Isaiah, XL-LV* (The Torch Bible Commentaries), pp. 138 ff.

Moreover, Deutero-Isaiah does not lay stress on the manner in which the Servant, in spite of his martyrdom, is going to experience the divine benediction; perhaps he was unable to put the resurrection of Yahweh's Chosen into words, perhaps he had not even given it a thought. After all, it matters little to him how the Servant is to be rescued from ignominy, so long as his vindication is certain, his reward sure, and his victory manifest.

More than this must not be read into the prophet's words, and we cannot say with certainty whether the writer of the fourth Song believed in the resurrection of the Servant.

Exegetes, however, lay stress on the fact that the proclamation of a victory over death—how gained, we cannot tell—is here seen as bound up with a preoccupation with righteousness. It is in His concern for justice that Yahweh promises His Servant a glorious future. Whatever form it may take, the new life proclaimed to Yahweh's Servant is the fruit and wages of his labours, the reward of his obedience. It is for this reason that F. Nötscher, among others, declares: "For the first time resurrection is connected with retribution." [37]

Doubtless it is essential to emphasise this relationship, which seems to be established by vss. 10 ff.; but, in our opinion, Deutero-Isaiah's concern is somewhat different. For him, the question is not primarily one of rendering recompense to a wretched man for his undeserved sufferings, but rather one of vindicating him, first of all in the eyes of his contemporaries, and thereafter in the sight of the whole world, so that all men may learn to know "the work of Yahweh." The paramount interest of the writer of the fourth Song is not to inform the Servant of the reward of his martyrdom; he is revealing to him that his entire destiny is part of the divine plan. The Servant's compensation is only one element in his vindication, and this latter is centred not on the person of Yahweh's Chosen, but on the comprehension of the purpose of the God of Israel. In other words, the resurrection, if resurrection there be, is not anthropocentric, its end is not to render to man what belongs to man, even although he has been a victim of human iniquity, it is theocentric, and its aim is to render to God what

---

[37] Nötscher, *op. cit.* (above, n. 22), p. 164.

I

belongs to God.   Its basis and aim alike are nothing other than the very revelation of the Living God.[38]

The reward of the Servant of Yahweh is merely a consequence of Yahweh's good pleasure.   It is not a question of strict justice being the cause of his final success, but of the will of the God of Israel to perform His work through the humiliation and glorification of His witness, that is to say, ultimately to reveal Himself in His essential nature to His creatures.

d. *Provenance of the Concept of the Humiliated and Glorified Servant*

It is possible, if not certain, that Deutero-Isaiah expected the resurrection of the Servant of Yahweh.   Some commentators do not hesitate to go further and to claim that the prophet, consciously or not, directly or indirectly, was inspired by the Canaanite or Israelite cults representing the operation of the forces of nature.   The destiny of the Chosen of the Living God, humiliated, then glorified, was only an echo of the myth of the god who dies in the dry season and rises again in spring. H. Gressman [39] has already stressed the striking analogy that exists between the lot of the Servant and the avatars of the god Tammuz, lamented every year in Palestine;   R. Kittel [40] connects Is. LIII with certain expiatory rites regularly performed by the Kings of Babylon;   M. Haller,[41] for his part, considers that Deutero-Isaiah is referring to his people, represented by the Servant, while making use of imagery borrowed from the Adonis-Tammuz cult.   Quite recently, I. Engnell has strongly emphasised the dependence of the final Servant Song on the myth of Tammuz, or that of Aliyan Baal, his counterpart

[38] In our discussion of Ezek. XXXVII, we have already established the fact of the relationship between the revelation of the God of Israel and the resurrection of His People;   this latter depends entirely on Yahweh, as He has made himself known to His own, and it is attested by the Living God's intention of glorifying His Name.

[39] H. GRESSMANN, *Der Ursprung der israelitisch-jüdischen Eschatologie*, 1905, pp. 301 ff., 323 ff.

[40] R. KITTEL, *Geschichte des Volkes Israel*, p. 257.

[41] M. HALLER, *comm. ad loc.*

among the Western Semites.[42]   He would find the key to the
mystery of the Servant and his destiny in the Tammuz ideology
and compares the sufferings of the first with the troubles of the
second, as they are enumerated in the Sumero-Accadian
liturgies or the Ugaritic texts; similarly, the resurrection of
Tammuz or Aliyan Baal, announced by a cry such as "Aliyan is
living," explains that of Yahweh's Chosen.[43]   According to
the same writer, his own interpretation of the Servant Songs
as being derived from the agricultural cults is "absolutely
inescapable." [44]   More subtle is the position of H. H. Rowley,
who suggests that Deutero-Isaiah was influenced not by an
alien cult, but by the cultic practices of the Temple.[45]

It is not, however, established that the prophet of the Exile
owes the essential elements of what he says about the Servant
to the myth, more or less modified, of the periodically dying
and rising god.   In spite of their number, I. Engnell's arguments are not entirely convincing; as H. Frankfort in particular
objects against him,[46] the Swedish scholar's conclusions are
over-schematised, and the texts which he cites, especially those
of Ras Shamra, are still under discussion; the parallels that he
adduces are often very remote, for instance the cry of "Aliyan is
living," which definitely has no counterpart in the last Song.
Moreover, it seems difficult to suppose that Deutero-Isaiah
drew his material so directly from a heathen source, since his
own attitude to Babylonian worship and ritual was one of
violent opposition.   H. H. Rowley's position would be more
tenable; but the Jerusalemite ritual is to this day still subject
to very different interpretations.[47]   Without denying all
possibility of connexion between the myth of the god of vegetation and Is. LIII, we must take into account the substantial
differences between the worship of the forces of nature and the
execution of God's plan by means of the absolute obedience

[42] ENGNELL, op. cit. (above, n. 22), pp. 4 f.
[43] ENGNELL, op. cit., pp. 7, 32, etc.
[44] ENGNELL, op. cit., p. 32.
[45] ROWLEY, op. cit., pp. 42 ff.
[46] Cp. FRANKFORT, Kingship and the Gods, esp. pp. 277 ff., 295 ff., and
p. 405 (Ch. I, n. 1).   This writer stresses the essential distinction subsisting
between the Egyptian and Mesopotamian conceptions and the individual
peculiarities of each cultus.
[47] Cp. below, pp. 199 ff.

of one who is called to bear the sins of his people. In the Tammuz, Adonis, or Baal cycle, the heart of the matter is the continuity of life, the continuance of the vegetation, and the maintenance and renewal—which are in some sense automatic —of a blind force upon which both man and the world are dependent; in the Song in Deutero-Isaiah, everything is centred upon the Servant's fulfilment of Yahweh's purpose, which involves the salvation of the sinner as well as the glorious revelation of the God of Israel.

Deutero-Isaiah had no need to make an extensive search among several myths, more or less foreign to the true traditions of Israel, to find a model for the Servant of Yahweh; in the history of the Chosen People one was already available. Though the cult may have played a more or less conscious part in the elaboration of the last Song, the determinative factor seems to have come from the historical traditions of Israel.[48]

W. Zimmerli [49] likewise rightly observes that there is no need to have recourse to the Tammuz ritual for an explanation of the Servant's sufferings, it is sufficient to consider the lives of the men of God, and doubtless, first and foremost among them, those of Jeremiah and Moses. It was not a king symbolically enacting the drama of nature at the New Year festival, but surely a witness to the Living God, who in the course of his mission met with general hostility and even martyrdom, who was the prototype of the portrait of the Servant in Is. LIII. H. S. Nyberg, cited by A. Bentzen,[50] lays stress above all on the role of the Prophets in this respect, and especially on that of Jeremiah, whose confessions and the closing chapters of whose book acquaint us with his tragic lot.[51] Following others (and particularly E. Sellin, who once wrote a sort of novel about Moses the martyr and model of the Servant of Yahweh), A. Bentzen draws our attention to the

---

[48] This is also the opinion of RIGNELL, *op. cit.* (above, n. 22), p. 89, who holds that historical facts and not a sacral-king ideology constitute the background of Deutero-Isaiah's message regarding the Servant.

[49] ZIMMERLI, in KITTEL, VOL. V, p. 666, n. 72.

[50] BENTZEN, *King and Messiah*, pp. 68 f.

[51] For GELIN also, *op. cit.* (above, n. 18), p. 104, the Servant is modelled on Jeremiah, although immeasurably greater than he. This writer connects Is. XLIX. 1 with Jer. I. 5, Is. XLIX. 1-6 with the confessions of Jeremiah, and the martyrdom of Yahweh's Chosen with Jer. XXVI, etc.

leader of the Chosen People at the time of the Exodus.[52]
Yahweh's Chosen appears to be the counterpart of Moses in
a wilderness journey which, according to Deutero-Isaiah himself, brings the flight from Egypt to mind; the circumstances
seem to be similar, the mission is almost the same; the second
Song already connects Moses and Joshua with the Servant
(Is. XLIX. 5 f., 8-12). Although Moses does not endure martyrdom, he is prepared to suffer it to save his people, for which he
never ceases to make intercession; [53] in short, he plays a part
similar enough to that which is assigned to the Servant in the
final Song.

Doubtless the Chosen People provided Deutero-Isaiah with
other examples besides those of Moses and Jeremiah; perhaps
we should go back in time as far as Abel, the first martyr, and
come down to Deutero-Isaiah himself, some passages of whose
work seem to be autobiographical,[54] without overlooking,
among the great body of faithful servants whose mission meant
suffering and humiliation, the "*Ḥasidim,*" the "pious men,"
known perhaps only to their God, if it be true, as B.D. Eerdmans
suggests,[55] that Is. LIII is a perfect representation of the destiny
of one of Yahweh's "clients."

Thus the history of Israel, or at least the lot of certain members
of it, more than heathen or Jerusalemite ritual, seems to have
given Deutero-Isaiah the material for his song about the destiny
of the Servant. Somehow we sense that, in the background of
the portrait in Is. LIII, the role, albeit unconsciously played, of
a Moses, a Jeremiah, or even a *ḥasid,* was far more important

---

[52] BENTZEN, *King and Messiah,* pp. 65 f., writes that the Servant is probably
a new Moses. The Danish scholar notes that the mysterious central figure
of the songs sometimes seems to be a king and sometimes a prophet; in his
view this would be (p. 68) easily intelligible if it were admitted that Deutero-
Isaiah was influenced by the ideology of the primordial man (*Urmensch*)
who is king and prophet at once. (Cp. also RUDOLPH, *op. cit.,* pp. 110 f.;
and, quite recently, G. VERMÈS, "Moïse au tournant des deux Testaments,"
and R. BLOCH, "Quelques aspects de la figure de Moïse dans la littérature
rabbinique," both in *Moïse,* Cahiers sioniens, Paris 1954, pp. 80, 152 ff.)

[53] Exod. XXXII. 31 ff.; Deut., IX. 17-20, 25-29; also Deut. I. 37, III. 26,
IV. 21.

[54] S. MOWINCKEL, cited by ROWLEY, *op. cit.,* pp. 7 ff.

[55] B. D. EERDMANS, "The Chasidim," Essays on Masoretic Psalms,
Oudtest. St., 1941-2, pp. 176 ff.

than any taken by a Tammuz or Baal. Both the sufferings and
the prospective glory of Yahweh's Chosen alike have historical
rather than mythological roots; in the final analysis, the
expectation of his ultimate triumph is based, not on the resurrection of an agricultural divinity, but on the self-revelation of the
Living God to Israel as that is recorded in time and space; the
ground of the last Song is strictly theological, not mythological.

e. Conclusion

In spite of its difficulties and obscurities, Is. LIII allows us to
make several important observations.

The prophet here seems to be informing us of the destiny
of an individual and not about the lot of a group; thus the
exaltation of the Servant implies more than the restoration of
Israel and the prospective greatness of the People of God.

The destiny of the humiliated and glorified Servant presupposes his resurrection; yet Deutero-Isaiah makes no
specific reference to this. Thus we cannot be sure that this
was the precise way in which he envisaged the ultimate glorification of God's Chosen. The text itself is not at all clear;
it appears that the writer does not possess the conceptual equip-
ment that would enable him to formulate the event that he
foresees; in any case, his concern is rather to assert the vindication of the Servant than to explain how he is going to survive
his martyrdom.

But, as the victory over death given to the Servant by
Yahweh's free grace must ultimately involve his resurrection,
it is the answer to his sufferings; along with these it forms part
of Yahweh's plan. Although some exegetes speak of his case
as involving retribution, it must not be overlooked that, in
fact, that is only one consequence of the divine purpose which
is being fulfilled through the Servant's abasement and exaltation; the Living God is thus at once both the cause and the end
of the ultimate chapter of his existence; the prospect of life,
granted to him who freely pours out his soul unto death, is
finally seen as the full manifestation of the divinity of Yahweh.

The lot of the Chosen remains exceptional. The promises
that Yahweh makes to him regarding his final state in no way
concern the whole body of the Israelites. Is. LIII may perhaps

enable us to obtain a glimpse of the resurrection of an individual unique in the annals of the Chosen People, but it does not allow us to make any general statement about the resurrection of the dead.[56]

Finally, the Servant's destiny is to be explained rather by the history of God's revelation in Israel than by the agricultural cults, by the destinies of Moses and Jeremiah in particular rather than by the avatars of Tammuz and Adonis. The Chosen of Yahweh, humiliated and glorified, seems to be both the successor and the perfected type of the servants of the God of Israel, who were His faithful witnesses throughout the centuries, rather than the embodiment of an ideology based on the recurrent appearance and disappearance of life.

Is. xxv. 8: "Death shall be no more. . . ."

a. Introductory: Is. xxiv-xxvii

The two passages (Is. xxv. 8, xxvi. 19) which we are about to study belong to four chapters in the Book of Isaiah which, in the opinion of the generality of the critics, constitute one of its latest component parts. On considerations whose character is at once literary, historical, and theological, Is. xxiv-vii, commonly called the Apocalypse of Isaiah, is not the work of the eighth-century prophet and dates from the period which followed the Exile. There the agreement of the exegetes usually ends; it is difficult, in point of fact, to assign an exact date to these chapters, to understand how they are inter-related and to what events they refer.[1] Thus, while J. Lindblom thinks that they were written in the fifth century, soon after the capture of Babylon by Xerxes, B. Duhm, K. Marti, and A. Lods believe they find allusions in these passages to the campaigns of Antiochus Sidetes and John Hyrcanus against the Parthians (129 B.C.); but the majority of commentators place this "apocalypse" in the fourth century, at the end of the Persian supremacy, at the time of the

---

[56] On the later use of Is. LIII in this connexion, cp. below, pp. 138-45 ff., i.e. the section of this chapter dealing with Dan. XII. 2 f.

[1] A. LODS, *Histoire de la littérature hebraïque et juive*, Paris 1950, pp. 853 ff.

conquests of Alexander and the disturbances they caused,[2] and it seems to us that this middle view is in greatest conformity with the few indications we can obtain from the text.

The question, moreover, is bound up with the identification of a town frequently mentioned in these chapters; here, too, exegetical opinion is divided: the enemy city was Babylon, devastated by the Persians in 486 (J. Lindblom), or captured by Alexander in 331 (W. Rudolph); or Carthage, destroyed in 146 (O. Procksch); or Samaria, razed by John Hyrcanus in 107 (A. Lods); or again Tyre, which fell to the Greeks in 332; or even the capital of the land of Moab. Other difficulties arise in connexion with the study of the content of Is. XXIV-VII, in which some find a series of passages that are independent of one another, and others, a well co-ordinated whole; thus W. Rudolph declares that we have to deal with the juxtaposition of half a score of more-or-less connected fragments which were the work of a third-century Judean; O. Procksch bases himself on considerations of a literary, poetical, and historical character, and finds two documents which originally were unrelated to each other in these chapters: one, belonging to the second century, celebrates the fall of a city hostile to the People of God and the glorification of Jerusalem; the other, from an earlier age, contemplating the future and no longer the past, proclaims the Last Judgment. J. Lindblom, for his part, considers that the historical elements distinguished by O. Procksch cannot be separated; they constitute an entity, a sort of liturgical canticle, composed shortly after the destruction of Babylon, which is viewed as the event that precedes the upheaval of the last days and the establishment of the Kingship of Yahweh.

In dealing with these passages, it is not easy to get beyond the stage of hypotheses, but nevertheless we can assert that Is. XXIV-VII is essentially post-Exilic, and apparently dates from the end of the Persian supremacy or from shortly after Alexander's conquests. Therefore passages are now before us which are definitely later than those that we have previously studied.

[2] Such is notably the opinion of R. Smend, A. Kuenen, T. K. Cheyne, C. Steuernagel, J. Skinner, etc.

b. *Is. xxv. 8: Text*

He [i.e. Yahweh] destroys death for ever.[3]

c. *Context and Meaning*

Is. xxv. 6 ff. follow after a song celebrating Yahweh's deliverances (xxv. 1-5). The God of Israel has accomplished His wonderful purpose, He has transformed the arrogant heathen city into a heap of rubble, and has revealed Himself as a protector of the poor. This song refers to some past event; it is followed by a section, definitely eschatological in character (xxv. 6 ff.), which appears to be the natural sequel to the end of CH. XXIV and especially to XXIV. 21-3: the end of the age is upon us; the earth is overwhelmed, the universe is melted away, while Yahweh establishes His reign on the mountain of Zion. Powers of the earth and stars of the heaven alike are

---

[3] (RSV, however, translates "He will swallow up death for ever.") R. SMEND, *Z. alttest. W.*, 1884, pp. 161, 224; K. MARTI, *K. H.-C. A. T.*, 1900; A. CONDAMIN, "Le livre d'Esaïe," *Et. bib.*, 1905; E. SELLIN, "Die alttestamentliche Hoffnung auf Auferstehung und ewiges Leben," *N. k. Z.*, 1919, p. 256; G. B. GRAY, *I. C. C.*, 1928; O. PROCKSCH, *Komm. A. T.*, 1930; W. RUDOLPH, *Jesaja xxiv-xxvii*, Beitr. z. Wiss. vom A. N. T., 1933; J. LINDBLOM, *Die Jesaja-Apocalypse, Jes. xxiv-xxvii*, Lund 1938; J. STEINMANN, "Le prophète Isaïe," *Lectio divina*, 1951, pp. 353 ff.; J. LINDBLOM, "Die Jesaja-Apocalypse in der neuen Jesajahandschrift," *Bulletin de la Société Royale des lettres de Lund*, 1951; NÖTSCHER, *op. cit.* (above, p. 55, n. 5), p. 154; EICHRODT, *Theol. des A. T.*, VOL. III, pp. 156 f., etc.

This text is cited by St Paul in 1 Cor. xv. 54; the Apostle's version κατεπόθη ὁ θάνατος εἰς νῖκος differs from the LXX translation, which reads κατέπιεν ὁ θάνατος ἰσχύσας, and, on the other hand, is nearer to Theodotion's κατέπιεν ὁ θάνατος εἰς νῖκος. In Paul, the verb has become a passive corresponding to בֻּלַּע, *bullā‘*, "to be destroyed, swallowed up," and לָנֶצַח, *lāneṣaḥ*, "in glory" or "to eternity," is rendered by εἰς νῖκος and not by εἰς τὸ τέλος.

In its primitive sense, נֵצַח, *neṣaḥ* conveys the idea of "victory, triumph, brightness, glory" (cp. the Greek translation of 1 Chron. XXIX. 11; Lam. III. 18); the LXX usually translates לָנֶצַח, *lāneṣaḥ*, by εἰς τὸ τέλος, but sometimes also by εἰς νῖκος. Aquila invariably renders this expression as εἰς νῖκος; cp. H. LIETZMANN, "1. Korintherbrief," *H. N. T.*, 1949, *comm. ad loc.*; A. RALHF, *Z. neutest. W.*, 1921, pp. 182 ff.

Rev. XXI. 4 has paraphrased these words accurately as ὁ θάνατος οὐκ ἔσται ἔτι, that is to say, "death shall be no more."

in thrall to the God of Israel; all glory pales before Yahweh's. The Living God comes to rule over the Holy City (vss. 21 ff.)

Then Yahweh invites the peoples of the earth to gather themselves together there (xxv. 6) to taste His blessings and praise His power. The greatness of the God of Israel, once revealed to the prophet Isaiah (Is. vi.), is now made manifest in the eyes of all the nations; "in that day" the glory of the God of Hosts in very truth fills all the earth, and His holiness streams forth from Zion (Is. vi. 3, xxiv. 23).[4]

As a king celebrates his coronation by a solemn festival at which all his vassals are present (1 Sam. xi. 15; 1 Kings i. 9 ff., 25), so Yahweh receives the peoples at an enthronement feast, in the course of which He sets שְׁמָנִים מְמֻחָיִם, *s⁰mānîm m⁰muḥayim*, "delicious meats," before them, and שְׁמָרִים מְזֻקָּקִים, *s⁰mārîm m⁰zuqqāqîm*, the "choicest of wines." Here the figure of the "Messianic Feast" makes its appearance, which is also found in other Old Testament passages, such as Pss. xvi, xxiii, lxxxvii, and cxvi, and is likewise employed by Jesus in the Parable of the Great Supper (Lk. xiv. 16-24; Mt. xxii. 2-14) or on other occasions (Mt. viii. 11, xxvi. 29; Lk. xxii. 29 ff.), of which the most important is the institution of the Lord's Supper on the eve of His death (Mt. xxvi. 26; Lk. xxii. 14 ff.)[5]

Whereas Jeremiah was commanded to offer the cup of Yahweh's anger to the peoples in token of their impending doom (Jer. xxv. 15 ff.; cp. also Ezek. xxiii. 31 ff.), the unknown prophet summons the nations to partake of His blessings at the hand of the Living God. It is to a banquet wholly devoted to

[4] The invitation extended to all the world (xxv. 6) is reminiscent of another prophecy, which may be the work of Isaiah himself, and which tells of the heathen streaming towards Jerusalem and pilgrims coming from every quarter of the earth to ascend the Holy Mountain there to hear the Word of Yahweh and learn to live in peace (Is. ii. 2 ff.)

[5] The metaphor of the meal plays an equally important part in the post-Biblical literature and is used to express the bliss of the Chosen Ones (cp. 1 Enoch lxii. 14; Ps. Sol. xvii. 40; ii Enoch ii. 5; ii Baruch xxix; cp. P. Volz, *Jüdische Eschatologie von Daniel bis Akiba*, Tübingen 1903, pp. 331 ff.); and in Rev. it becomes the Marriage Supper of the Lamb (Rev. xix. 9). In the Biblical perspective, the meal is a sign of communion; to partake of food with someone means to enter into fellowship with him, to participate in his destiny; similarly, to drink of a cup with someone, is to identify oneself with him, to share his lot.

rejoicing that Yahweh is calling men; suffering and sorrow cannot intrude there; and Yahweh removes the mourning veils and wipes the tears from their faces (vss. 7 ff.)

O. Procksch thinks that the reference here is to the veil of ignorance that for so long has blinded the nations, and especially the People of God, to Yahweh's work and will. In answer to this deficiency in spiritual understanding, the God of Israel sends His Spirit to enable the nations to draw near to Him. Is. xxv. 7, then, was the reply to an Isaianic oracle in which the prophet informs his rebellious contemporaries that God has resolved to cause their minds to grow dull (xxix. 9 ff.); this passage was to be a formative factor in the Apostle Paul's treatment of the theme of the veil that rests over the Old Testament and can only be taken away in Jesus Christ (ii Cor. iii. 12 ff.)

Doubtless the writer did not see as far as that, and is saying something simpler. The veil to which he refers is a sign of mourning and of distress in general. Yahweh renders its presence unnecessary by removing all occasion of trouble and trial from those He invites. All cause of sadness is taken away from the Living God's guests, and, in particular, Yahweh looks in favour upon His own People and turns His anger aside, that is to say He puts an end to its exile and especially to the racial animosity that it appears to arouse (O. Procksch). The solemn closing affirmation of vs. 8 is like God's counter-signature to His witness's declarations, His guarantee that they will be brought into effect. Vss. 9, 10*aa* voice the joyful and confident response of the People of Yahweh, whose hand rests on the mountain of Zion.[6]

We must emphasise the "catholic" outlook of this prophecy. The whole world is called to live in the Living God's presence and to share in His gifts. God intervenes to remove all cause of suffering in the holy place where all the peoples are expected. Nevertheless, this universalism does not exclude a certain particularism: Yahweh, whose coronation is celebrated by all the world, remains the God of Israel; He does not forget His

---

[6] The reference to Moab is not in keeping with the context, the judgment of the world is already over, and now it is the time for the Messianic Feast, and not for the settling of scores between neighbouring nations. Thus vss. 10*aβ*, ff., are a gloss.

own People or the place He has chosen for Himself, where the destiny of mankind is being wrought out. The Biblical revelation follows a specific course, leading by way of particular places and times and individuals, even although it is ultimately concerned with the whole of creation; this short fragment by an anonymous writer is a perfect illustration of the characteristic manner in which God is working for the salvation of the world.

d. *Is. xxv. 8aα and its context*

Up to the present we have not taken account of the opening words of xxv. 8, "He abolishes death for ever," which the Apostle Paul cites in his argument in favour of the resurrection of the body (1 Cor. xv. 54). We hold that they could not in fact have formed part of the original text. Writers like K. Marti and H. Guthe believe them to be a marginal note that was subsequently incorporated into the text; W. Rudolph proposes to excise them and to place them at the end of the oracle, whose climax they would then become.

In point of fact, Is. xxv. 8aα interrupts the rhythm of vss. 6 ff. and the entirely natural sequence of vss. 7 and 8aβ: "Yahweh removes the veil that covers the peoples and dries the tears that course down their cheeks." A reader probably supposed that these verses were telling, not only of the end of all sorrow whatever, but also of the decisive destruction of that which is seen as the first and final cause of human suffering: death. The commentator therefore went further than the writer of Is. xxv. 6 ff., and anticipated St. Paul in sensing the collapse of the last enemy of mankind. To hold that verse 8aα is a later gloss, and in actuality the first exegesis of this passage, is in no way to detract from its importance; the text of the Bible is no dead letter, but a living witness in which every generation in its turn receives the message it needs. To reckon up the glosses and then discard them is not enough; we must rather welcome them as a valuable commentary on a dynamic Word through which God never ceases to speak to men.[7]

[7] On this point, cp. H. W. HERTZBERG, "Die Nachgeschichte alttestamentlicher Texte innerhalb des Alten Testaments," *Wesen und Werden des A. T.*, Beihefte z. *Z. alttest. W.*, Berlin 1936, pp. 110-21.

For the believer who has read Is. xxv. 7 ff., Yahweh, in this passage, promises to do away with death which causes the tears that course down human cheeks; it is no longer a question of mere prolongation of life as that is envisaged in a somewhat similar context: "No more shall be heard in it the sound of weeping and the cry of distress . . . for the child shall die a hundred years old . . ." (Is. LXV. 19 ff.); no more is it a question of resurrection: an entirely new situation is created, in which, as the Book of Revelation puts it, death is no more, in which it loses all reality and no longer subsists alongside the Living God, whose life takes possession of the whole universe. Prospects undreamed of are opened up by this brief marginal note; the New Testament will define them with precision when it comes to proclaim: "Death shall be no more. . . . God shall be all in all! . . ."

e. Conclusion

It is probable that the words "He destroys death for ever" (xxv. 8*aa*) did not form part of the original text, but are a sort of interpretation of vss. 7-8, and are very early. If we grant that Is. XXIV-VII dates approximately from the fourth century, the oracle may have assumed its present form in the third century: we must not assign it too late a date, because of the Qumrân manuscripts.

This comment proclaims God's final victory over death, which will disappear. Death will become of no more account for man, it will at last cease from imposing its power upon him. The commentator is not speaking about those who have died during its reign, and therefore is not referring to their resurrection.

Death is destroyed, not because man has somehow recovered his original righteousness—in that case there would be no reason for its continued existence since it is the wages of sin—but because it is impotent to oppose the absolute power of the God of Israel. The reign of Yahweh entails the destruction of all other dominion. The Living God who manifests His sovereign rule in the judgment of the universe, and His care in the assembling of all nations together in the place where His glory shines forth, no longer permits death to mar the rejoicing of His guests. Here hope of immortality is bound up with expectation of the coming of the Kingdom of God.

Is. xxvi. 19: "May thy dead revive!"

a. Text

In the Apocalypse of Isaiah we find the first text that deals, not with the restoration of Israel, but with the resurrection of the members of the Chosen People. According to the consensus of exegetical opinion, Is. xxvi. 19 proclaims that the faithful Israelites will live again through the renewing action of their God.[1]

> *May thy dead revive, may their bodies arise,*
> *May they awaken and sing for joy who dwell*
> *in the dust,*
> *For Thy dew shall be a dew of light*
> *And the earth shall bring forth the R e p h a i m.*[2]

The writer of Is. xxvi. 19 hopes that the dead will live again; a true Israelite, he has no conception of disembodied human life. The soul sundered from the body perhaps exists, it does not live; thus its body must be restored to it. Return to life presupposes the re-animation of the corpse, or even of the skeleton. This is at rest, it will arise; it seems asleep, it must be awakened, and the new life thus appears to be a

---

[1] For C. LARCHER, however, "La doctrine de la résurrection dans l'A. T.," *Vie et lumière*, 1952, p. 19, Is. xxvi has a symbolical character: the resurrection is a picture of the repopulation of the Holy Land, and the resurrected are the exiles who are going to be repatriated.

[2] Cp. (above, p. 125, n. 3) the bibliographical references given in connexion with Is. xxv. 8 to which must be added A. LODS, "La victoire sur le Léviathan," in "Deux notes relatives à la mort et à ce qui la suit," *C. r. Ac. Inscr.*, 1943, pp. 284 ff.

נְבֵלֹתָם, *niḇlōṭām*, "their bodies," must be read, and not נְבֵלָתִי, *n°ḇēlāṭî*, "my body," with the Syriac version and the Targum.   O. Procksch and W. Rudolph propose to read נְבֵלֹתֶיךָ, *niblōṭeyḵā*, that is to say, "thy dead bodies."   Instead of the imperative, D.S. (Is.), like Aquila, Symmachus and Theodotion, has יָקִיצוּ וִירַנְּנוּ, *yāqîṣû wîrann°nû*, fut., "they shall awaken and sing for joy."   The LXX seems to have read אֲרוּכָה, *'°rûḵâ*, "restoration, healing," instead of אוֹרֹת, *'ōrōṯ*, "lights," which gives the meaning that the dew of Yahweh would have healing power.

continuation of the former existence; moreover the verbs "to awaken, to arise, to keep alive," are employed as technical terms in connexion with the resurrection.[3]

Is. xxvi. 19 voices a prayer rather than a certainty; the prophet desires that the shades should live again; he believes the miracle possible; he knows that it depends on the God to whom he is speaking. Here he is not, like Ezekiel, envisaging the political revival of the nation; he is not even speaking about an event that would concern all Israel; he is thinking only of certain members of the Chosen People, of those to whom the words "thy dead" refer, that is to say, he is doubtless thinking first and foremost of Jews who died for the sake of remaining faithful to Yahweh—in short, of the martyrs.

The resurrection referred to here is not universal, nor indeed does it concern the whole body of the Israelites; the Living God will restore life only to those whom He recognises as His own, and uppermost of these in the writer's mind are the victims of the persecutions; so Jerome interpreted his thought long ago, when he rendered his words as "Mortui tui, qui interfecti sunt propter te"—that is to say, "Thy dead, who were slain for Thy sake."

This passage apparently dates from a time of difficulty for the People of Yahweh, during the great upheavals that preceded and followed the conquests of Alexander the Great, probably in the fourth century. At that period, Palestine was invaded on several occasions by foreign armies and was threatened with famine. In Jerusalem, the Jewish community had increasing difficulties with the Persian authorities and with the neighbouring peoples; and faction, in the very midst of the Holy Nation, helped to make the plight of the "pious," the *Ḥasidim*, a precarious one, and, beyond question, some of them paid for their faithfulness to Yahweh with their lives. It is primarily to them that the resurrection is promised. Yahweh recognises those who endure to the end as His own; He, the Living God, will not leave them in the dust for ever.

Ezekiel (xxxvii) described the miracle of the Resurrection of the Dry Bones in minute detail. Here the believing writer is sketching out a somewhat similar description; he is indicating

[3] A. T. NIKOLAINEN, "Der Auferstehungsglaube in der Bibel und ihrer Umwelt," *Ann. Ac. Sc. Fen.*, 1944, p. 99.

how, under the hand of Yahweh, the return to life will be wrought. He pictures the God of Israel causing the dew to descend to the ground; thanks to its life-giving power the earth will bring forth the shades. "The comparison with the dew that revives the plants is very fine. The night of death fallen on the departed is fleeting. The dawn will follow, bringing the dew, and the earth will give birth to the bodies again, just as in the morning the flowers revive under the shining dew of the dawn." [4]

Here the writer is making use of ancient mythological traditions which he adapts to the revelation of Yahweh. In this passage, the dew plays the part fulfilled by the Spirit in Ezekiel's vision; it is, as in the Book of Hosea (VI. 4, and esp. XIV. 5: "I will be as the dew to Israel, he shall blossom as the lily"), and as in other Old Testament passages (Mic. V. 6; Ps. CX. 3; and again Is. LXVI. 14), and in the Ras Shamra texts, associated with the idea of renewal of life; [5] here it is entirely at Yahweh's disposal as the expression טַלְּךָ, *talleḵā*, that is to say, "thy dew," attests; it has no independence of action. It is characterised by the term אוֹרֹת, *'ōrōt*, "lights," which must be a plural of intensity; this word calls to mind the two great lights set by God in His creation (Gen. I. 15 ff., cp. Gen. XXVII. 28, 39). Thus the shining dew of which the prophet speaks is a bringer of life, it is as life-giving as the light or the rain, it is the opponent of the dark and the dust.

Then the earth, fertilised by the divine power, shall bring forth the *rephaim*. This figure belongs to the Mother Earth theme, which plays an important part in human imagination; [6] we find echoes of it even in the Old Testament (Pss. CXXXIX. 13 ff.,

---

[4] J. STEINMANN, *op. cit.*, p. 356.

[5] Cp. above, pp. 74 ff. It will also keep this meaning in later Jewish tradition: cp. 1 Enoch LI. 1 ff.; Bab. Ḥag. 12b, Bab. Sanh. 90b, etc., cited by P. KARGE, *op. cit.* (above, p. 36, n. 18), 1917, p. 568. The Talmudic texts refer to dew of God stored up in the Seventh Heaven, which is to descend at the resurrection of the dead. Neo-Hebrew poetry voices the prayer that it may be sent down by God upon the dry bones. In the Qaraite literature, as in Christian texts, it is often referred to, according to Karge, as the instrument of the resurrection (cp., for example, Ephraem Syrus in his homily "On the Resurrection of the Dead," ch. v).

[6] ELIADE, *op. cit.* (above, p. 2, n. 2), ch. vii: "La terre, la femme, la fécondité," pp. 210 ff.

xc. 2); "the rebirth of the dead is accomplished through a new motherhood, and in particular through the motherhood of Mother Earth." [7]

In the myths, birth is often represented as the fruit of conjunction between Heaven and Earth, the issue of the union of some celestial divinity with the latter; here the resurrection is a new birth, effected by the intervention of Yahweh alone, but somehow compelling the earth to deliver up its spoil; it takes the form of a gigantic labour.

To sum up, this verse proclaims the resurrection. This, reserved for Yahweh's dead, is the work of the Living God, and seems to be accomplished through a sort of earth-motherhood under the influence of the dew of heaven.

b. Context

These indications are confirmed and established by the information afforded us by the context of Is. xxvi. 19, even although it is difficult to obtain critical agreement about the interpretation that should be given to Is. xxvi as a whole. [8]

Though the commentators are far from being in agreement as to how the first part of the chapter ought to be divided up,

[7] Morin, *L'homme et la mort dans l'histoire*, Paris 1951, pp. 110 ff.

[8] In the twenty-one verses composing ch. xxvi, P. Lohmann finds a catena of brief fragments with no actual interrelationship; on the other hand, K. Marti considers that vss. 1-19 constitute a single prayer that can be sub-divided into several strophes. O. Procksch would separate a song celebrating Yahweh and Jerusalem (vss. 1-6) from a prayer of the community in its trouble (vss. 7-19), which is answered by an oracle (vss. 20 f. and xxvii. 1, 12-13). W. Rudolph asserts that following upon a hymn glorifying the God of Jerusalem (vss. 1-6), we have a song expressing confidence and not distress (vss. 7-12, 15-16*ba*, 13-14*b*); he holds that, vss. 14*a*, 16*bβ*, and 19 did not belong to the original text.

J. Lindblom divides ch. xxvi up in yet another way and thinks that vs. 19 is not original. Vss. 1-14 form a song of thanksgiving in which the classical themes of thanksgiving hymns (the call to worship God, the motifs of thanksgiving, confession, and supplication) are to be found. This passage is followed by a lament (vss. 15-19), whose closing words contain Yahweh's reply; Lindblom holds that this was a late text dating from the Maccabean period. He considers that references to events mentioned by the Jewish historian Josephus (massacres, spoliations, famines, with the consequent decimation of the people), which are to be placed in the time of Jonathan, are to be found in this passage.

K

in general they emphasise that its closing verses (vss. 20-1, with XXVII. 1) have hardly any connexion with the preceding passage.

The variety of the hypotheses advanced on these passages show us the difficulties that the exegetes encounter when they come to expound them in detail. It must be admitted that many points are still obscure and that our explanations remain contingent. It is manifestly clear that vss. 1-6 celebrate the salvation that God gives to His City and the victory that He has just gained over a city that arrogantly arrayed itself against Him. The rest of the chapter contains a sort of long supplication offered to Yahweh, in which the expectation of the righteous who are looking for His judgments (vss. 7 ff.), the certainty that the Chosen People definitely belongs to Yahweh alone (vss. 11 ff.), and, since trouble seems to be constantly increasing, the hope that Yahweh will accomplish the miracle of resurrection for His own (vss. 15 ff.) are expressed.

The people appears to be torn between trust and impatience; it sees the tokens of the liberating interventions of its God, but it demands a fuller deliverance. In spite of Yahweh's presence, the times are hard; will not the God of Israel bestir Himself now on behalf of His own? We do not necessarily require to come down as far as the Maccabean period to discover the reason for a prayer like that. As we have already pointed out, long before the persecutions of Antiochus Epiphanes the Jews were confronted by a multitude of difficulties, particularly at the time of Alexander's campaigns; the Books of Ezra and Nehemiah show us how delicate the situation after the return from the Exile was for the true worshippers of Yahweh; subsequent events only added to their sufferings; the more the centuries went on, the more fate seemed to assail the community of faithful Yahwists. The crisis that rent the People of God in the second century is the culminating point of a struggle that was prepared for long before; the martyrs of the time of Antiochus Epiphanes are neither the first, nor the last, among the Chosen People.[9]

[9] Notwithstanding all the problems raised by Zech. IX-XIV, it is possible to discern in these anonymous oracles an echo of the struggles and suffering of the Jewish community immediately after the campaigns of Alexander the Great.

The faithful Jews demand that Yahweh's righteousness should be made manifest; the difference between the righteous and the ungodly must be made apparent to the eyes of all the earth (vss. 7 ff.), and, if need be, even after death. The *Ḥasidim* who have paid for their faithfulness to the God of Israel with their lives cannot suffer the same lot as their adversaries, who are Yahweh's enemies as well; the latter vanish for ever, the former will be restored to life. The divine righteousness involves the resurrection of "God's dead," vs. 19 is the answer to vs. 14, the ultimate destiny of the departed is dependent on the attitude that they adopted to God during their lifetime.

Therefore it seems to us to be erroneous to separate vss. 14 and 19, as J. Lindblom does. The second is intelligible in the light of the first; together they show that the distinction between the pious man and the ungodly does not end with this life, it remains as real for the future as it is for the present; thus death—and this point is of capital importance, for it will radically transform the Chosen People's traditional conceptions of life and death—no longer brings all men together into a shadowy existence common to all; it is eternal only for those whom God punishes, for Yahweh's dead it becomes a passing state. The resurrection reveals that the righteousness of God discriminates between those who serve Him and those who oppose Him. Among those of the perished whose remembrance Yahweh blots out for ever are probably the enemies of the Chosen People, the foreign tyrants who usurped a place which belongs to the God of Israel alone, and doubtless also the renegade Jews who made common cause with the heathen and showed themselves to be perhaps the worst enemies of the faithful observers of the Law.

In his prayer the believer importunes Yahweh to rebuild His People decimated by famine, war, and persecution, to extend the ridiculously small territory on which the Holy Nation now lives (vss. 15 ff.); the sufferings of Israel are like those of a woman in labour: but will they (as O. Procksch supposes [10])

---

[10] O. PROCKSCH, *comm. ad loc.*, emends vs. 18 to read רוּחַ יְשָׁעוֹת, *rûaḥ yešu'ôt*, " (a) wind of salvation," and makes it refer to the eschatological woes that, according to the apocalyptic tradition (cp. Mt. xxiv. 8; Mk. xiii. 8, etc.), are going to herald the end of the world and the advent of the Messianic Kingdom.

bring forth salvation, or (as the actual Massoretic text implies) are they in vain? In any case, the intervention of Yahweh is required to repeople His Nation and to show forth His righteousness and power.

Contrary to the opinion of the majority of the critics, XXVI. 20-1 constitute, together with XXVII. 1, a veritable answer to this prayer, if we are to give credence to an ingenious study of them by A. Lods.[11] The God of Israel tells the *Ḥasidim* that the judgment of the world is about to begin. He advises His faithful people to hide themselves while His divine wrath passes upon the earth, as it formerly did upon the cities of the Egyptians (XXVI. 20). For Yahweh is coming forth from His dwelling in heaven to punish the crimes of mankind; the earth must disclose the transgressions of men; the blood of the slain is crying aloud for vengeance, it is in vain to cover it with dust. The very ground bears witness against the guilty (vs. 21). This verse suggests that innocent blood has been shed in the land, doubtless that of the faithful Jews, wickedly slain, but whom Yahweh recognises as His dead and for whom He will accomplish the miracle of the resurrection.

The fact is that, according to the exegesis of A. Lods, Is. XXVII. 1 proclaims that the gate of the nether world is no longer closed, the monster guarding it has disappeared, and so the dead may have open access to the land of the living. Leviathan has been smitten by Yahweh Himself; this monster, long regarded by the critics as a political power, or even as the three Empires of the Middle East: Assyria, Egypt, and Persia, was, in point of fact nothing else than a demonic force which, according to certain Phoenician traditions of which Is. XXVII was an echo, kept the dead in Sheol, a sort of Cerberus who would imprison the departed in the realm of shades for ever. The God of Israel deals the beast a mortal blow and then the *rephaim* can emerge from Hades and the earth bring forth the new-born of God.

Thus XXVI. 20-1 and XXVII. 1 exactly correspond to the believers' prayers: God avenges the blood of the martyrs; Yahweh forces the gate of the nether world, overcoming Leviathan; His faithful are able to arise from the earth.

[11] LODS, "La victoire sur le Léviathan," in *C. r. Ac. Inscr.*, 1943, pp. 284 ff.

Notwithstanding the many problems that it presents, which are far from being solved, Is. xxvi, as a whole, confirms the interpretation of vs. 19; this verse assumes its full significance when it is read as part of the prayer of the Yahwists, which is favourably received by God.

c. Conclusion

In reading Is. xxvi. 19, we must bear in mind its context, and especially xxvi. 8, 14, 21, and xxvii. 1. It dates from the same period as the Apocalypse of Isaiah and therefore probably from the fourth century.

In the form of a prayer, Is. xxvi. 19 proclaims the resurrection of the dead; this is still reserved for certain members of the Chosen People, perhaps only for the martyrs; it is denied not only to the heathen, but doubtless also to the impious Jews whose remembrance Yahweh blots out (xxvi. 14).

Here the resurrection is concerned with the actual renewal of the life of the departed and is doubly the work of Yahweh; for, on the one hand, the God of Israel puts forth a life-giving power upon the earth, and, on the other, He destroys the monster that guards the gateway of Sheol.

The concept of resurrection does not appear to be absolutely novel to the writer of the prayer; here he is probably voicing the thought of the pious Jews. The resurrection is seen as a possibility already glimpsed and now defined with precision, rather than as a *creatio ex nihilo*. Is. xxvi. 19 thus implies that in the fourth century there were believers who could admit the possibility of a new life after death.

The resurrection is particularly bound up with a requirement of justice; the lot of Yahweh's dead cannot be identical with that of His enemies. It is, in the first instance, concerned with the martyrs. It is primarily to secure not, as some think, the increase of the people, but the retribution of the faithful; it also bears witness to the power of Yahweh over the forces of death; at the same time it reveals the care of the God of Israel who does not forget His own, even when they are lying among the dead, and His righteousness, which is to be made manifest in striking fashion on the last day; it is thus at the service of the Living God.

The resurrection depends on Yahweh alone. In seeking to give expression to the inexpressible, the action of God on the dead, the writer of Is. xxvi. 19 makes use of images that belong to the mythological speech of all ages; dew, Mother Earth, and Leviathan are so many concepts borrowed from the world round about him, which perhaps enrich the prophet's vision, but do not determine it. The resurrection derives, not from the forces of nature, but uniquely from the intervention of the Living God, and is finally a decisive event belonging to the eschatological drama.

IN DANIEL

Dan. xii. 2 f.: "Many shall be raised. . . ."

a. Introduction

Generally speaking, Old Testament specialists concede that the Book of Daniel, as a whole, was composed about the year 165 B.C. before the Purification of the Temple in Dec. 164, when the revolt of the Maccabeans against Antiochus Epiphanes had already broken out, but had not as yet gained any decisive successes.

The writer is doubtless relying on many traditions, some of which are exceedingly ancient and may be of Babylonian or Persian provenance; he works over his material, using it to compose a book designed to encourage the orthodox Jews persecuted alike by the Seleucid authorities and by those of their own brethren who are inclined to Hellenism. The purpose of his work is to remind them that the God of their fathers is in control of the history of the world; in spite of all the contradictions of the times, the end of the tyrants is near, and a glorious salvation is in store for those who endure to the end in the way of faithfulness.

Daniel himself appears as the typical pious man, the example of the *ḥasid* whom Yahweh delivers from dire dangers. To a community that is liable to lose heart in the midst of mounting difficulties, the writer issues the word of command to hold fast since the ultimate victory of the God of the Jews is beyond question; to bring this home to them, he paints, several times, a picture of the events of the past and the present that are inevitably leading on to the manifestation of the kingship of the Living God and to the triumph of those who are faithful to Him to the end.

The various problems, literary, linguistic, and theological, that are raised by the Book of Daniel have been extensively studied, but no final solution of these can as yet be claimed; this will become evident if we consider some recent conclusions.[1]

There is general agreement among the critics that CHS. X-XII constitute one of the major subdivisions of the book. It opens with the recollection of a series of events, whose character is sufficiently clear to permit of their identification, and it closes, in CH. XII, with a brief description of the end of the age, which re-echoes other eschatological imagery, in particular that of CH. VII. It is thus within a context definitely bearing upon the final consummation of human history that the resurrection of the dead, for the first time becomes, no longer merely an aspiration as in Is. XXVI. 19, but an assurance. The resurrection is bound up with the coming of the Kingdom of God, or, in the words of a statement in CH. VII, with the giving of dominion over all the earth to the people of the saints of the Most High (VII. 18, 27 ff.):

> And the kingdom and the dominion
> and the greatness of the kingdoms under
>   the whole heaven
> shall be given to the people of the saints
>   of the Most High;
>   their kingdom shall be an everlasting
>   kingdom. . . .

It thus coincides with the decisive victory of the cause of Yahweh and His own.

---

[1] W. BAUMGARTNER, "Ein Viertel Jahrhundert Danielforschung," *Th. R.*, 1939, pp. 59-83, 125-44, 201-28; A. LODS, *Histoire de la littérature hébraïque et juive*, 1950, pp. 830 ff.; H. H. ROWLEY, "The Unity of the Book of Daniel," in *The Servant of the Lord, and other Essays on the O.T.*, London 1952.

Some writers, such as P. Volz, M. A. Beek, F. Nötscher, and
W. Baumgartner, hold that Dan. xII. 1-3 has no particular
connexion with its context; these verses, then, were either a
fragment of an earlier apocalypse subsequently interpolated
into CHS. x-xII (P. Volz, W. Baumgartner), or else a marginal
note showing Persian influence (B. D. Eerdmans, cited by
M. A. Beek). Be that as it may, here we have a text that, for
the first time, unequivocally proclaims the resurrection of
the dead; [2] this passage, unique in the Old Testament, marks,
at one and the same time, the end of a long quest and the
beginning of a new way of understanding human destiny.
The declaration contained in Dan. xII. 2 f. was forthwith
adopted by a section of Judaism. This fact indicates that men's
minds were ready to receive it, for, although it meant the
overturning of long existent ideas, it answered to the deep
aspirations of the Chosen People.

b. Text

[2] And many of those who sleep *in the land of dust* shall awake,
some to everlasting life, and some to shame and everlasting
contempt. [3] And those who are wise shall shine like the brightness of the firmament; and those who turn many to righteousness,
like the stars for ever and ever.[3]

[2] For some writers, such as W. Baumgartner, and J. Lindblom, Dan.
xII. 2 f. is the earliest testimony in favour of the resurrection of the dead;
they consider that Is. xxvi. 19 was of later date.

[3] G. Behrmann, *Hk. A. T.*, 1894; K. Marti, *K. H.-C. A. T.*, 1901;
M. Haller, *Schr. A. T.*, 1914; J. A. Montgomery, *I. C. C.*, 1927;
P. Volz, *Die Eschatologie von Daniel bis Akiba*, 1903, pp. 9 ff. (new edition,
1934); M. A. Beek, *Das Danielbuch*, Leyden 1935, pp. 45 f., 89 f.;
A. Bentzen, *Hb. A. T.*, 1937, 2nd edn., 1952; F. Macler, *B. Cent.*, 1947;
H. L. Ginsberg, "The Oldest Interpretation of the Suffering Servant,"
Vet. test., 1953, pp. 400 ff. (cp. also *Vet. test.*, 1954, p. 274); P. I. de
Menasce, *B. Jerus.*, 1954; Eichrodt, *Theol. des A. T.*, vol. III., pp. 150 ff.;
Sellin, *op. cit.* (above, p. 55, n. 5), pp. 262 ff.; Nötscher, *op. cit.* (above,
p. 55, n. 5), pp. 163 ff.

In vs. 2, אַדְמַת־עָפָר, *'admat-'āpār*, should be translated as "in the land
of dust," that is to say, Sheol, where the dust is all-prevailing (עָפָר, *'āpār*,
often denotes the dominion of the dead), and not, as Segond's French
version and also Père de Menasce render it, "in the dust of the earth."

חֲרָפוֹת, *ḥᵃrāpôt*, "shame," may be a gloss. דִּרְאוֹן, *dir'ôn*, "contempt,

c. Meaning

The expression "at that time" at the beginning of Dan. xii denotes a new element in the development of Dan. x ff.; history suddenly gives place to eschatology. Henceforth, the subject is the last hours of a crumbling world upon whose ruins a new order is built. The writer sketches out a schema that is going to be repeated interminably by the Jewish and Christian apocalyptists: evil continues increasing, the forces of Hell are unleashed, tribulation comes to its climax. All at once, the situation is utterly changed, the end of the oppressors is near, the faithful or the chosen are saved, and the glory of God the Victor shines forth upon them.

Xii. 1 calls the final scene in human history to mind: the unprecedented distress of the time,[4] the presence among the believers of one sent from God,[5] the salvation of those who, like burgesses of their city,[6] are enrolled in the record of God.[7]

abhorrence," is found only here and in Is. lxvi. 24. In this passage the pious are contemplating the dead bodies of the unrighteous that are decomposing before their eyes, doubtless in the valley of the sons of Hinnom, גֵּיא בֶן־הִנֹּם, *gê' ben-hinnōm*, "valley of the sons of Hinnom," (Jer. vii. 31 f.; cp. also Neh. xi. 30), an accursed place because human sacrifices were formerly offered there (Jer. vii. 31 f.; ii Kings xxiii. 10), and which gave its name to Gehenna (Mt. v. 29).

The idea that the righteous will shine like the stars (vs. 3), or even be transformed into stars, is found again in post-Biblical Judiasm (i Enoch civ ff.; iv Ezra vii. 97, 125; ii Baruch li; ii Enoch lxvi. 7 ; cp. also Wisd. iii. 7; i Enoch li. 5, cviii. 11 ff.; Ps. Sol. iii. 12; Mt. xiii. 43), and may be derived from an astral religion. הַמַּשְׂכִּילִים, *hammaśkîlîm*, are the wise, the "erudite," as Père de Menasce calls them (*doctes*); we propose to adopt his translation, bearing in mind the expression "the teachers of righteousness"—הַמַּצְדִּיקִים, *hammaṣdîqîm*, literally "those who lead to righteousness" (in the lxx, οἱ συνιέντες and οἱ κατισχύοντες τοὺς λόγους μου), not only those who have taught righteousness, but those who by their speech and their behaviour, perhaps even by their martyrdom, have led many to righteousness (cf. xi. 33 f.) Volz raises the question as to whether this phrase is to be understood in terms of vicarious suffering, or of a treasury of merits (cp. ii Macc. vii. 36 ff.)

[4] Joel ii. 2; Jer. xxx. 7; Mt. xxiv. 21; Mk. xiii. 19; Ass. Mos. viii. 1; Rev. xvi. 18.

[5] Dan. x. 13; Zech. iii. 1 ff.; Rev. xii. 7 ff.; Jude 9.

[6] Jer. xxii. 30; Ezek. xiii. 19; cp. the lists in the Books of Ezra and Nehemiah.

[7] Ex. xxxii. 32; Ps. lxix. 28; Is. iv. 3; Ps. cxxxix. 16.

On the last day, a separation is going to be made among the living, all will not perish with the former world, a certain number of them will be saved.

Vss. 2-3 are concerned with the lot of those who died before the judgment. They postulate the resurrection of some of these. It is probable, but in view of the brevity of the text not certain, that these include, on the one hand, those who remained faithful to Yahweh to the end and sometimes paid with their lives for their devotion to the divine Law, and on the other, those who, whether intentionally or not, by apostatising from the traditions of their fathers, had provoked the persecution of the *Ḥasidim*.

Here again, as in Is. xxvi. 19, the justice of the Living God requires that the final state of the righteous shall be other than that of the renegades. The resurrection makes retribution possible, and, in view of the circumstances, this is deferred to the world to come. Sooner or later, the difference between the man who has given up safety or life itself for the sake of the God of the Jews, and the man who has chosen to yield to the seductions of the world, is to shine forth. In the time of the Maccabees, it becomes unthinkable that when so many martyrs have fallen in Yahweh's cause, persecutors and persecuted should be found together in the same dismal Sheol. Dan. xii. 2 f. goes even further than the text in Is. xxvi. 19: it shows that the *Ḥasidim* are demanding the chastisement of the guilty; the impious cannot merely be deprived of life like every other human being, they must be punished in a positive way. Thus they rise to suffer unending shame. The wrath of the God whom they have despised no longer visits them only in their offspring or in their dead bodies, it smites them personally and directly.

The concise character of the passage does not allow the nature of that everlasting contempt, דְּרָאוֹן, *dir'ôn*, (the expression is doubtless derived from Is. lxvi. 24), which the wicked will suffer, to be defined with precision. Moreover, the writer does not lay stress on this point; he is more concerned with the believer's lot. The later apocalypses will not be so restrained and will revel in depicting the atrocious sufferings in store for the damned in Hell; their descriptions will strike the popular imagination and, especially in the

Middle Ages, will pervert men's understanding of the message of the Bible.[8]

The righteous will be recalled to life,[9] they need have no more fear of death, their resurrection is final, לְחַיֵּי עוֹלָם, *leḥayyê ʿôlām*, "to everlasting life." It appears that a particular class, enjoying special honour, must be distinguished among them; for in fact the מַשְׂכִּילִים, *maśkîlîm*, "those who are wise," and the מַצְדִּיקֵי הָרַבִּים, *maṣdîqê hārabbîm*, "those who turn many to righteousness," will shine like the stars. In this way, they, like the Messiah, will have part in the glory of Yahweh, and the splendour of the God of Israel will be reflected upon them as upon Yahweh's Chosen One.[10]

Doubtless the מַשְׂכִּילִים, *maśkîlîm*, "those who are wise," and the מַצְדִּיקִים, *maṣdîqîm*, "those who make righteous," are the "teachers of righteousness," those who taught the faithful Israel to live in righteousness, that is to say, to observe the laws of God, and, in spite of all kinds of pressure, to follow the footsteps of the fathers in the way of the statutes established by the Covenant uniting the Chosen People to Yahweh.[11] Their speech and even more their stand led the believers upon the right road; their martyrdom (Dan. XI. 33 ff.; II Macc. VI. 18 ff., VII. 1 ff., etc.) conferred an unimpeachable authority upon their teaching; it is not impossible that the believers regarded it as having atoning power.

It is striking to note that the terms מַשְׂכִּילִים, *maśkîlîm*, מַצְדִּיקִים, *maṣdîqîm*, and רַבִּים, *rabbîm*, the "many," are to be found, in one form or another, in the last of the Servant Songs. The writer of Dan. XII. 2 f. doubtless bases himself on this text, he identifies the Servant with the group of the faithful who, enlightened by Yahweh, instruct the people and even go as far as to sacrifice themselves to purify it—with those "teachers of righteousness" who, despite the persecutions, expect their cause to triumph, and see the mysterious prophecy of Is. LIII actualised in their own destiny; Dan. XII. 2 f. was thus an early interpretation of

[8] J. HUIZINGA, *The Waning of the Middle Ages*, London 1924, p. 198.
[9] Daniel will be among them (Dan. XII. 13).
[10] EICHRODT, *op. cit.*, VOL. III, pp. 158 f.
[11] The "Justifying Wise" are, for the Talmud, the teachers of Israel; for Eben Ezra, the men of the Mishna; for J. A. Montgomery, the Assideans, the "pious," the party of the Pharisees.

this song; it shows where the *Ḥasidim* found their special assurance of their glorious future. The Book of Isaiah, in fact, made both their present trouble and their final triumph clear to them.[12]

The writer of Dan. XII. 1 ff. says little about the resurrection. He asserts the fact, but he does not enlarge upon its realisation. This brevity suggests that his readers are aware of what he is referring to. The proclamation that the dead will awaken does not appear to be an absolute novelty in Maccabean times.

This text is concerned with the resurrection of a certain number, מִן, *min*, "some," of the perished. Only belatedly, and not without hesitation, will the Jews reach the idea of a universal resurrection.[13] The perished summoned to everlasting life or to everlasting shame are probably Jews, the best and the worst elements among the Chosen People; the mass of the people does not appear to be interested in an event which will enable the *Ḥasidim* to be rewarded and the impious punished; the indifferent will thus remain in the dust. Justice requires the resurrection, for only the resurrection provides the one answer to the problem raised by the death of the most faithful servants of the Living God. "The martyrs will be raised," such is the truth that comes home, then, to the persecuted *Ḥasidim*; the sacrifice of the witnesses sets them free from the bonds of Sheol; he who loses his life for Yahweh's sake shall find it again.[14] Yahweh's final victory will not leave His worshippers in the land of dust; those who have served Him here below will be reunited with Him to live in the splendour of His presence.

d. Conclusion

The first definite assertion of the resurrection of the dead is found in Dan. XII. 2 f., but the way in which the writer speaks

[12] H. L. GINSBERG, "The Oldest Interpretation of the Suffering Servant," *Vet. test.*, 1953, pp. 400 ff. Points of contact between Is. LIII and the Qumrân Community have also been established recently (M. DELCOR, *Vet. test.*, 1954, p. 219); thus it seems that for those Jews who in spite of the difficulty of the times remained faithful to Yahweh the Servant Songs assumed a special significance, of which we find many echoes in Biblical and extra-Biblical Judaism.

[13] H. STRACK and P. BILLERBECK, *Kommentar z. N. T.*, 1928, vol. IV, *excursus*, "Allgemeine oder teilweise Auferstehung," pp. 1166-98.

[14] II Macc. VII. 9, 11 f., 13 f., 23, 29, 36 f., XII. 43 f., XIV. 46.

about it allows us to conjecture the conception to be less novel than it appears. Preoccupation with a victory over death existed before the text in Daniel.

According to this passage, the resurrection is not universal; it primarily concerns the Chosen People, and only some of its perished members, the *Ḥasidim* deceased before the triumph of the God of the Jews, and the renegades who have escaped His wrath.

The resurrection makes retribution even after death possible, and in particular it allows of the chastisement of Yahweh's adversaries and the glorification of His most faithful adherents, and especially of the "teachers of righteousness" who taught the people to observe the commandments of God.

The resurrection thus particularly concerns the faithful worshippers of the God of Israel; here Dan. xii. 2 f. appears to be an interpretation of the last Song of the Servant of Yahweh affording a glimpse of how the account of the ultimate lot of God's Chosen was understood in the Maccabean period; Yahweh will pluck His servants out of the shadows and cause them to dwell in His glory.

Finally, the resurrection asserted in Dan. xii. 2 f. is not the outcome of academic reasoning, it is a consequence of the martyrdom of the *Ḥasidim*, the fruit of the struggles and sufferings of a people oppressed for its faith; it was not elaborated by the theologians, but was impressed upon men by the martyrs who, dying, dared to declare: "My bodily parts I received from God, for His laws I offer them, and from Him I hope to receive them again" (ii Macc. vii. 11).

We shall have occasion to revert to the connexion between martyrdom and the resurrection, which we have already sensed in Is. xxvi. 19 and which at the present we are discussing with reference to Dan. xii. 2 f. and the victims of Antiochus Epiphanes.[15]

GENERAL CONCLUSIONS

In the course of this chapter, we have been considering several important texts, each of which, in its own way, asserts the possibility or even the actuality of a conquest of death by the

---

[15] Cp. doubtless also Is. liii; cp. below, pp. 218-21 ff.

Living God, and the resurrection of some though not all of the
perished. We shall discuss these testimonies again in the third
part of this book. Let us note, however, their extreme variety
in form and in substance alike. As they are, we observe that
they span six centuries of history in the course of which the
Chosen People underwent many changes. Thus Hos. vi and
xiii date from the royal period; Ezek. xxxvii and Is. liii were
written during the Exile; and Is. xxv and xxvi and Dan. xii
are among the latest documents in the Old Testament, belonging to the fourth or even to the second century b.c.

Moreover, these texts answer to different interests; the
contemporaries of Hosea and of Ezekiel are concerned about
the future of the Holy Nation; the writers of the Apocalypse of
Isaiah and of the Book of Daniel are thinking about the lot of
the faithful members of the Chosen People deceased before
their God's final victory; Deutero-Isaiah is exercised about the
vindication of the Servant of Yahweh. Let us also note that
Is. xxvi and Dan. xii are at one in envisaging the resurrection
of the *Ḥasidim*, since, in His righteousness, Yahweh cannot
condemn His worshippers and His enemies to the same Sheol;
but what the first passage expresses in the form of a yet hesitant
prayer, the second clearly asserts as an indisputable fact. Let
us remember another difference; the circumstances of Hosea
and Ezekiel are entirely antithetical: the former has to struggle
against the facile optimism of his interlocutors, who confuse the
God of Israel with some sort of agricultural divinity; the latter
is contending with the deep-rooted despair of the exiles, who
refuse to admit the possibility of revival for the Chosen People.
In the first case, the theme of the resurrection is borrowed from
the surrounding heathenism, and Hosea rejects it; in the
second, it is based on the creative power of Yahweh, of which
Ezekiel paints a striking picture.

In short, we have to take this diversity into account when
we seek to understand how the People of God was led to believe
in the resurrection of the dead. Every interpretation that would
ignore the variety of the witness of the Old Testament seems
to us to be, *a priori*, false; the texts themselves invite us to
acknowledge many causes for the birth and growth of belief in
the revival of the perished.

Chapter III

"Nothing can Separate us from the Living God . . ."

Certain passages in the Old Testament, whose interpretation has been and still is a subject of much controversy, remain to be examined: these are Pss. XVI, XLIX, and LXXIII, and Job XIX. Some exegetes consider that in these—which, it should be borne in mind, present textual difficulties—either the hope of resurrection or the believer's assurance of immortality is expressed; others think, on the contrary, that the verses in question say nothing more than the Old Testament as a whole asserts, namely, that God is able to rescue His faithful from death at the eleventh hour; His saving interventions thus take place here and not hereafter. Each case must be examined on its own merits before we can attempt to offer a general answer to this question.

IN THE PSALMS

Ps. XVI. 9-11: "I dwell secure"

Most of the commentators, for example B. Duhm, H. Gunkel, C. A. Briggs, A. T. Nikolainen, etc., consider this psalm to be post-Exilic; in A. Weiser's opinion, however, it presupposes the existence of the First Temple. J. Steinmann connects some of its expressions with the Egyptian cult, holding that its writer belonged to a Jewish community living in the Delta of the Nile.

a. Text

9 Therefore my heart is glad, and my soul
     rejoices;
  my body also dwells secure.

10 *For thou wilt not give up my soul to Sheol,*
  or let thy godly one see the Pit.

¹¹ Thou dost show me the path of life;
in thy presence there is fulness
of joy,
in thy right hand there are pleasures
for evermore.[1]

b. *Psalm xvi as a whole*

This song is a psalm of confidence. The writer is voicing his happiness at being in communion with the Living God; thanks to this he has tasted a serene joy, he has discovered the wellspring of a veritable and inexhaustible felicity. Yahweh is his Lord, his chiefest good, his refuge, and his portion. In short, He is his all; and so, for this *ḥasid*, the presence of the God of Israel is the ground of his assurance and joyfulness.

[1] C. A. and E. G. BRIGGS, *I. C. C.*, 1906-07; W. STAERK, *Schr. A. T.*, 1911; B. DUHM, *K. H.-C. A. T.*, 1922; P. VOLZ, "Zum Verständnis von Psalm 16 und Psalm 130," *Marti-Festschrift*, Beihefte z. *Z. alttest. W.*, 1925, pp. 287 ff.; H. GUNKEL, *Hb. A. T.*, 1926; E. KÖNIG, *Die Psalmen*, 1927; R. KITTEL, *Komm. A. T.*, 1929; H. SCHMIDT, *Hk. A. T.*, 1934; C. MERCIER, *B. Cent.*, 1947; E. PODECHARD, *Le Psautier*, VOL. I, 1949; A. WEISER, *A. T. D.*, 1950; R. TOURNAY and R. SCHWAB, *B. Jérus.*, 1950; G. VON RAD, "Gerechtigkeit und Leben in den Psalmen," *Festschrift A. Bertholet*, 1950, pp. 432 ff.; J. STEINMANN, *Les Psaulmes*, 1951; H. J. FRANKEN, *The Mystical Communion with JHWH in the Book of Psalms*, Leyden 1954, pp. 70 ff.; EICHRODT, *Theol. des A. T.*, VOL. III, pp. 165 ff.; C. BARTH, *op. cit.* (above, p. 1, n. 1), pp. 153 ff.; SELLIN, *Theologie des A. T.*, p. 282; NIKOLAINEN, *op. cit.* (above, p. 131, n. 3), p. 121, etc.

Vs. 9: כְּבוֹדִי, *kᵉḇôḏî*, may mean "my soul." Certain critics, such as H. Gunkel, have emended it to כְּבֵדִי, *kᵉḇēḏî*, that is to say, "my liver."

Vs. 10: שַׁחַת, *šaḥaṭ*, R.S.V. "pit," originally means "snare"; here it denotes Sheol. The LXX translated it as διαφθορά, that is to say, "corruption."

It was in that sense that the N.T. writers understood this term (Acts II. 25-31, XIII. 35); while the Psalmist envisages that Yahweh will not allow His worshipper to die, the versions suggest that God will not let his body decompose.

Vs. 11: אֹרַח חַיִּים, *'ōraḥ ḥayyîm*, "the path of life," is also found in the Israelite Wisdom literature (Prov. v. 6, x. 17, xv. 24), and could be of Egyptian provenance.

The LXX read πληρώσεις, that is to say "תַּשְׂבִּיעֵנִי, *taśbîʿēnî*, "thou wilt satisfy me," instead of שֹׂבַע, *śōḇaʿ*, "fulness." נֶצַח, *neṣaḥ*, "for ever," lays stress on the fact that the pleasures bestowed by God are far from being exhausted.

The psalm opens with a petition, the believer prays God to guard him, in the midst of the devastating idolatry by which he is surrounded, he seeks shelter and counsel in Him.

The song, which expresses the absolute devotion of the faithful to the God of Israel, is divided into three strophes. In the first (vss. 1-4) the writer tells Yahweh: "Thou art my all." He calls upon Him, separating himself from those who are giving themselves over to heathen practices, seeking instead the fellowship of men who are dedicated to God (vs. 3); [2] two groups seem to be face to face: the one is composed of the Israelites who have been seduced by heathenism, the other of Yahweh's adherents, among whose number the psalmist is to be counted.

The second strophe develops the assertion of the believer who, to indicate what Yahweh means to him, makes use of imagery borrowed from the cultic and juridical language of his people. He declares that the Living God is חֶלְקִי, *ḥelqî*, lit. "my portion." The expression refers to the institution of the allocation of the arable land and brings the names given to some members of the Chosen People to mind, such as Jeremiah's father (Jer. I. 1), and the high priest in the reign of Josiah (II Kings XXIII. 4), [3] which may have a confessional significance. This declaration, precisely stated in Ps. XVI. 6, recalls the ritual portioning-out of the Holy Land among the tribes of Israel (Num. XXVI. 55 ff., XXXIV. 13; Josh. XIII. 7), and particularly the situation of the Levites, who did not receive a share of the land, but whose inheritance and possession is Yahweh Himself (Deut. X. 9; Num. XVIII. 20 ff.) Here the psalmist is spiritualising an ancient tradition; he is indicating that the supreme good, the presence of the Living God, has been given to him without money and without price.

Yahweh is also his cup. This second comparison reinforces the first. "To partake of the cup" with someone means, in a

---

[2] It must be borne in mind that Ps. XVI. 3 is interpreted in various ways. For example, E. Podechard holds that the expression "the saints" is applied ironically to the idolaters, and there is no reference to the *Ḥasidim*; according to R. Tournay, it meant the holy places where more or less magical rites were performed; conversely, for W. Staerk, E. König, C. A. Briggs, etc., the קְדוֹשִׁים, *qᵉḏôšîm*, "saints," are the followers of Yahweh; cp. also H. J. FRANKEN, *op. cit.*, pp. 71 ff.

[3] Cp. also II Kings XVIII. 18; I Chron. VI. 13; Neh. VIII. 4, etc.

very special sense for the Semite, "to unite one's lot" with his. Thus the believer is showing how strong the bonds binding him to Yahweh are; between the *hasid* and his God there subsists a veritable intimacy. The psalmist, fortified by this communion, goes on his way in peace, and has fellowship day and night with the God of Israel.[4]

The final strophe (Ps. 9-11) returns to the same theme, joy, rest, blessing, but contemplates it in terms of the future. Tomorrow as well as today, Yahweh's presence will shed light on the life of the faithful; for this reason, he has fear of nothing, not even of death, he goes on in the way of life and his joy has no end.

We must now define with precision the scope of the expressions contained in vss. 9 ff.

c. Vss. 9-11: Meaning

Let us remember that the writer of the Acts of the Apostles cites this text on two occasions: first in Peter's sermon on the Day of Pentecost (Acts II. 25 ff.), and again in Paul's apologia at Antioch in Pisidia (Acts XIII. 35).

According to the Apostolic interpretation, the writer of the psalm, who is David, is here foretelling the resurrection of Jesus Christ. Peter definitely states that the King of Israel is predicting that He will not see, not death, but corruption, as the Greek version indicates; thus he is not referring to himself, since he is dead and his sepulchre is known, but to one of his descendants (Acts II. 29 ff.) Paul understands the text in the same way, and actually says: "For David, after he had served the counsel of God in his own generation, fell asleep, and was laid with his fathers, and saw corruption. But He whom God raised up saw no corruption" (Acts XIII. 36 f.) Thus for the primitive Church, reading this psalm in its Greek translation, this passage refers to Easter.

Exegetes are far from being agreed among themselves as to

---

[4] According to H. J. FRANKEN, *op. cit.*, pp. 71 ff., 74, vss. 7 and 8 referred to a certain technique "in order to create religious experience . . . to perceive the reality of God functioning as an inward light. . . ." He states that, with this intention, certain of the *Hasidim* used to practise the cultivation of the spiritual life.

the precise significance of these verses.   Some, at variance with
the traditional view of the Church, consider that, according
to the Hebrew text, the writer is only expressing his assurance
that Yahweh will not suffer him to die prematurely.   He does
not dread "evil" death;   in some way his piety is a guarantee
against it.   There is absolutely no question of resurrection or
immortality here;   such is the opinion of H. Gunkel in particular,
and, more recently, of C. Barth.

Other critics think that this psalm expresses more than the
simple hope of dying at a ripe old age;   the psalmist was in
advance of most of the believers in Israel: his desire is that
death may not break the bonds that unite him with Yahweh.
Thus, according to C. A. Briggs, the *hasid* was desiring to have
his abode in a special region in Sheol, in communion with the
God of Israel.   For E. König and R. Kittel, these verses imply
the presentiment, if not the assertion, of a blessed life in the
Beyond;   J. Steinmann calls this prayer "the Psalm of Immortality," and thinks that the writer is regarding Yahweh as the
Egyptian dead regard Osiris.

It seems that the psalmist does not have the resurrection
in mind;   that remains outwith his interests.   No more is he
picturing a sort of translation into the Beyond, as P. Volz
suggests,[5] but is putting his trust in God for the future as for
the present.   As A. Weiser justly observes, his understanding
of how it will be is less important to him than the fact that
Yahweh will remain in communion with him.   He does not
dread a sudden brutal death;   we must go even further;   he
has no fear of death at all, not because he considers that he
must have everlasting life, but because of the presence of the
Living God the problem of death becomes secondary;   in some
sense death is blotted out, it retreats.   The *hasid* who is living
by God, for God, and in God, no longer looks upon death as a
threatening present reality;   in the presence of the Living God
it loses its importance.   The believer is so attached to Yahweh,
so fully taken up with Him, that his life no longer unfolds

[5] VOLZ, *op. cit.*, pp. 289 f., thinks that the *hasid* is distinguishing himself
here from a community of more or less heathen mystics, and is setting his
faith in Yahweh, who is his *summum bonum* over against their religiosity,
while at the same time making use of expressions or imagery borrowed
from mysticism.

under the sign of death, but rather in the radiance of the glory
of God; in a sense, he finds himself back where Adam was
before the Fall. His life is full, and he does not imagine that
one day his joy may end: his blessing cannot be taken away
from him, since Yahweh is keeping him safe.

In the expressions inspired by the faith of the *ḥasid*, a sort
of immortality is implicit; this word may, of course, lend
itself to misunderstanding, but here it suggests that the divine
presence has neither beginning nor end. As G. von Rad
rightly emphasises,[6] the problem is not one of knowing whether
the bonds that unite him to Yahweh concern his earthly life
or his life in the Hereafter, as commentators on these verses
too often suppose. To lay down such an alternative is to
ignore the fact that, for the believer, communion with the
Living God is a reality transcending the limits imposed on the
creature, it brings Yahweh's inexhaustible power of life into
the daily existence of the faithful; he who has the God of
Israel for his portion possesses a never-failing joy; in some
sense he lives in a sort of eternal present.

d. *Conclusion*

This psalm is the work of a Yahweh-worshipper who has
found his supreme happiness and his sovereign good in God.
He lives in fellowship with the Living God and ardently gives
expression to his joy and his peace, and he knows that these
will have no end, since he can count on the faithful presence
of his God.

There is no question of the resurrection here. The psalmist
is not actually thinking about dying, and is not looking to God
to rescue him from the grave. In some sense, death has already
been overcome by him, not of course in principle, but in fact,
by the bonds that unite him to Yahweh.

This psalm is speaking neither of the immortality of the
faithful, nor of his translation into the Beyond; the *ḥasid* is
not really concerned about what will happen after death,
his sole interest is in praising his chiefest good: Yahweh, God
of Israel.

The real question in Ps. xvi is that of communion with the

---

[6] G. VON RAD, *op. cit.*, 1950, p. 435.

Living God; the writer foresees no end to this; he does not understand how its persistence will be possible, but that does not trouble his mind, because it depends on God. Even now, all things are his, since Yahweh is with him. God will not leave the man for whom He is all far from Himself; after Easter, the faith of the psalmist became the great certainty that the Church has to proclaim to the world.

1 Ps. XLIX. 15: "My God will receive me. . . ."

According to the consensus of critical opinion, Ps. XLIX is a Wisdom psalm which, like Pss. XXXVII and LXXIII, has for its theme the prosperity of the ungodly and the tribulation of Yahweh's servants.

a. *Text*

But God will ransom my soul from the
power of Sheol,
for he will receive me.[1]

b. *Ps. xlix as a whole*

The subject of this psalm is the problem of retribution. The Chosen People has learned, especially from the teaching of Ezekiel, that in this life Yahweh rewarded the righteous and punished the wicked (Ezek. XVIII). Prosperity ought therefore to be the fruit of piety, and adversity the result of iniquity; now this assertion is daily denied by the facts, so much so that wealth tends to become identified with ungodliness, and

---

[1] C. A. and E. G. BRIGGS, *I. C. C.*, 1906-07; W. STAERK, *Schr. A. T.*, 1911; R. KITTEL, *Komm. A. T.*, 1914; H. GUNKEL, *Hk. A. T.*, 1926; E. KÖNIG, *Die Psalmen*, 1927; H. SCHMIDT, *Hb. A. T.*, 1934; P. VOLZ, "Ps. 49," *Z. alttest. W.*, 1937, pp. 235 ff.; J. LINDBLOM, "Die Eschatologie des 49. Psalms," in *Horae Soederblomianae, Mélanges J. Pedersen*, I, 1944; P. HUMBERT, *B. Cent.*, 1947; E. PODECHARD, *Le Psautier*, I, 1949; A. WEISER, *A. T. D.*, 1950; R. TOURNAY and R. SCHWAB, *B. Jérus.*, 1950; M. STENZEL, "Ps. 49. 14-16a," *Th. Z.*, 1954, pp. 152 ff.; SELLIN, *op. cit.* (above, p. 55, n. 5), p. 284; EICHRODT, *Theol. des A. T.*, VOL. III, p. 164; NIKOLAINEN, *op. cit.* (above, p. 131, n. 3), p. 125; C. BARTH, *op. cit.* (above, p. 1, n. 1), pp. 158 ff., etc.

poverty with keeping God's commandments. The manifest success of those who scorn Yahweh is a stumbling-block for the believer. Like others before and after him,[2] the writer of Ps. xlix tries to resolve this difficulty and reconcile doctrine with reality.

His work is divided into two parts (vss. 1-12 and 13-20), each ending with the same refrain (vss. 12, 20), which lays stress on the stupidity, or even the brutishness, of the great of this earth, loaded indeed with honours and possessions, but devoid of understanding—that is to say, of piety. The psalmist begins his meditations on an emphatic note, he has a message for all the world and has particular disclosures to make to the rich and the poor, who are equally concerned in the enigma whose solution he claims to bring (vss. 1-4).

After this solemn introduction, the first strophe (vss. 5-12) offers an answer to the question of the prosperity of the un-righteous by asserting that this is only ephemeral. The human situation must therefore be viewed *sub specie aeternitatis*. Wealth does not last, it does not ensure length of days. None can redeem his life with money (vss. 7-8). The wicked perish, and, as must be borne in mind, so do the righteous (vs. 10). No man is immortal, no man can keep his possessions for ever. Thus the psalmist's theme is simple: death overtakes every man, the prosperity of the rich is not everlasting, it disappears in the hour of death.

In the second part, the writer repeats and develops his earlier assertions. The interpretation of vss. 13 ff. is necessarily dependent on what meaning we give to vs. 15. This still refers to the rich, upon whom death battens: when they die they take neither riches nor honour with them (vs. 17), and they will never see the light again (vs. 19). The reasoning does not seem very original; if vs. 15 is not taken into account, the meditations of the psalmist in the long run offer only cold enough comfort to the oppressed and suffering righteous.

c. Vs. 15: Interpretation

The few words that constitute this verse have been the occasion of many commentaries. Some exegetes, as F. Baethgen and

---

[2] Cp. esp. Pss. xxxvii, lxxiii, and Job.

F. Schwally, consider that the writer is speaking in the name of the faithful community; this will survive, under Yahweh's protection (vs. 15), while the wicked will vanish away. For other expositors, this fifteenth verse did not form part of the original psalm, but was an addition made, doubtless, under the influence of Ps. LXXIII. Such is the opinion of W. Staerk, A. Bentzen, and H. Gunkel; for this last, the central idea of Ps. XLIX is that death reduces all men to the same lot and levels out all inequalities.

But if this fifteenth verse be excised, the second strophe merely repeats the opening assertions of the psalm, there is no progression in its thought, whose jejuneness is in contrast with the psalmist's solemn declarations. Thus most of the commentators view this verse, which is found even in the earliest of the versions, as authentic and indeed as marking the culminating point of this Wisdom poem.

Here the writer was expressing not only his assurance of not being overtaken by premature death, which is the view of W. Nowack, J. Wellhausen, and more recently C. Barth, but also, according to E. Podechard, his hope of being preserved from Sheol and received into the presence of God. For P. Volz, death, instead of being the great leveller, as H. Gunkel imagines, on the contrary, according to this psalm, effects an absolute separation between the wicked and the righteous: the former go into the world of shades for ever, the rich man has no power against Sheol; the latter dwell with God, and Sheol is impotent in face of the bonds that unite them to Yahweh.[3]

Critics observe, in general, that the verb לָקַח, *lāqaḥ*, "to receive, take," is found in Ps. LXXIII. 24, and, in particular, in Gen. v. 24 and II Kings II. 3 ff.; since these last passages deal with the translations of Enoch and Elijah, the psalmist, by this term, was expressing the hope of escaping death and of somehow experiencing the extraordinary lot of these men of

---

[3] P. Volz, following Theodoret and the Vulgate, draws particular attention to the relationship subsisting between Ps. XLIX and the Parable of the Rich Man and Lazarus (Lk. XVI.); in this psalm the abode of the dead is already transformed into a sort of infernal region, and retribution is postponed until after death. The revolutionary conceptions of the psalmist, the result of a special revelation, the commentator concludes, thus justify his preamble.

faith. Here, too, לָקַח, *lāqaḥ*, had the technical meaning of "to translate" (to the presence of the Living God) and not merely that of "to guard, to protect." [4]   For B. Duhm, this event was to take place after the death of the believer; according to R. Kittel, instead of it. A. Weiser considers with some justice that the fact is of more importance than its modality: in his faith, the psalmist was certain that he would overcome death; he was ignorant of whether he would be translated or raised; but in any case that mattered little to him, he was content to put his trust in Yahweh. "Faith's assurance," A. Weiser sums up, "consists not in knowledge but in power."

Doubtless it is irrelevant to say that this psalm refers to resurrection or immortality. On a closer study of the text, we must note, with J. Lindblom, that the second strophe merely recapitulates the ideas expressed in the first. The writer, after having declared that the rich are not going to escape death, describes the end that awaits them; it takes the form of a violent and utter catastrophe; [5] it smites all the wicked with one fell blow, swiftly and fearfully, it mows them down or devours them implacably. Vs. 14 suggests that Death leads its flock as in a sort of Dance of the Dead; in the morning, לַבֹּקֶר, *labbōqer*, that is to say, in the hour of judgment, the greatness of the mighty vanishes away and the righteous are triumphant. [6]

It seems that, according to certain Israelite traditions referred to by J. Lindblom, the righteousness of Yahweh is made manifest by a judgment which overtakes the wicked all at once; in this way, their dreadful end eradicates their ephemeral prosperity. History preserves the memory of such signal chastisements: the Egyptians perish in the Red Sea; [7] the confederates of Korah go down to the dwelling-place of the dead alive; [8] the Assyrians are decimated outside Jerusalem. [9] Ps. XXXVII similarly suggests that the wicked will be

---

[4] Cp. above, p. 69.

[5] Lindblom says "eine summarische Katastrophe."

[6] לַבֹּקֶר, *labbōqer*, "in the morning," means not only "soon," "quickly" (K. Budde, B. Duhm), and "every morning"(C. A. Briggs) but, according to E. König, "in the morning, the great morning (of the Day of the Lord)."

[7] Ex. XIV. 17 f., 26 ff., XV. 5, 10; Deut. XI. 4; etc.

[8] Num. XVI. 28 ff.; Ps. LV. 15.   [9] II Kings XIX. 35; Ps. LXXVI. 5.

smitten suddenly, wiped out for ever,[10] while Yahweh protects
the righteous in time of tribulation.

Thus the psalmist states firstly that all men die, riches do
not redeem any man's life (Ps. XLIX. 5-12); and then that the
wicked will meet with death suddenly, brutally, fearfully, on
Yahweh's appointed judgment-day, but the faithful can then
count on the protection of his God. He will not fall with the
wicked, Yahweh will receive him to Himself, He will preserve
him alive (vss. 13 ff.)

This psalm thus asserts, on the one hand, that neither power
nor fortune is of any avail for the creature in its perishing hour,
and, on the other, that in death itself the difference between
the man who serves God and the man who scorns Him is
made apparent. The psalmist is sure that his God will not
let him suffer the fate of the impious; through faith, he asserts
that God will be with him, the hand of Sheol is impotent
against the presence of Yahweh with those who are His own.
Perhaps he goes even further and envisages the possibility of
being received by the Living God, either before or after his
death; we cannot dogmatise upon this point. In any case, for
the psalmist, the heart of the matter is that it is impossible that
the divine retribution will not, sooner or later, be made
manifest.

d. Conclusion

Ps. XLIX does not refer to the resurrection, at least not in an
obviously explicit way. Its starting-point is the manifest
scandal of the prosperity of the wicked. It gives a twofold
answer to this, recalling that no man is immortal, and that
wicked men will meet a fearful end, while the *ḥasid* remains
assured of the protection of Yahweh.

It is possible, but not certain, that the believer thinks that
he will escape not only premature death or the judgment that
is going to smite all the ungodly, but, by some special dispensation, death itself as well. He would then go to live in the
presence of the God whom he served in this world. Yahweh
would take him—יִקָּחֵנִי, *yiqqāḥēnî*, "he will take me"—to dwell

---

[10] Ps. XXXVII. 2, 9 f., 13, 20, 22, 28, 35 f., etc., and 19, 28, 33, 39 f., etc.;
cp. also Pss. LV. 15, 23, LXIII, 9 ff., CIV. 35; Ps. Sol. IV. 6, XIII. 2, XV. 7, etc.

with Him for ever.   We may have some hesitation over this.
The study of Ps. LXXIII will doubtless enable us to come to a
more positive conclusion.   One thing is obvious: the faith of
this Old Testament believer enables him to wait for the Day
of Judgment unafraid, his piety bids him consider the prosperity
of the wicked in the light of his knowledge of Yahweh, and
choose the fellowship of the Living God in its stead.

Ps. LXXIII. 23-8: "With God in Heaven and on Earth . . ."

In Ps. LXXIII we will find again the theme of the prosperity of
the ungodly and the sufferings of those who would remain
pure in heart (vs. 13).   The solution proposed by the writer
is appreciably the same as that offered in Ps. LXIX; here,
however, the psalmist lays even more stress upon the privilege
of the man who lives close to God (vs. 28).

a. Text

23 Nevertheless I am continually with thee,
      thou dost hold my right hand.
24 Thou dost guide me with my counsel,
      and afterward thou will receive me to
      glory.
25 Whom have I in heaven but thee?
      And there is nothing upon earth that I
      desire besides thee.
26 My flesh and my heart may fail,
      but God is the strength of my heart
      and my portion for ever.
27 For lo, those who are far from thee shall
      perish;
      thou dost put an end to those who
      are false to thee.
28 But for me it is good to be near God;
      I have made the Lord GOD my
      refuge,
      that I may tell of all thy works.[1]

---

[1] Lit. (24*b*) "And after . . . glory . . . thou wilt receive me."   B. DUHM,
K. H.-C. A. T., 1899;   C. A. and E. G. BRIGGS, *I. C. C.*, 1906-07;   W.
STAERK, *Schr. A. T.*, 1911;   R. KITTEL, *Komm. A. T.*, 1922;   H. GUNKEL,

b. Ps. lxxiii as a whole

Like Pss. XLIX and XXXVII, this Wisdom psalm thus deals with
the success of the wicked and the tribulation of the believers.
What answer the psalmist offers to the agonising question of
retribution is largely contingent on the meaning attributed
to vs. 24; nevertheless, we may in any case affirm that the
writer sets another kind of satisfaction, grounded on communion with the Living God, over against the well-being of
the ungodly. There are, in point of fact, two sorts of prosperity:
the one, plain to be seen, but ephemeral and ending in frustra-
tion, is that of the rich—bloated, proud, and sheltered from
the hardships of other men—who mock at God and unlawfully
amass countless possessions: the other is reserved for the faithful, it is the fruit of a life that is filled with the presence of
Yahweh, it goes with an existence of which God is the constant
guide and refuge; true blessing consists in having the God of
Israel as one's portion and in being able to draw near to Him.

Such are the meditations of the believer who composed
Ps. LXXIII; after long seeking and sore striving, he remains
faithful to his people's heritage, and declares (vs. 1): "Truly
God is good to the upright. . . ." But this assertion is a cry of
faith struggling with doubt, it is the "Nevertheless" with which
the *hasid* bids defiance to the world scene.

Like his brethren, the psalmist was scandalised by the insolent
triumph of those who forget God and His laws, it seemed to
him that it was of no avail to follow the divine commandments,

Hk. A. T., 1926; E. KÖNIG, *Die Psalmen*, 1927; H. SCHMIDT, *Hb. A. T.*,
1934; L. RANDON, *B. Cent.*, 1947; E. PODECHARD, *Le Psautier*, I, 1949,
R. TOURNAY and R. SCHWAB, *B. Jérus.*, 1950; G. VON RAD, *op. cit.* (above,
p. 148, n. 1), 1950, pp. 433 ff.; A. WEISER, *A. T. D.*, 1950; E. WÜRTHWEIN;
"Erwägungen zu Psalm 73," *Festschrift A. Bertholet*, 1950, pp. 532 ff.;
H. RINGGREN, "Einige Bemerkungen zum LXXIII Psalm," *Vet. test.*, 1953,
pp. 265 ff.; SELLIN, *op. cit.* (above, p. 55, n. 5), pp. 275 ff.; EICHRODT,
Theol. des A. T., VOL. III, pp. 162 ff.; NIKOLAINEN, *op. cit.* (above, p. 131, n. 3),
p. 127; C. BARTH, *op. cit.* (above p. 1, n. 1), pp. 161 ff.

Vs. 24 will be explained later. In vs. 25, the Greek and Syriac versions
and Jerome read מָה, *mâ*, "what," instead of מִי, *mî*, "who," that is to say,
"What is there for me (apart from Thee)?" "The strength of my heart"
(vs. 26) may be taken to be a gloss, as also the closing words of vs. 28 "That
I may tell of all thy works." Idolatry is a form of adultery (vs. 27; cp.
Hos. II. 7; Jer. III. 6 ff.; Ps. CVI. 39; Ezek. XVI. 15 ff., XXIII. 2 f.)

and that all went well with those who shamelessly and continually say (vs. 11), "How can God know? Is there knowledge in the Most High?" and that he ought to have copied the man whose portrait he so vividly paints; but on his way to denial, a thought gives him pause, he did not desire to betray the heritage of his fathers, he remembered the ancestral faith, he felt that in spite of all he was one of the Chosen People. Nevertheless his struggles went on until the solution was revealed to him.

He himself says (vs. 17) that he was sorely perplexed until he went into the "sanctuaries of God," and realised the final lot of the wicked. This seventeenth verse has been variously interpreted; the solutions proposed are contingent upon how vs. 24 is understood.

Thus, for certain writers, מִקְדְּשֵׁי־אֵל, *miqdeše-'ēl*, the "sanctuaries of God," denotes quite simply the Temple at Jerusalem; [2] this is what the Greek and Syriac versions already suggest. H. Schmidt, for example, thinks that in making his way to the Temple, the psalmist witnessed some extraordinary occurrence —perhaps the sudden death of a rich man as the result of a heart attack! This sudden death showed him where true prosperity was to be found. A. Weiser considers that the change of outlook in the writer of Ps. LXXIII derives not from an inward light but from an encounter with the Living God in the course of a cultic ceremony in the Temple. It was a theophany that caused the reversal of the believer's conceptions and made Him look on reality as Yahweh saw it. H. Ringgren develops this idea further: he believes that the psalmist was present, during a festival, which might have been the New Year festival, at a ritual performance in which the ephemeral triumph of the wicked and the decisive defeat of the enemies of the God of Israel were successively represented. The Scandinavian scholar thus interprets Ps. LXXIII in the light of the myth of the dying and rising god, whose destiny is enacted by the king, who has periodically to engage in combat with the powers of Chaos, and puts them to flight only after having given ground before them. This comparison is ingenious, but ultimately improbable; it may explain the psalmist's terminology, not his work as a whole. It is not likely that it was through a representation, albeit a cultic one, that the

[2] Jer. LI. 51; Ezek. XXI. 7; Ps. LXVIII. 5.

believer discovered the answer to the problem of retribution.
E. Podechard is doubtless nearer to the truth when he writes:
"It was within Temple circles that the psalmist was enlightened,
doubtless when he was admitted to one of the guilds of
singers. . . ." In point of fact, it does seem that the writer of
Ps. LXXIII has a particular and quasi-constant connexion with
the Temple, since he appears to be able to draw near to
Yahweh with ease (vs. 28). Père Tournay thinks, for his part
that "the divine sanctuaries" means simply the teaching contained in the Holy Scriptures.[3]

Certain commentators, as E. König, J. Meinhold, and R.
Kittel, connect vs. 17a with the "mysteries of God," τὰ μυστήρια
θεοῦ, referred to in the Book of Wisdom (Wis. II. 22). God had
revealed the solution of the problem that was perplexing the
psalmist, not in consequence of a cultic ceremony or a study of
the Torah, but by a mystical illumination, perhaps even in the
course of an ecstasy (II Cor. XII. 2 ff.) This explanation does
not take sufficient account of the fact that far from being
steeped in Hellenistic thought like the writer of the Book of
Wisdom, the psalmist behaves as a true Israelite; his "mysticism" scarcely brings that of the mystery cults to mind, it is
grounded on the revelation of Yahweh to His People.

We do not know exactly how this faithful man arrived at the
truth, but one thing is certain. An intervention by the Living
God was required to make him realise, on the one hand
(vs. 17b), the frailty and vanity of the well-being of the impious,
threatened by inevitable calamity and summoned to sudden
destruction, and, on the other (vss. 23 ff.), his own privilege,
since, in His faithfulness, Yahweh has preserved him in the
hour of temptation, and guides him today with His counsel,
and since nothing will be able to separate him from Him. God
is his portion, his chiefest good, in Heaven and on earth.

c. Vs. 24b: Meaning

We are now concerned with the interpretation of the following
words: וְאַחַר כָּבוֹד תִּקָּחֵנִי, *weʾaḥar kābôd tiqqāḥēnî*, the literal meaning
of which is "and after glory thou wilt take me." The word

---

[3] Ps. CXIX. 130; Prov. IX. 1 ff.; Ecclesiastes XIV. 23 f.; XXXIX. 1.

כָּבוֹד, *kāḇôḏ*, "glory," in particular, can be understood in different ways.

For Kimḥi, cited by E. Podechard, it denotes the soul; vs. 24*b* then means "after thou shalt take my glory," that is to say my soul; in short, the psalmist knows that he must die, only his death will not be the same as that of the ungodly.

H. Gunkel allows that the text of vs. 24*b* makes sense as it stands; he connects it with I Tim. III. 16, ἀνελήφθη ἐν δόξῃ; it would then be concerned with a translation into glory. But he prefers to emend it, holding that it has been corrupted in consequence of a confusion between כָּבוֹד, *kāḇôḏ*, "glory," and כָּבֵד, *kāḇēḏ*, "liver," and again between אַחַר, *'aḥar*, "after," and אֹרַח, *'ōraḥ*, "path." Thus he reads vs. 24*b*: וּבְאֹרַח כָּבֵד תְּחַזְּקֵנִי, *úḇā'ōraḥ kāḇēḏ teḥazzepēnî*, that is to say, "Thou wilt strengthen my liver on the way." [4] Thus for H. Gunkel, the psalmist is envisaging neither a salvation after death nor an assumption; he is only voicing his certainty of being guided and strengthened by Yahweh; vs. 24*b* follows naturally after vss. 23 and 24*a*.

For most of the exegetes, however, כָּבוֹד, *kāḇôḏ*, means "glory," and is to be construed adverbially; the Greek and Latin versions add a preposition as well, μετά or *cum*, and thus read "in glory" or "with glory." [5] For B. Duhm, the psalmist was proclaiming here that Yahweh is going to receive him into Paradise after his death. R. Kittel more simply declares that the bonds uniting the Living God and His worshipper will not be severed by death. [6] E. Sellin considers that this vs. 24*b* is the high-water-mark of the Old Testament, since, by a sheer act of faith, death is here transcended and vanquished.

For C. Barth, however, this exegesis is much too extravagant. The believer knows that he must die, he is referring neither to resurrection nor to immortality, but he is no longer afraid

---

[4] G. Beer proposes as his suggested reading: וְאֹרַח כָּבוֹד תּוֹרֵנִי, *we'ōraḥ kāḇôḏ tôrēnî*, that is to say, "and Thou wilt show me the path of glory."

[5] E. Podechard cites the various Latin renderings: "*et cum gloria suscepisti me*"; or "*et post gloriam tuam rege me*"; or again "*et postea in gloria suscipis me*." The writer was referring to some glorious event, either in the past or still to come.

[6] "Communion with God is everlasting," writes L. Randon, following the same line of thought, "it survives the destruction of the flesh and the heart."

of a premature death; "evil" death is impotent against him, just in so far as he is in God.[7]

It is unnecessary to enumerate the many hypotheses to which this vs. 24*b* has given rise. The critics are divided into two groups: the minority consider that here the psalmist is thinking only of his life on earth and in no sense of the Beyond; the majority hold, on the contrary, that the writer is proclaiming the fulfilment of the divine retribution, not before death, but by means of and after it; the wicked will lose their possessions and life, while the righteous will be received to the presence of Yawheh and will dwell in His glory.

It was particularly observed long ago that the verb לָקַח, *lāqaḥ*, "to take, receive," with "God" as subject and "man" as object, which is found in vs. 24*b*, is similarly employed in Ps. XLIX. 15 and in the accounts of the translations of Enoch (Gen. v. 25) and Elijah (II Kings II. 3, etc.) This was therefore a technical term for assumption. R. Kittel, W. Staerk, A. Bertholet, and G. von Rad have stressed this point; [8] it is possible that the writer of Ps. LXXIII envisaged a sort of translation for himself.

Yet it does not seem to be, for him, the heart of the matter to know whether his days on earth will be prolonged, or whether he has a prospect of life in the Beyond, but to live for ever in the presence of the Living God, in whom he has found his chiefest good. The solution of the problem of retribution, so long a stumbling-block to him, is to be found in God alone: that is to say, in a life lived in communion with Him. This is not a matter of giving an academic answer to a question that has haunted so many minds, but of a living experience which has been a sort of revelation to the believer. He now sees his own life and that of sinners as God sees them.

For the psalmist, the God of his people is all his joy. To live

---

[7] E. Würthwein proposes another interpretation; he adopts and modifies the collectivistic exegesis formerly held by Hitzig and Ewald. In his view it is the King of Israel who is speaking in this psalm; the future of Israel depends on his lot, and he is waiting for his enemies to be crushed, and for himself, and consequently the Holy Nation, to be covered with glory.

[8] R. KITTEL, *comm. ad loc.*; W. STAERK, *comm. ad loc.*; A. BERTHOLET, "The Pre-Christian Belief in the Resurrection," *Am. J. Th.*, 1916, p. 22; G. VON RAD, *op. cit.* (above, p. 148, n. 1), p. 435.

in His fellowship is security for tomorrow as for today. To depart from Him is to be doomed to disappear, and to draw near to the Living God is a privilege of which he does not foresee the end. Yahweh fills his whole mind and heart, and, in face of his faith, death seems to withdraw or at least lose its power to harm.

The conviction born in the *ḥasid's* soul in consequence of the intervention of his God, involves the beginning of the breaking-up of the constricting framework within which the Old Testament confined creaturely existence, and it prepared the way for Paul's assertion: "If God is for us, who is against us? . . . Neither death, nor life . . . will be able to separate us from the love of God . . ." (Rom. VIII. 31 ff.)

Thus, to an even greater degree than Ps. XLIX, and in the manner of Ps. XVI, Ps. LXXII lays stress on the significance of Yahweh for the believer. He praises Him as his sovereign good, his refuge, and his portion; his confidence and his joy most particularly bring to mind the tones of the *ḥasid* singing of his inheritance and cup in God (Ps. XVI. 5 ff.) In emphasising all that the Living God bestows on him, the psalmist develops the positive aspect of the divine retribution at greater length than the writer of Ps. XLIX does; of course, sharing as he does in the tradition of his people, he knows that a chastisement, as terrible as it is sudden, is in store for the impious, but above all he knows the privilege of the wise man who tastes the joy of the friendship of God. Similarly it seems that he is more positive in speaking about his own future; the expressions that he employs suggest that death could not separate him from his Lord, Yahweh is watching over him from the height of Heaven, he meets Him likewise at every step of his earthly way (vss. 25); perhaps he foresees the hour when, bereft of even his heart and flesh, he will be still with the Living God (vs. 26).

Though the psalm does not speak explicitly of either immortality or resurrection, though it does not specifically state that the believer will be translated to heaven but primarily tells of his present and ultimate blessing which infinitely transcends all that the ungodly greedy for worldly wealth can imagine, the manner in which the psalmist speaks about his life in some sense implies a transcending of the human situation as it was defined for centuries by the Old Testament.

d. Conclusion

In common with Pss. xxxvii and xlix, this psalm speaks of the scandal of the prosperity of the ungodly and the sufferings of the righteous; it attains not only to the assertion of the punishment of the former and the salvation of the latter, but also to the discovery of the imperishable blessedness of the man who lives in God.

The believer sees himself satisfied by the presence of Yahweh, in Him he finds peace and plenty, he knows that, come what may, God will remain his guide and his good; all may be taken from him, yet he possesses all things, since the Lord is at his side.

Here there is no question, at least explicitly, either of the resurrection of the righteous or of his immortality; the psalmist is content to sing of his joy in the goodness of Yahweh, and to declare his faith in the God of whom nothing can deprive him. It is possible, but not certain, that he envisages being received, before or after his death, into the presence of God; but for him the heart of the matter remains, not this unprecedented occurrence, but the actual and, as it were, definitive presence of Yahweh in his daily life.

Wherever the Living God is accepted, death is effaced, its power is blunted, and it is rendered irrelevant; in the psalm, this truth is understood rather than expressed; the psalmist has no intention of proclaiming a universal abstract law, he is confessing a living personal experience.[9]

[9] Certain exegetes would find references to the resurrection of the dead in Pss. xvii. 15 and xxvii. 13. In the former, we read (vs. 15):

> "As for me, I shall behold Thy face in righteousness;
> When I awake, I shall be satisfied with beholding Thy form."

According to several commentators, *e.g.* R. Kittel, F. Nötscher, E. Sellin, C. A. Briggs, and O. Schilling, the expression בְּהָקִיץ, *bᵉhāqîṣ*, "on awakening," would imply the re-awakening of the departed. This is by no means the case, and E. Podechard rightly recalls that the psalmist, exposed to the malice of the wicked, and convinced of the justice of his cause, is waiting to behold Yahweh, i.e. to take part in worship, at the hour of its celebration, in the morning. In H. Schmidt's opinion, the term בְּהָקִיץ, *bᵉhāqîṣ*, is to be connected with another custom: judgment in court used to be pronounced at the first hour of the day, the hearing of cases taking place during the night. The writer of Ps. xvii was therefore, on this view, thinking of justice being granted him soon. As for Ps. xxvii, it makes no reference to a life

M

IN JOB

Job xix. 25-7: "My defender is living"

The last passage that we are to study, like many of the others dealt with in this work, presents so many difficulties that the exegetes are far from being in agreement as to its exact meaning. In particular as the variety of the proposed translations shows, Job xix. 26 raises problems that are not yet solved, which confirms the justice of this observation by Knabenhauer, cited by C. Kuhl: "Versiculus brevis, septem constans voculis, at undequaque difficultatibus septus." [1]

a. Text

The following translation is merely an attempt to render intelligible a text in which—as the subsequent discussion will show—almost every word is capable of various interpretations:

> 25 *But I, I know that my defender is alive,*
> *And the last, he will stand up on the*
> *earth,*
>
> 26 *And after they have torn my skin to shreds,*
> *this [?]*
> *rent from my flesh, I shall see God.*
>
> 27 *I myself shall see Him, myself, my eyes*
> *will see Him, not another,*
> *my reins are wasting within me.*[2]

in the Beyond. The believer is expressing his hope that Yahweh will answer him in his trouble; he can count on Him alone; therefore he beseeches Him to intervene without delay, "in the land of the living," that is to say, in this world, before his death.

In conclusion, Pss. xvii and xxvii make no reference at all to the resurrection of the departed, and only Pss. xvi, xlix, and lxxiii are relevant to our study—not because they make any explicit proclamation of victory over death, but because they stress with particular intensity the abiding consequences of the presence of God in the life of believers.

[1] On the history of the interpretation of this passage, cp. esp. the commentary by N. Peters (1928), and Sperr's art. in *Z. alttest. W.*, 1905, pp. 47-140.

[2] E. Renan, *Le livre de Job*, 1865; K. Budde, *Hk. A. T.*, 1896; B. Duhm, *K. H.-C. A. T.*, 1897; W. Staerk, *Schr. A. T.*, 1911; A. Ehrlich, *Randglossen zur hebraischen Bibel*, 1913, vol. vi, pp. 257 f.; P. Humbert, *L'Ancien*

b. Meaning of xix. 25-7

Vs. 25 presents comparatively little difficulty. In translating the word גֹּאֵל, *gō'ēl*, the French writers Segond, Dhorme, and Renan take it respectively as meaning "redeemer" (Segond), "defender" (Dhorme), and "avenger" (Renan); according to A. R. Johnson, the essential function of the גֹּאֵל, *gō'ēl*, is the protection of the individual and of the community to which he belongs. The primitive sense of the root גָּאַל, *gā'al*, was "to cover." The *Goel* is thus the protector, the guarantor of normal life, and therefore the defender as much as the avenger or redeemer. The גֹּאֵל, *gō'ēl*, is charged with the גְּאֻלָּה, *ge'ullâ*, the "duty of protection," which ensures the continuance of the family group. This is a matter of duty rather than one of law, as J. J. Stamm emphasises (Lev. xxv. 24 ff.; Jer. xxxii; Ruth).[3] It seems, as J. J. Stamm, C. Steuernagel, G. Hölscher, etc., hold, that in Job xix. 25, God is primarily Job's defender and

---

Testament et le problème de la souffrance, Lausanne 1918; S. R. DRIVER and G. B. GRAY, *I. C. C.*, 1921; S. MOWINCKEL, *Hiobs go'el und Zeuge im Himmel*, K. *Marti Festschrift*, Beihefte z. Z. alttest. W., 1925, pp. 207-12; P. DHORME, *Et. bib.*, 1926; J. HEMPEL, "Das theologische Problem des Hiobs," Z. *syst. Th.*, 1929, pp. 221-39; F. BAUMGÄRTEL, *Der Hiobdialog*, Beitr. z. Wiss. vom A.N.T., 1933; G. HÖLSCHER, (1) "Hiob 19. 25-27 und Jubil. 23. 30-31," Z. *alttest. W.*, 1935, pp. 277 ff.; and (2) *Hb. A. T.*, 1937; J. LINDBLOM, "Ich weiss, dass mein Erlöser lebt," *St. th.*, 1940, pp. 65 ff.; J. J. STAMM, *Erlösen und Vergeben im A. T.*, Berne 1940, I, pp. 27 ff.; M. GEHMANN, "סֵפֶר," an Inscription, in the Book of Job," *J. Bib. Lit.*, 1944, pp. 303 ff.; R. DUSSAUD, "La *Nephesh* et la *Rouach* dans le livre de Job," *R. h. r.*, 1945, pp. 17 ff.; J. STEINMANN, *Job*, Témoins de Dieu, 1946; E. MONTET, *B. Cent.*, 1947; J. J. STAMM, "Versuche zur Erklärung von Hiob 19. 24," *Th. Z.*, 1948, pp. 331 ff.; C. LARCHER, *B. Jérus.*, 1950; E. F. SUTCLIFFE, "Further Notes on Job, Textual and Exegetical," *Biblica*, 1950, p. 377; A. R. JOHNSON, "The Primary Meaning of √גאל," *Vet. test.* (supp.), Leyden 1953, pp. 67 ff.; A. WEISER, *A. T. D.*, 1951; C. KUHL, "Neue Literarkritik des Buchs Hiob," *Th. R.*, 1953, pp. 271 ff.; L. A. SIJNDERS, "The Meaning of זר in the O.T.," *Oudtest. St.*, 1954, pp. 70 f.; SELLIN, *op. cit.* (above, p. 55, n. 5), pp. 275 ff.; NÖTSCHER, *op. cit.* pp. 237 ff.; EICHRODT, *Theol. des A. T.*, VOL. III, pp. 161 f.; PEDERSEN, *op. cit.* (above, p. 2, n. 2), VOLS. I-II, pp. 363-74, etc.

[3] At critical moments in the history of His People the God of Israel appears as a גֹּאֵל, *gō'ēl*, especially at the time of the Exodus and of the Babylonian Exile (Ps. LXXVIII. 35; Is. XLIII. 1, XLIV. 6; etc.); He similarly reveals Himself as the protector of the weak and the small (Ps. LXIX. 18; Hos. XIII. 14; Prov. XXIII. 10 f.); He is the advocate of the defenceless.

not his avenger; Job has not, in point of fact, been murdered; he is shamed by his misfortune and demands vindication; [4] so we shall adopt the translation proposed by P. Dhorme: גֹאֲלִי, *gō'ªlî*, means "my defender."

In vs. 25*b* we find the word אַחֲרוֹן, *'ahªrôn*, the "last." This term assumed a distinctly eschatological significance in the Vulgate, which renders it "in novissimo die"; but Job is by no means contemplating a prospective event at the end of the age, he is hoping that his advocate will take conclusive action on his behalf, when all his friends have abandoned him; וְאַחֲרוֹן, *weʾahªrôn*, "and the last," thus indicates the moment of the divine intervention and perhaps, according to A. Weiser, its manner as well. The last word is with Yahweh.[5]

עַל־עָפָר, *'al-'āpār*, "on earth," emphasises that Yahweh is going to reveal Himself here below. The witness whom Job has in Heaven (XVI. 19) will at last come to this world to vindicate him.

As in XLI. 33, עַל־עָפָר, *'al-'āpār*, "on earth," may be translated as "on earth"; it is neither the dust of Sheol (as some including Jerome, Luther, and, still more recently, Ridderbos, have maintained) nor Job's grave, that is the subject here. Therefore it is erroneous to hold that these words are proclaiming the resurrection of Job.[6]

Thus vs. 25 informs us that Job is confidently expecting the intervention of Yahweh even at the eleventh hour; he sees his defender arise, the term brings to mind the theophanies of the God of Israel and His actions on behalf of those who are without resource,[7] when all other support fails him. His vindication will be effected here on earth; this verse makes no reference to the Hereafter; Job is certain of his God's appearing,

---

[4] S. Mowinckel holds that it is not God Himself, but a guardian angel that would be Job's witness and advocate before the Almighty.

[5] We may note, without adopting it, the theory held by various critics, including E. Kissane, who is cited by C. Kuhl, according to which אַחֲרוֹן, *'ahªrôn*, "last," which can also mean "hinder," is synonymous with גֹאֵל, and denoted Yahweh in so far as He is "He who stands behind," the "Hintermann," that is to say, the surety, he who assumes the responsibility of others.

[6] Cp. especially K. BUDDE, *comm. ad loc.*

[7] Pss. III. 7, VII. 6, IX. 19; etc. (cp. A. WEISER, *comm. ad loc.*)

the dialogue, moreover, is to end with a theophany (Job xxxviii. 1 ff.)

Vs. 26, particularly in its opening words, is a *crux interpretum*. It may be literally translated: "And after (or 'behind') my skin, they have torn this[8] to shreds and from (or 'without') my flesh, I shall see God."

One point is certain: Job is counting upon seeing God, but the difficulty is to understand exactly when and in what circumstances. Is it to be before his death, when he will no longer have even skin on his bones? Or in spite of his death, although only his resurrection or the intervention of the Living God in the world of the perished makes this vision possible? Critical opinion is divided, and that all the more because the text, obscure in itself, should probably be emended; the versions themselves have interpreted it in many different ways.[9] For according to the Septuagint, here Job is thinking of his return to life, or at least of his healing; the Vulgate is more definite still, since it distinctly refers to the resurrection of the body, מִבְּשָׂרִי, *mibbᵉśārî*, becoming "in carne mea."[10]

The expressions וְאַחַר עוֹרִי, *wᵉʾaḥar ʿôrî*, and וּמִבְּשָׂרִי, *ûmibbᵉśārî*, are obviously ambiguous. אַחַר, *ʾaḥar*, may be a preposition, an adverb, or a conjunction, and וְאַחַר עוֹרִי is sometimes rendered as "behind my skin," that is to say, "under my skin" (A. Ehrlich); and sometimes as "after my skin," meaning "after I have been deprived of my skin" (E. König, cited by E. F. Sutcliffe). In the same way מִן, *min*, generally indicates provenance, "from,

---

[8] According to E. Montet, at this point Job was displaying his ailing body.

[9] The LXX for example reads: "(vs. 25) I know that he is eternal who is to deliver me on earth (vs. 26) to restore (ἀναστῆσαι, which is ambiguous and can imply either healing or resurrection) my flesh which is suffering this. For that which has been wrought for me is of the Lord (vs. 27) that I will know myself, that my eye has seen, and not another."

[10] "On the last day I shall be raised from the earth and be clothed once more with my skin, and in my flesh I shall see God." Jerome, writing with reference to this text, says: "Here Job is prophesying the resurrection of the body in such a way that no one else has written on this subject as definitely and explicitly as he." All the Fathers do not hold this opinion; Chrysostom, for example, considers that here Job is only referring to his healing; Irenaeus, Tertullian, and Justin Martyr do not use this text as a proof-text for the resurrection (cp. C. LARCHER, *B. Jérus.*, 1950, Introduction, p. 29).

out of," but may also denote absence and have the sense of
"without"; therefore, in the one eventuality, Job would only
see God when deprived of his flesh and skin, that is to say when
dead, whereas, according to the other, Yahweh would appear
to him in his utter extremity, but while he still has flesh and
skin, that is to say, while he still breathes.

E. Dhorme rightly considers that the expressions employed
here indicate that Job means to be present in person at the
Last Judgment; his vindication, which could not but take
place, must be effected in this world, and Yahweh's servant
himself must be there. This expectation seems to be in keeping
with the whole series of Job's speeches.

K. Budde observes that, although without flesh and skin,
Job would still have his bones (Lam. IV. 8), that is to say a
vestige of life; even when reduced to this pitiful plight, he
would not give up counting on divine intervention. E. F.
Sutcliffe, for his part, proposes to emend the order, not the
words, of vs. 26; he reads וְעוֹרִי נִקְּפוּ מִבְּשָׂרִי וְאַחַר זֹאת אֶחֱזֶה אֱלוֹהַּ,
weʿôrî niqqepû mibbeśārî weʾaḥar zōʾt ʾeḥezeh ʾelôah, meaning
"and when my skin is torn from my flesh, even after this I shall
see God." We are still faced by the same assertion; whatever may be Job's prospective state, he is quite sure that God
will take action on his behalf before he dies.

The words נִקְּפוּ־זֹאת, *niqqepû-zōʾt*, raise other difficulties. נִקְּפוּ
is generally connected with נָקַף, *nāqap*, "to surround," or with
נקף, *n-q-p*, "to cut down" (Is. x. 34), which here has the
meaning of "to destroy, to tear, to pull to pieces." K. Budde
and G. Hölscher read נִקַּף כָּזֹאת, *niqqap kāzōʾt*, that is to say, "after
my skin has been torn like this." [11]

It is not necessary to cite the great number of theories to
which this verse has given rise; their very diversity is enough
to show how weak many of them are. We must, however, draw
attention to the ingenious interpretation of G. Hölscher, who
holds that Job is certainly expecting some event which must

---

[11] P. DHORME reads נִזְקַפְתִּי, *nîzqapetî*, the *niphal* of the verb זָקַף *zāqap*, "to
erect," "to set up," and translates as "and behind my skin" as behind a
curtain (!), "I shall stand erect." Similarly, F. BAUMGÄRTEL emends
עוֹרִי, *ʿôrî*, "my skin," to עֵדִי, *ʿēdî*, "my witness," and נִקְּפוּ־זֹאת, *niqqepû-zōʾt*,
"they have torn this," to יִזְקֹף אוֹתִי, *yizqōp ʾôtî*, "he will raise me again,"
which gives: "And then my witness will raise me up again."

follow his death, but which could not be the resurrection as
Jerome and Luther conceived of it.

G. Hölscher, in fact, considers that Job is hoping to be
vindicated even after his death. God will come down to this
world, even when Job no longer possesses either flesh or skin,
that is to say, when he has perished; He will justify him in the
eyes of the living, and the sufferer will be present then, in
spirit, at his own exoneration. It is true that Job dismisses
the possibility of a resurrection (xiv. 10 ff.), he pictures the
abode of the dead in the darkest of hues, but it is possible that
he shares the primitive belief of the Israelites according to which
the departed, that is to say their spirits, are endowed with a
certain understanding and know what goes on in the land of the
living. G. Hölscher bases himself particularly on the Book of
Jubilees, xxiii. 30 ff., which in his view also expresses the same
conception (cp. further 1 Enoch xciii. 1 ff.) Thus Job was to
witness his posthumous vindication.[12]

It does not seem possible to sustain this exegesis. In the
course of this dialogue Job peremptorily requires Yahweh to
give him justice while he is still alive; it is not sufficient for
him that he should be a shadowy presence at the favourable
resolution of his case. It is in this world that judgment must
be granted, not in the Beyond.

J. Lindblom reminds us that Job is a sick man; what he is
primarily looking for is healing; this will be the token of divine
blessing and the proof of his innocence. Moreover, according
to this Scandinavian scholar, vs. 26 does not necessarily refer
to the sufferer's death; מִבְּשָׂרִי, *mibbᵉśārî*, certainly means
"without my flesh," but it must not be forgotten that the
unfortunate man's body, sorely stricken, is gradually decaying
and giving off a noisome smell; Job's desire is to be relieved
of it, as he is looking to being set free from a disease-ravaged
skin; in short, in vs. 26, the sick man is giving expression to
his ardent wish for his troubles to end, he is wanting to be
healed. He is hoping to see his God, and this does not necessarily mean to encounter Him in the Temple or to find Him in
some ecstatic experience, but to know Him in the new blessings

---

[12] LARCHER adopts this theory and thinks that Job is to be present, *post
mortem*, at the judgment that will vindicate him. He holds that, by
special sanction, Job was going to return from Sheol on that occasion.

with which God will satisfy him. When the Creator hides
His face, He makes man feel His wrath; thus, to see God is
tantamount to tasting His goodness. Vs. 26, then, according
to Lindblom, simply expresses the sick man's hope of regaining
his health, and, with it, his reputation (Job xxxiii. 25 ff.)

In conclusion, this verse, despite its obscurities, enables us
to say that Job is counting on seeing God, even in his last hour.
All having been taken from him, he would cherish the hope of
still meeting his Lord. From the beginning of his suffering to
its end, he is crying aloud for this personal encounter with the
Most High; he knows, with a conviction that nothing is able
to shake, that sooner or later it is bound to be, even although
neither his flesh nor his skin should remain. Job wants
vindication here in this world, and before he dies; in this text
he is referring neither to his resurrection, nor (as G. Hölscher
believes) to a judgment of which he would be a far-off and
posthumous witness; doubtless he *is* calling for healing, which
will be the token of honour restored: but he is going further
than J. Lindblom thinks, he is looking for God to appear to
him, and to being able to come to an understanding with Him
once and for all. His prayer will be answered at last and he
will see the Creator, as he has never ceased to desire
(Job xlii. 1 ff.)

Vs. 27 continues in the same strain; its primary declaration
is that the sufferer will see the Lord personally. אֲשֶׁר, *'ašer*,
rel. pron., here = "whom," connects the assertion that follows
to the previous verse; אֲנִי, *'anî*, emphasises the fact that Job
will look upon the Most High with his own eyes, and may be
translated by "myself."

The main difficulty lies in the meaning that should be
assigned to וְלֹא־זָר, *we� lō'-zār*, that is to say, "and not another . . .
a stranger . . . an adversary . . . ," which may refer either to
Job or to God. On the first interpretation, the writer is
repeating again that Job, in person, is going to see God; none
but he will be granted the theophany which he implores; this
is the opinion of E. Dhorme, A. Ehrlich, and others. On the
second, it is God Himself who is the stranger, the adversary,
and who, at last, will no longer appear to Job in this inauspicious
light; this point of view is shared by F. Baumgärtel, A. Weiser,
and J. Lindblom. Lindblom, for example, lays stress on the

fact that Job, in the course of his sickness, is contending with a God whom he understands no longer and who is hiding His true face from him. God has become unknowable; His servant is at grips with a sort of demon who, for no apparent reason, has destroyed all that made his life worth while. Throughout the whole of the dialogue, Job is making appeal to the God he formerly knew, the righteous sovereign whose equity was evident in all His actions; he wants to find Him again; he is hoping that his enemy of today will become his friend once more, as yesterday He was. Here Job is certain of being reconciled to his Lord, in anticipation he is welcoming the hour when he will no longer have to do with an hostile and strange divinity, but with his constant defender.

This exegesis is possible; the first appears to be more natural; both seem to be preferable to L. A. Snijder's theory, according to which וְלֹא־זָר, *wᵉlō'-zār,* "and not another," denotes Job, in so far as he was considered, by the community and by Yahweh Himself, as an "outsider," a non-initiate, or even as excommunicated. At the end of his trial, Job was to be re-admitted into the circle of the pious.

This verse confirms our exegesis of those that precede it; the writer is proclaiming that Job will see God, in person, with his own eyes; it seems that the expressions he uses imply the appearance of the Most High to him while he is still alive, and not in the Beyond.

c. *The meaning of ch. xix as a whole*

According to vss. 25-7 of this chapter, Job is proclaiming an inevitable and ardently-desired encounter between God and himself; he is not expecting an intervention by God after his death; he is not counting on his resurrection; he wants to see his Lord before he breathes his last, and he knows that this vision will be granted to him, even were he to be bereft of his flesh and his skin. He is consumed with impatience as he calls upon his defender to intervene at the eleventh hour. The whole of CH. XIX is compatible with this interpretation.

In the course of a long speech, which is nothing but a bitter complaint, Job replies to his friends and reproaches them, first of all, for overwhelming him with their words. He tries to make them understand him and appeals to their friendship (vss. 2, 5), They ought to know that it is God Himself who is persecuting him, that he is hemmed in on every side, caught in a trap, that every avenue of escape is closed to him. Job begs for justice but encounters silence. God has cast him down to destruction: He has despoiled him, broken him up, taken away his hope (vss. 8-12). He has estranged his friends and kindred from him (vss. 13); Job has become a stranger to his own family, unrecognisable to his own kinsmen; he is an object of revulsion to his own wife, he is reduced to skin and bone (vss. 13-20). Therefore he implores his companions to take pity on him. He is so miserable that his friends should sustain him instead of crushing him more (vss. 21 ff.)

But his interlocutors remain deaf to his wailings; Job's heart-rending plea does not move them. One resource alone remains to the unhappy man, one single way out: to cast himself directly upon the God who is afflicting him, "to appeal from God ill-informed to God informed better" (J. Hempel).

But before envisaging this eventuality, Job contemplates another possibility (vss. 23 f.) Today, no one understands him; tomorrow perhaps posterity will do him justice, sooner or later his innocence will be made manifest, and the coming generation will vindicate him. He desires then that his plea may be engrossed in some indestructible document. There is, of course, no reference here to writing a book, but only to some text that will bear irrefutable testimony to his integrity.[13] His words must not perish with him.

But he sets this idea aside, he prays for more than a posthumous vindication; he accepts death, but not before his innocence is established. In the very moment that all men forsake him, he finds one who will take his part. His friends renounce him, God will receive him; his companions turn a deaf ear to his pleadings, His Lord will hear him; his family flees him, Yahweh will come down from Heaven to bear witness to his integrity and restore his reputation.

Job passes from the deepest despair to the boldest hope, and all at once the situation is transformed: the God who has crushed him is coming to defend him, his advocate is the very one who has deprived him of all (vss. 25 ff.) The closing

---

[13] G. Hölscher, P. Dhorme, A. Weiser, J. J. Stamm.

words of his discourse are directed to his hearers, not to move
them to pity, but to give them a warning; he no longer appeals
to their compassion, he declares that God will punish them
since they have not listened to him. "Know that there is a
judgment." The accused becomes the accuser. Vss. 28-9
proclaim that God will punish Job's interlocutors at the same
time as He acquits him; his trial will thus be concluded in this
world and not in the Beyond.

d. The meaning of the Book of Job

In Job XIX. 25-7, Job foresees that God will arise at last to
plead his cause; he has no doubt that, before he dies, he will
see the Most High and his innocence will be established. This
passage has no reference at all to an intervention by God after
his death.

This exegesis is consistent with the indications that we
find throughout the whole of the Book of Job. It is not our
present concern to offer an answer to all the problems raised
by these forty-two chapters, nor even to make any intensive
study of the message of this book; we shall confine ourselves to
outlining its general theme.[14] Let us, however, point out
that the original dialogue was doubtless completed, and also
that the relationship between the narrative framework and the
discourses is not clear; nevertheless, the Book of Job, written
and conceived by a Semite, is not to be judged according to
our standards. Its writer may have purposely allowed a
certain break between the prologue and the body of the work.
The problem that he is dealing with, which may be called the
problem of suffering in general and the trouble of the righteous
man in particular, must, in his view, be approached in different

---

[14] For questions of introduction, for example, the connexion between the
prologue and epilogue and the dialogues, the place in the work of the
speeches of Elihu and God, and the extent of the original work, we refer to
the article by C. KUHL, *Th. R.*, 1953, or to studies such as those by A. LODS,
Histoire de la littérature hébraïque et juive, 1950. Cp. also the following recent
works: P. HUMBERT, "Le modernisme de Job," *Wisdom in Israel and in the
Ancient Near East, to H. H. Rowley*, Leyden 1955, pp. 150 ff.; J. DANIÉLOU,
Les quatres visages de Job, Etudes, Sep. 1955, pp. 145 ff.; R. DE PURY, *Job
ou l'homme révolté*, Geneva 1955.

ways, by a sort of dialectic, and not in a schematic and ultimately superficial manner.

Thus, in the first chapter, Job appears as a servant of God
who is going to suffer for his Master's honour. God is
represented as the accused, Job is to be the witness for the
defence; on his martyrdom, in the twofold sense of the word,
depends the honour of the Living God. Here suffering is
bound up with the glory of God.[15]

But, on the other hand, in the body of the book, Job seems
to be suffering for his sins; yet he refuses to connect his troubles
with his transgressions. In spite of his friends and their erudite
orthodoxy, he protests his innocence, and even dares appeal to
God. He counts on justice being rendered him. Here Job
is at the heart of the controversy, his suffering is bound up with
the problem of retribution. Job is in distress, but he is unable
to account for his trouble; the whole of the drama lies there.
His misfortune is unexplained and inexplicable. The book
closes with the long-expected intervention of God, but Job
receives no academic answer to the question of the origin of his
sufferings; he has encountered the Living God, his prayer has
been heard, which is equivalent to vindication; overawed, he
bows down before the mystery of God, who is infinitely beyond
his understanding.

Job is suddenly stricken by an evil that breaks him, body and
soul. According to good orthodox Judaism, his shattering
trouble has a cause: exceptionally serious sin committed by the
man who claims to serve God. Job rebels against this inference,
he considers that there is no common measure between his
faults and what has happened to him. He certainly doubts
neither God nor His righteousness; not for a moment can he
concede that God may be unjust, but he also holds with all his
power to his own righteousness, so much so that he can understand nothing about his misery, and his ignorance plunges him
into despair.[16]

---

[15] J. HEMPEL, *op. cit.* (above, n. 2), pp. 643 ff., lays stress on this point.

[16] BAUMGÄRTEL, *op. cit.* (above, n. 2), pp. 170 ff., ably presents the
dramatic situation of Job who, as a true Israelite, claims not prosperity
but his rights. He holds so tenaciously to justice being granted him only
because he holds so tenaciously to God Himself. His "wherefore" is not
the "wherefore" of reason, but of faith.

He refuses to renounce either of the affirmations upon which his life is built; he does not reject God, but he cannot deny himself; he is torn between his faith in the righteous God and his certainty that he is being wrongfully punished.[17]

His friends confine themselves to repeating a well-learnt lesson; he spurns their commonplaces, appeals to God, and boldly claims to be heard at His judgment seat. He renounces neither God's righteousness nor his own right, and demands that the Lord explain to him the reason for his suffering. He requires God to reply.

But the point is that God holds His peace, God hides Himself. What troubles Job is not the rationalisations of his friends, nor their condemnation, but the silence of the Most High, His withdrawal, and ultimately His enmity. God confronts him as a hostile power; God has changed, He is no longer his friend, and yet he can do no other than appeal to Him, he has none but Him as defender. Time is pressing, Job grows impatient; he knows that his days are numbered, the hours pass swiftly on, death is at hand; God remains silent, his friends continue to utter empty words. Job is feeling more and more at bay, his voice grows shriller, his utterances become more violent, they border on blasphemy; he wails, he hopes, laments again, recovers his confidence; all is confused again, again all is clear; in his torment there is one sole fixed point: he beseeches God. "Oh, if he could but see God, were it only for an hour . . . for a single moment!" Thus Job alternates between the heights and the depths, sometimes he reaches a crest, almost gets a finger-hold on the solution, only to fall back and sink into an abyss of perplexity and despair.

Job XIX. 25 is one moment of the crisis, and not its end. In this passage, Job sees God coming towards him, but soon finds himself alone once more, and when he begins to speak again, his accusations become harsher, he is bold enough to assert that his case is not unique; indeed on the contrary, the world situation reveals the universality of the reign of unrighteousness (CH. XXI).

[17] J. PEDERSEN, *op. cit.* (above, p.2, n. 2), VOLS. I-II, pp. 363 ff., notes that the life of the Israelite is based on the harmony between God's righteousness and man's. If God is unrighteous then the foundation of the Covenant is destroyed; everything falls in ruin.

In CH. XIII Job is already asking to plead his cause in the presence of God, he is ready to face Him, he demands that He give him his due (XIII. 3 ff., 13 ff.) A little later he is wishing that the earth will not cover his blood—that is to say, that his trouble will not be hidden from sight; he desires that his cry will rise up to Heaven, where his witness is to be found. He beseeches God to justify Himself against him (XVI. 18 ff.) All at once Job knows that God is going to answer him, his defender will arise and vindicate him (XIX. 25 ff.), but his certainty soon gives way to bitterness as he considers the shameless prosperity of the wicked (XXI. 5 ff.)

Job continues to call on his Lord, he does not wish to die before having encountered Him. "Oh, that I knew where I might find him . . .! I would lay my case before him and fill my mouth with arguments" (XXIII. 3-4). Again he cries, "Oh, that I had one to hear me?" (XXXI. 35 ff.) The silence of God obsesses, overwhelms him, for his defence is all prepared.[18]

At last God breaks down the wall of silence within which He has been enclosed; at last the sufferer sees Him towards whom he has so long stretched out his hands in vain; at last God intervenes. Job may depart in peace, his conflict has come to an end; he bows himself down, a broken man, but with peace restored to his heart. He is reduced to skin and bone, but his honour is safe. His recovered health, his renewed fortune, his refounded family, are simply the signs of the restoration of fellowship between God and himself. Nothing is theoretically resolved, but Job is able to lead a new life in the sight of God and men: that is the heart of the matter. Life becomes possible for him again, and death itself has no more importance.

There is no place in this for the resurrection of Job. He does not ask that he may live again, but to see God. He prays that justice may be rendered to him, and considers his innocence will be evident as soon as he can speak with the Most High. The resolution of the crisis is thus bound up for him with a divine revelation before his death; he does not defer it to the Hereafter. The interpretations of Job XIX. 25-27 by Jerome

---

[18] J. STEINMANN, *op. cit.* (above, n. 2), p. 61: "For the further the drama unfolds, the further does Job set his faith in the divine righteousness and feels that it would prevail (that is to say, that he would be acquitted) if God were willing to take up his cause."

and Luther are not consistent with the Book of Job as a whole; this does not end with the proclamation of its hero's return to life, but it unfolds itself at length until it comes to the point where the intervention of God breaks the silence that He had observed till then.

The possibility of the resurrection is not Job's proposed solution of the problem of suffering. The unhappy man has even had a fleeting glimpse of this eventuality of human rebirth but has set it aside. A tree that is cut down, he declares, may sprout again, but man lies down and rises no more, he is doomed to eternal sleep (XIV. 7 ff.) In his distress he even desires to descend into Sheol, but only for a time, till the wrath of God is over. He would return to the world again when his Lord remembered him, but that is an unrealisable prayer. If only a man could live again, he adds (XIV. 14), how easy everything would then be, how much more easily would he endure his troubles! But this hope is denied Job, this eventuality is dismissed, and the wretched man finds himself alone with a God who is attacking him relentlessly.

Thus the question of the suffering of the innocent is not answered in another world; divine righteousness does not have the Hereafter at its disposal for its manifestation, the sufferer has no prospects after death. Therefore his rights must be recognised before he breathes his last.

e. *Conclusion*

From our exegesis of Job XIX. 25-7, and from our further discussion of CH. XIX, and our cursory commentary on the book as a whole, we can see Job as a believer clinging to God in his trouble. His Lord is at once his scourge and his only resource; he inveighs against Him and at the same time makes his appeal to Him. His existence is meaningless apart from communion with God; he expects His intervention, seeks His presence, and demands His verdict; he can live only by Him and ceaselessly strives to prevail upon the Most High to draw near to him. He expects all things to result from this encounter for which he constantly prays.

Job neither doubts God nor denies His righteousness. His

faith, far from solving his trouble, is itself the cause of the crisis that he is passing through; the more he believes in God the more incoherent his life seems to him, and the greater the scandal of his suffering appears. Like the psalmists whom we have discussed, who found their sovereign good in God, Job confesses his utter need of Him; but, in contrast with those who can sing of His presence, he has to deplore His absence; while others draw near to Him freely, he himself struggles against His silence and calls on His name in vain; whereas Yahweh is the portion of those who wrote Pss. XVI and LXXIII, Job is bereft of His blessing and fellowship. Job sees all that other believers have received rudely snatched from him, and nevertheless, for him as for his brethren, his life is without meaning apart from God.

So the Most High eludes Job, but he refuses to give up as long as He hides Himself from him. "I will not let you go, unless you bless me" (Gen. XXXII. 26). God cannot be God unless He answers His servant. Before he dies—for the whole drama originates and is enacted in this world—Job will hear his Lord's voice, and behold His majesty. The cry of the faithful is answered at last.

GENERAL CONCLUSIONS

In the course of this chapter we have heard the voices of some believers in Israel rejoicing in their communion with God. For each of them, the Living God is seen as the ground of their life and the pledge of their joy. These faithful men live by God and in God; the psalmists, it would appear, cannot conceive that this communion can ever be broken, even by death; in contrast with this, Job, in his flesh and his heart is tortured because of the absence of the Most High, his life has no more meaning, he is no longer alive, he is as good as dead. For all of them, the heart of the matter is not so much the question of everlasting life, as that of life with God; they are less concerned about the length of their days than about the relationship that should unite them to Him; they are more preoccupied with belonging to God than with their existence.

In this perspective, the problem of death remains secondary; are not the divine righteousness for Job, and the goodness of Yahweh for the psalmists, worth more than life, that is to say, than a prolonged earthly existence? Are not these still manifested beyond death? Is the question merely that of continuing to exist, of not being destroyed?

Because they have part in the life of God, the believers who, for example, wrote Pss. XVI, XLIX, and LXXIII, or the dialogues of Job, feel that their existence is thereby radically transformed; the former conceptions are implicitly questioned, the ancient values upon which the Israelite bases his life are assailed, and the limits imposed on the condition of man by age-old beliefs are shown to be doubtful.

In short, without actually being aware of it, the *Ḥasidim* are battering the gates of the kingdom of the dead; without reaching the positive assertion of the immortality or resurrection of the believer, being primarily concerned with tasting or seeking the fullness of the presence of their Lord, they are preparing the way for future generations to proclaim that death is impotent against those who are living in communion with the Living God.

The texts studied in this third chapter do not as yet sing of the victory over Sheol, they in no way envisage a resurrection which would be the lot of all mankind, they belong to personal experience which, little by little, is opening new vistas to the eyes of Yahweh's worshippers, by setting before them, rather than the return to existence of the departed, a sort of immortality for the man who shares in the very life of God. In the eyes of faith, the gift of Yahweh's presence is seen as a blessing that cannot be taken away.

N

PART III

FROM DEATH TO RESURRECTION

IN Part I, death was seen as the final event in human existence; it imposes itself upon every man as an inevitable and decisive fact. Sooner or later the creature goes down to rejoin its fathers and the world that receives it is a prison from which it will never emerge; the few exceptions known to the Old Testament only serve to confirm the general rule. We saw that the human being falls completely into the power of death; all that is in it is given over to that power which the Scriptures call "the king of terrors" (Job xviii. 14), for if its shade lives on in Sheol, the travesty of life that it then leads in no way involves what is usually meant by the immortality of the soul. Man, in his totality, is condemned to "being-only-for-death."

But in Part II we observed that the rule of death seems sometimes suspended or even finally broken. For Israel at the beginning this is only a matter of a more or less vague intuition, which, nevertheless, reaches fulfilment in the very definite assertion that death is destroyed. With the passing of the centuries, the Chosen People, not without hesitation, discovers this new aspect of the sovereign power of its Lord: Yahweh is able to give life to the departed. As N. Söderblom rightly puts it, "by their faith, the faithful in Israel, little by little, are opening the gates of the kingdom of the dead"; [1] the various texts which we have expounded bear witness to that slow advance towards a truth by which believers are thenceforth going to live.

Here, in Part III, we shall define with precision the reasons that, step by step, brought those who believed in Yahweh to proclaim that He would break the bonds of Sheol; we shall follow them on the way that leads from death to resurrection,

---

[1] N. SÖDERBLOM, *La vie future d'après le mazdéisme, à la lumière des croyances parallèles dans les autres religions,* Paris 1901, p. 342.

in other words from the affirmation of death's absolute power over the perished to the assurance that God will effect the resurrection on behalf of His own, thereby making manifest His glory, His righteousness, and His mercy together.

Let us now briefly recall the results of our exegetical investigation. The Old Testament passages which, in one way or another, proclaim the temporary or definitive limitation of death's power over mankind are few; nevertheless, certain of them have a significance which is enhanced by their coincidence with the important factors in the history of the Chosen People, in particular with its occupation of Canaan, its exile in Babylon, and its struggle with Hellenism in Maccabean times. Thus belief in the resurrection of the dead does not arise of itself, it is bound up with historical circumstances, within a particular context which is quite as much social and political as religious; it was not born of the brains of the scribes, but of the very life of the People of Yahweh; it involves a development, and is the consequence of the conjunction of several factors which now fall to be defined.

We have observed three sorts of evidence. In a first group of texts, the God of Israel's sovereign power over death is expressed: but this power is made manifest only occasionally and sporadically; Yahweh not only grants life but also preserves and restores it to His creature. Thus eleventh-hour deliverances, extraordinary translations, and sensational healings show the transcendence of the Living God over the forces of destruction; nevertheless, these are, in general, only exceptional actions, and, moreover, their effect is only transitory; the law demands that the sons of Adam do not ultimately escape Sheol.

Again, several Old Testament passages assert the possibility or even the certainty of the departed returning to life; yet at the beginning this is merely a matter of picturing the restoration of the Chosen People condemned by successive misfortunes to a miserable existence: Israel will recover its power, think Hosea's contemporaries; the Holy Nation will be re-established, Ezekiel declares. Later, the symbol becomes reality and the parable fact: anonymous preachers foretell the posthumous vindication of the Servant of Yahweh (Is. LIII), the rebirth of the Rephaim (Is. XXVI), and the awakening of those that sleep in the dust (Dan. xii). The resurrection of the dead thus appears in widely divergent contexts and its scope varies from one text to another; sometimes it is bound up with the contemplation of the laws of nature, sometimes it is a consequence of the creative power of the God of Israel; here it simply concerns the restoration of the Chosen People at some particular point in its history, there it becomes a unique and decisive event placed at the end of the age; finally, it makes manifest the ultimate triumph of Yahweh over His enemies as well as the care of the God of Israel for the *Ḥasidim*, who thus receive life again for having lost it for His sake.

A third group of evidences brings to mind not the return of the faithful to life, but the permanence of the bonds that unite them to their God. The believer, strictly speaking, is not expecting his resurrection, he lives in and by the presence of Yahweh; the nearness of the Living God drives back or disarms death. The fellowship of God involves a sort of immortality; it is, in any case, a pledge for the future; the *ḥasid's* worship of his God is overturning the traditional Old Testament conceptions of human existence. One day, Jewish piety is going to find an expression adequate to its assurance and hope that nothing, not even death, is able to separate the faithful believer from his Lord, in the assertion of the resurrection of the dead.

Belief in the return of the departed to life makes its appearance only at a late stage among the Chosen People, at the very moment when the Old Testament comes to a close. Certain specialists consider that it has no particularly Israelite characteristics, and that it cannot be explained except as a borrowing from a foreign faith; and in our first chapter we shall see what is to be thought of this point of view. According to other scholars, the emergence of this new doctrine in the midst of the Jewish nation is intelligible without recourse to a theory of extraneous influence, in the light of Israel's own historical and religious evolution; we will examine their opinions in a second chapter and will conclude by briefly recalling how the Jews, following the Maccabean martyrs, reacted to the proclamation of the resurrection of the dead.

Chapter I

Possible Foreign Influence on the Formation of the Old Testament Belief in the Resurrection of the Dead

Many critics hold that Israel did not attain to the conception of the departed returning to life by itself; the fundamental principles of its faith seem in fact to preclude, or at least render difficult, the belief to which Is. xxvi and Dan. xii bear particular witness. For the explanation of such passages the intervention of doctrines foreign to the true Israelite traditions must be conceded; two religions in particular may have influenced the Chosen People in this respect, that of the Persians with whom the Jews were in contact from the period of the Exile onwards, and that of the Canaanites which never ceased to exert a strong attraction upon the new inhabitants of the country.

The thesis of the Persian origin of the Old Testament belief in the resurrection of the dead has long been maintained and debated; that which lays stress upon the role of the agricultural cults in Palestine, without being new, is at present in particular favour, especially among the Scandinavian school; we shall study them consecutively.

IRANIAN INFLUENCE

At the beginning of the present century, H. Gunkel defined the Judaism contemporary with the commencement of the Christian era as a "syncretistic religion"; [1] with him, many other writers have laid stress on the transformation that was wrought in the Jewish beliefs, after Alexander the Great's conquests, and have indicated many resemblances between later Jewish writings

[1] Cited by A. Causse in *Les dispersés d'Israël*, Paris 1929, pp. 130 ff.

and Babylonian, Iranian, or even Greek traditions, particularly in texts dealing with the origin or the end of the world.[2] The specialists have noted that through its Diaspora, for the most part settled in Babylonia and Egypt, the Chosen People was in contact with new ideas which were at work throughout the Ancient East after the downfall of the Achaemenid Empire, overturning age-old conceptions of the destiny of man and the universe. The Jews were thus caught up in the many currents that disturbed the ancient world; by these, their piety and their doctrines alike were profoundly modified and in some respects manifestly enriched. In particular, belief in the resurrection was one of the acquisitions of Jewish syncretism.

W. Bousset, for example, considers that the role of Iran was of capital importance in this sphere. The Persians taught the Jews to believe not in the immortality of the soul but in the resurrection of the body, and to connect it with the universal cataclysm at the end of the age which must take place at the time of the Last Judgment. Of course, W. Bousset does not deny that there had been a preparation in Israel for the new doctrine, which, however, did not assume its full significance till it was influenced by Persia.[3]

H. Schmidt, for his part, declares that at the time when Ezekiel is writing CH. XXXVII of his book, the Chosen People is on the verge of believing in the resurrection; but for Judaism to attain to real certainty, the intervention of Persian religiosity will be required.[4]

Still more recently, H. Birkeland [5] has maintained the same point of view against the Scandinavian school and in particular against H. Riesenfeld. He declares that the decisive impulse comes from Persian religion.[6] In his opinion the idea of the

---

[2] E. Meyer, W. Bousset, H. Gressmann, R. Kittel, etc., cited by A. Causse, *op. cit.*, pp. 131 f.

[3] W. Bousset, *Die Religion des Judentums*, 2nd edn., 1904, pp. 540 ff.; 3rd edn. revised by H. Gressmann, 1926, pp. 510 ff. H. Gunkel claimed to have found that the faith in the resurrection had its origin in an astral cult; E. Meyer laid stress on the part played by Egypt; cp. Nötscher, *op. cit.* (above, p. 55, n. 5), pp. 173 ff.

[4] H. Schmidt, *Schr. A. T.*, 1915, *comm. ad loc.*

[5] H. Birkeland, "The Belief in the Resurrection of the Dead in the O. T.," *St. th.*, III/1, 1950.

[6] Birkeland, *op. cit.*, p. 74.

resurrection of the body derives from a special interest taken
in the physical aspect of the final restoration; this attention
devoted to the material is evidence of an Iranian origin.

This position has been disputed by other Old Testament
specialists such as W. von Baudissin, W. Eichrodt, and F.
Nötscher, to cite only a few of them. We must therefore
examine its tenability.

One fact is certain: the resurrection of the dead, in the form
not of an exceptional and restricted intervention by Yahweh on
behalf of one of His faithful, but of an event concerning, if not
all men, at least a great number of them, only appears in a late
period, after Israel had been in contact with the Persians. In
the earliest texts in the Old Testament we can find pregnant
indications of the later development of the belief in the return
of the departed to life, but there is a gap between these in-
frequent signs and the proclamation of a general, if not universal,
resurrection such as we find in Is. xxvi and Dan. xii, two texts
that were definitely written after the Exile. The return of the
departed to life, which for centuries was only hypothetical or
exceptional, as the Book of Job still testifies, became, when the
Jerusalemite community was living under Achaemenid rule,
a hope, and then a certainty.

The possibility of Iranian influence on the Jews is entirely
admissible. The Persian authorities and their Jewish subjects
were for long on excellent terms with one another, as the Books
of Ezra and Nehemiah attest; Israel did not forget that it was
indebted to Cyrus for its restoration. The religion of a great
empire pursuing a fairly liberal policy towards the Jerusalemite
community was doubtless held in high esteem by the Jews who
had returned to Palestine as well as by those who had remained
in Babylonia. This influence of Zoroastrianism upon Judaism
is, moreover, perfectly understandable, because there is a
certain affinity between them, especially in their moral emphasis;
Zarathustra has more than once been likened to the Prophets
of Israel. The thesis, maintained by W. Bousset, H. Schmidt,
H. Birkeland, and others, is all the more feasible since it is
generally admitted that, in many respects, the Jews were
influenced by Iran. They were, in fact, indebted to it for their
angelology, their Satanology, and in particular their eschatology
which, especially after the Exile, assumes the character of a

cosmic drama which is concerned not only with the lot of the Davidic Kingship or even with that of the earth, but also with the destiny of the entire universe. Thus the belief in the resurrection of the dead was far from being an isolated phenomenon, it was connected with a general tendency in Judaism, under the influence of its contacts with the Achaemenid Empire.

Against these arguments in support of a Jewish borrowing of the Iranian doctrine of the return of the perished to life, some scholars advance views tending to uphold the independence of Old Testament thought. Their main contention is that it is not easy to place the various scriptures that constitute the Avesta in chronological order; among the mass of Iranian texts, there are some that date from the Christian era, while others are anterior to it by several centuries. It is particularly difficult to discover what the religion of the Persian monarchs was during the period when Jerusalem was under their rule; for example, according to H. S. Nyberg,[7] the Achaemenids were not followers of Zarathustra, while, for E. Herzfeld,[8] Darius and his two immediate successors were certainly faithful champions of Zoroastrian doctrine; as long as these problems are unsolved, the question of the relationship between the Persian and Jewish faiths remains complex.

Further, after having long admitted the great indebtedness of Judaism to Iran, the critics now seem to be more cautious; they frequently declare that the innovations, allegedly borrowed from Zoroastrianism by the Jews, appear to be the natural development of a doctrine the seeds of which are to be found in the Old Testament itself; this is particularly the opinion of a recent writer J. Duchesne-Guillemin, who concludes a chapter entitled "Resemblances in Judaism to the Iranian faith" thus: "To sum up, in the evolution of post-Exilic Judaism, the definitely-established Iranian influence appears to be less than that of Hellenism." [9] Moreover, a distinction has to be made here between Biblical Judaism and post-Biblical Jewish doctrines; the reading of a study such as that by E. Böklen is a

---

[7] H. S. Nyberg, *Die Religion des Alten Iran*, Leipzig 1938.

[8] E. Herzfeld, "Die Religion des Achemeniden," *R. h. r.*, 1936, pp. 21-41.

[9] J. Duchesne-Guillemin, *Ormazd et Ahriman*, Paris 1953, p. 83.

revelation in this respect; [10]   parallels between the Old Testament and the Persian texts are relatively rare, but they become more and more numerous when we reach the extra-canonical literature. Thus the specialists are tending considerably to reduce the role of Iran in the formation of Judaism; with J. Scheftelowitz,[11] some writers even go so far as to hold that it was the Jews who, in more than one sphere, influenced the descendants of Zarathustra. Finally, the problem of the relationship between Persian and Jewish doctrines is more complex than it appeared to W. Bousset; therefore scholars are at present inclined to adopt more flexible views on this subject than their predecessors.

With regard to the resurrection itself, the sacred texts of Iran reveal different and contradictory conceptions superimposed on one another. In the Gathas, as H. S. Nyberg has shown, we find no reference to this doctrine; immediately after death, the soul of the departed enters the heavenly world or goes down to Hell; in point of fact, the judgment of the dead man takes place at once, in crossing the bridge of the "Separator." [12]   In reality, the lot of the corpse has absolutely no importance for the Gathas, and therefore its return to life would be without significance; only the soul matters, and all interest is centred on its journey to Heaven. The funerary rites in themselves are evidence of the small part played by the body in the Persians' view, since it is not even buried but, as a general rule, is simply left lying on the ground to be torn apart by the wild beasts. According to H. S. Nyberg, belief in the resurrection entails other funerary customs, and in particular it involves the burial of the corpse; this usage must have been observed by some Iranian tribes before being officially banned. Zarathustra's successors had abolished this rite while retaining its underlying conception. For H. S. Nyberg, the idea of the resurrection was ultimately a daring innovation and not the result of a normal development from the postulates of the Persian faith; it had, in point of fact, originated in popular eschatology,

---

[10] E. Böklen, *Die Verwandtschaft der jüdisch-christlichen mit der parsichen Eschatologie*, Göttingen 1902.

[11] J. J. Scheftelowitz, *Die altpersische Religion und das Judentum (Unterschiede, Übereinstimmungen, und gegenseitige Beeinflussungen)*, Giessen 1920.

[12] Nyberg, *op. cit.*, p. 310.

according to which the founder of the religion is to return at the end of the age. If the head of the community is to be raised, this means the simultaneous resurrection of the community itself.[13]

Thus the expectation of the resurrection appears to be a late doctrine in Iran; nevertheless, we must not go so far as to deny its priority in comparison with Jewish conceptions; this is confirmed by the testimony of Theopompus, who lived about 350 B.C., and of whose work two passages have been preserved for us by Plutarch and Diogenes Laertius; Iran certainly seems to have believed in the return of the departed to life before Israel did. In this connexion, A. Dupont-Sommer's declaration is true: "The doctrine of the resurrection of the dead, and that of the last judgment which is to be effected by fire, were Iranian conceptions before they became Jewish." [14]

This question of date being decided, other problems arise. The way in which the Jews envisage the resurrection scarcely brings the Persian conceptions to mind and appears to bear witness in favour of the Old Testament beliefs being independent of Iranian traditions.

Thus for the Persians the resurrection is universal, whereas for the Old Testament, in which it remains primarily a hope for the faithful, it concerns only a particular group of creatures. Is. xxvi proclaims that only Yahweh's dead will leave Sheol; Dan. xii states that only a certain number, and not all, of the departed will be awakened, some to be punished and others to be rewarded. The Psalms of Solomon and the Rabbinical texts that date to approximately the beginning of the Christian era similarly desire no more than the resurrection of the righteous; the passages that represent the resurrection as an event concerning all the dead are rare and late, and are generally subsequent to the beginning of the Christian era, like the Apocalypse of Baruch and the Fourth Book of Ezra. N. Söderblom considers that the discrepancy between the Jewish and Persian conceptions of the extent of the resurrection arises from the difference in their fundamental presuppositions. In Iran, eschatology is based on the natural scene; it is centred

---

[13] NYBERG, *op. cit.*, p. 311.

[14] A. DUPONT-SOMMER, "L'Iran et Israël," *La civilisation iranienne*, Paris 1952, p. 74.

on the destruction and renewal of the world. The resurrection of the dead is part of the physical re-creation of the universe. For Israel, the starting-point is faith in Yahweh, in the holy and righteous God who intervenes in history and establishes His kingship; here the resurrection is the answer to a religious and moral requirement and primarily concerns not mankind in general, but the lot of the *Ḥasidim*; thus it necessarily remains restricted, while from the Iranian point of view it is naturally universal, since it is connected with the destiny of the whole of the cosmos.[15]

After carefully comparing the Persian and Jewish eschatologies, N. Söderblom concludes that the latter borrowed only some insignificant details from Mazdaism, and adds: "There is only one capital point in which Judaism could have been influenced in any way by its contact with Mazdaism, and that is in its idea of the resurrection. But even this idea has a Jewish origin, and was developed independently, if not without having been influenced, at least without having been borrowed." [16]

A. Bertholet, following W. von Baudissin,[17] lays stress on another point.[18] The terminology employed by the Jews in discussing the resurrection in no way brings Iranian expressions to mind and is typically Semitic. Indeed, the Biblical texts speak about an awakening which is connected with sleep, to which death is often likened.[19] This way of speaking is alien to the Persians; for them, the resurrection is conceived not as a reanimation of the corpse (which, it should be borne in mind, does not exclude its transformation), that is to say, not as a return of vital force into an already existing organism, but as a veritable re-creation; it consists in a reconstitution of the body through the reunion of its several component elements; a characteristic text declares: "The spirit of earth gives the bones, water the blood, vegetation the

---

[15] SÖDERBLOM, *op. cit.* (above, p.183 , n. 1), p. 318.

[16] SÖDERBLOM, *op. cit.*, pp. 320 f.

[17] VON BAUDISSIN, *op. cit.* (above, p. 55, n. 5), pp. 418 ff.

[18] A. BERTHOLET, "Zur Frage des Verhältnisses vom persischen und jüdischen Auferstehungsglauben," in *Festschrift C. Andreas*, 1916.

[19] Is. XXVI. 19; Dan. XII. 2; IV Ezra VII. 32; Mt. IX. 24; Jn. XI. 11; I Thess. IV. 13, etc. The Phoenicians of Tyre similarly call the festival of the resurrection the festival of awakening, ἔγερσις.

hair, and fire the life." This essential difference shows that the Jews lay the stress on the new life granted to man, whereas the Persians emphasise the physical reconstitution of the creature.

Finally, like W. von Baudissin, A. Bertholet recalls that the resurrection was known in Israel before the Chosen People came into contact with the Persian Empire, since, as we shall see later, the Semitic world was by no means unaware of it.

What conclusions are to be drawn from these contradictory statements? It seems that Iranian influence on the formation of the Old Testament belief in the resurrection must be neither exaggerated nor denied. It is certain that this belief becomes clearly expressed, with the characteristics that it would thenceforth possess, at a time when the Jews have already been long in contact with Persian thought. Moreover, in Judaism as in the Iranian conception, the return of the departed to life is connected with the end of the world and the Last Judgment, and is thenceforth an eschatological conception.[20] Viewing the matter from another angle, for the Chosen People the resurrection remains restricted; only seldom and belatedly is it extended to embrace all mankind; this feature is characteristic of the Jewish conception; further, it is expressed in definitely Semitic terms, and is set in a distinctively Old Testament conceptual framework. W. von Baudissin justly writes that "Judaism had a Jewish conception of the resurrection," of which it knew before the Exile.[21]

Zarathustra's followers did not hand on an entirely unknown idea to the Jews; it is incorrect to speak of borrowing here and even questionable to say, as H. Birkeland does, that the decisive factor in the formation of the Jewish belief in the resurrection came from Persian religion. The Iranian doctrine helped the Jews to adopt a conception whose essential elements had already been provided by their own tradition, and perhaps to widen it, or even to transfigure it, so that it might give the answer to a question which, for generations and especially after the Exile, had haunted the minds of the Israelites, namely the question of the fulfilment of the righteousness of Yahweh and the final lot of the Ḥasidim. When Is. xxvi and Dan. xii were

[20] The Persians consider that this will be the work of the Saviour; the Jews expect it from Yahweh Himself and not from the Messiah.

[21] VON BAUDISSIN, *op. cit.* (above, p. 55, n. 5), p. 422.

written, belief in the return of the departed to life was doubtless
in the air, and Persian thought probably tended to spread it;
the Jews had known of it for a long time already, but, in the
light of recent events to which we shall return, and stimulated
by the new ideas that were spreading through all the former
empire of Alexander, they were reconsidering it and are dis-
covering its latent implications.   In conclusion, Persia did not
give the doctrine of the resurrection of the dead to Israel, and,
through Israel, to the world, but it enabled the Chosen People
to formulate its faith in the victory won for believers by its God
over the powers of death.

   There is nothing surprising in the indirect role of Iran in
revealing Yahweh's power over death.   This is not the first
time in the course of its history that Israel, through its contact
with other peoples, discovers the extent of the power of its God.
The Old Testament shows us that as a result of its encounters
with the heathen nations the People of Yahweh had its conception of the lordship and work of the Living God continually
enriched;   the role of Yahweh never ceased to become greater
nor His interventions to extend into spheres hitherto reserved
for other divinities.   Several assertions, implicitly contained in
the ancient beliefs, were rendered explicit and defined with
precision through resistance to the claims of rival faiths;   little
by little, the God of Israel took possession of all the world.

   Thus it is that, at the beginning, Yahweh appears as the
Lord of a semi-nomadic clan, He is the "jealous God," violent
as the thunderbolt, and haughty as the bedouin, master of a
rocky stronghold somewhere in the wilderness;   but after Israel
has taken possession of Canaan and the crisis brought on by
the competition of the agricultural cults with Yahweh occurs,
He is then manifested as the true master of the soil of Palestine,
the God who alone provides water and rain and bread and
wine, He upon whom Israel depends day by day in the land
that has been given to it;   thus Yahweh appropriates to Himself
prerogatives that belonged to Baal, but without becoming
identified with any form of vital force.

   Still later, through the contact with the mighty Assyrian and
Babylonian Empires whose tutelary god is Marduk, Yahweh,
when His People is dispersed among the nations, is revealed
no longer as a divinity whose power is confined within the

frontiers of Palestine, but as the absolute sovereign of the earth whose will determines the lot of Egypt and Assyria as well as that of Israel, as the creator of the universe who holds all things in the hollow of His hand, and before whom the glory of the heathen gods dwindles and dies away.

But one realm remains in which the God of Israel has not yet constantly and absolutely exerted His power; alongside His creation, the Living God has permitted the dominion of the dead to subsist. He has created neither Chaos nor Sheol, but He has long tolerated them; at the very moment when Iran is proclaiming the destruction of the world and its total renewal, Yahweh makes Himself known as He who is going to put an end to the power of death and utterly shatter the power of Sheol. He will raise the departed from the dust, He will awaken His faithful from the sleep of death, He will break open the gate of Hell.

Thus the Old Testament ends with the proclamation of Yahweh's victory over the last enemy; the revelation of the God of Israel begins in the wilderness, goes on to the conquest of nature, continues by taking posession of the universe itself, and ends in the annihilation of the forces of Chaos; the *Nihil* itself disappears before the Living God. "He will swallow up death for ever" (Is. xxv. 8).

CANAANITE INFLUENCE

The Chosen People did not wait until it was subject to the Achaemenids before becoming acquainted with the concept of resurrection; the texts confirm the fact that already before the Exile and from the time of its occupation of Canaan onwards, this idea was, in some sense, a familiar one. The starting-point of the assurance that finds its final expression in Dan. xii is to be found neither in the wilderness, where Israel met its God, nor in Mesopotamia, where the Chosen People were exiled and came into contact with Persian thought, but on the very soil on which Yahweh had settled it for centuries, in Palestine. It was the former inhabitants of the land who taught Israel to hope for return to life, but the difficulty is in understanding to what extent the Canaanites actually deter-

mined the Chosen People's expectation of the resurrection of
the dead.

Many writers have laid stress on this point; among them let
us cite I. Engnell, who, in his work on the Songs of the Servant
of Yahweh, notes that it is mistaken to claim that this belief
only dates from the Persian period. Far from having been
borrowed by the Jews from the Persians after the Exile, it is
rooted in the myth of the dying and rising god which is
indigenous in Canaan.[1] W. von Baudissin observed some time
ago that the concept of the resurrection derives from the
natural scene, in particular from the appearance and disappearance of some star, or, more probably of the vegetation;
it is originally Canaanite and not Israelite, and at the outset
has no specifically religious connotation.[2]

It is a matter of fact, as we have already indicated in
connexion with our study of Hos. VI. I ff. and repeated when
expounding Ezek. XXXVII, Is. LIII, and Ps. LXXIII, that the
People of Yahweh lived surrounded by nations among whom
the idea of a divinity who went down to the nether world
annually to return from it after a lapse of time played a
prominent part. The myth of a young god, periodically overcome by the powers of death, but nevertheless reappearing
among the living year after year, was celebrated almost
universally in the Near East. Festivals were observed in his
honour nearly everywhere, in accordance with almost identical
formulae. Although they bore different names and retained
individual characteristics, Osiris in Egypt, Tammuz at
Babylon, Attis in Phrygia, Adonis or Eshmun in Phoenicia,
Baal at Ras Shamra, and Melqart at Tyre, all ultimately
fulfilled the same function: by their own resurrection to
sanction, in every sphere, the renewal of life perpetually
threatened by hostile powers, and, in particular, to ensure the
food-supply of beast and man alike, since the destiny of these
divinities was supposed to reflect the succession of the seasons
and to represent the unending struggle between life and death.

Long ago the writers of antiquity pointed out the existence
of cults based on the cycle of nature; in the third century before
Christ, Theocritus refers to a belief in the return of Adonis,

---

[1] I. ENGNELL, *op. cit.* (above, p. 107, n. 15), 1948, p. 37.
[2] VON BAUDISSIN, *op. cit.* (above, p. 55, n. 5), pp. 428 ff. and 441 ff.

which is also known to Lucian. The recently-discovered Ras Shamra texts have abundantly confirmed these scanty evidences; thanks to them, we know of the role played by Baal among the near neighbours of the Israelites; his descent to the nether world is lamented in the dry season, his death is celebrated during the period when his enemy Mot—that is to say Death (or, according to R. Dussaud, the Warrior)—is triumphant. But in the end Baal, or his son Aliyan Baal, is discovered and set free; his victory and return to the light of the day ensures new fertility for the land.[3]

To this myth, widespread in various forms throughout the whole of the ancient world, there are corresponding rites, particularly the New Year festival, in the course of which the King, or his substitute, symbolically enacts the lot of the god, conquered at first by his enemies and finally overcoming the powers of chaos. The purpose of this ritual representation is to renew the forces of nature and of the nation for the coming year; it is a guarantee of peace, that is to say of prosperity, success, and abundance.[4]

Thus, on entering into Palestine, Israel found the cult of the annually dying and rising god; we have already observed its significance for the contemporaries of Hosea who confuse the God of Israel with Baal and picture Him as, like the latter, being bound to succumb to Mot continually; Hosea himself, while opposing the Ephraimites, betrays, by the expressions he

---

[3] C. VIROLLEAUD, in various articles published in *Syria*, especially in 1931, 1935, 1937, etc.; R. DUSSAUD, "La mythologie phénicienne d'après les tablettes de Ras Shamra," *R. h. r.*, 1931, pp. 353-408; "Le mythe de Baal et Aliyan d'après des documents nouveaux," *R. h. r.*, 1935, pp. 5-65; "Aliyan Baal et ses messages d'outre-tombe," *R. h. r.*, 1937, pp. 121-35; etc. Cp. also the important summary by W. BAUMGARTNER, "Ras Shamra und das A. T.," *Th. R.*, 1940, pp. 163-88; 1941, pp. 1 ff., 85 ff., 157 ff.

[4] About the beginning of the Christian era, these practices were transformed into mystery cults which, under the Roman Empire, underwent an extraordinary development; through their agency ordinary individuals, and no longer only the king, could now become one with the divinity, and, like the divinity, pass through death to experience thereafter the joys of new life and know a salvation which for long impeded the advance of the Gospel of Christ. Nevertheless, at the time when the Old Testament comes to its close, the mystery cults do not appear to be exercising an influence in Palestine strong enough to have inspired such texts as Is. xxvi and Dan. xii.

o

employs as well as by the content of his oracles, the influence of this nature-mysticism in his own life. It is to be borne in mind that the struggle between Yahweh and Baal does not date from the eighth century; it goes back to the Chosen People's occupation of Canaan—in particular it explains Elijah's interventions—and it continued throughout the whole history of Israel as numerous Old Testament texts confirm.[5]

A. Bertholet [6] points out that, as excavations have brought to light, Osiris thus was known in Palestine at a very early date; and, adopting an ingenious hypothesis of Lagarde's, he finds traces of him in Is. x. 4; [7] moreover, Is. XVII. 10 f. refers to the gardens of Adonis which, forgetting Yahweh, the Chosen People planted, doubtless in the heart of the Holy City; Is. I. 29, Jer. XXII. 18, XXXIV. 5, and 1 Kings XII. 24 (LXX) similarly make allusion to the cult of Adonis, and particularly to the ritual wailing associated with the god's death. In Jersusalem itself, Ezekiel is aghast to observe women weeping for Tammuz at the gate of the Temple of the Living God (cp. Ezek. VIII. 14; and perhaps also Dan. XI. 37). As for Jeremiah, he deplores that in the streets of Jerusalem, parents and children are preparing offerings for the Queen of Heaven, Ishtar, whose "descent to the nether world" is famous (Jer. VII. 18). It was not only before or even at the time of the Exile that the influence of the agricultural divinities made itself felt in the City of God itself; post-Exilic texts like Zech. XII. 11 (which refers to the God Hadad, often connected with Adonis) and Is. LXV. 4-5 (which alludes to the idolatrous practices indulged in by the Israelites) bear witness to the persistent hold of a worship offered to the forces of nature upon the Chosen People, notwithstanding all the efforts of the prophets and their followers.[8] Very much later, in the time of the Roman Emperors Hadrian and Constantine, the people of Bethlehem, according to Jerome, worshipped an agricultural divinity.

---

[5] W. BAUMGARTNER; cp. on this point: "Ugaritische Probleme und ihre Tragweite für das A. T.," *Th. Z.*, 1947, pp. 81 ff.

[6] A. BERTHOLET, "The Pre-Christian Belief in the Resurrection of the Body," *Am. J. Th.*, 1916, pp. 1 ff.

[7] Cp. also O. PROCKSCH, *Jes.* 1-39, 1930, *comm. ad loc.*

[8] Cp. also Song of Sol. IV. 8; Ecclesiasticus XLVI. 12, XLIX. 10, etc.

Additional items of evidence could doubtless be brought together,[9] but the texts that we have just pointed out are sufficient to indicate the constant presence in the very midst of the People of Yahweh of myths and rituals depicting the operation of natural forces and involving the death and resurrection of the god who represents them. It therefore seems to be established that the Israelites found the concept of resurrection before the Exile and in Canaan; and in some sense the Canaanite religion prepared the way for the belief which Iran later enabled to develop more easily in the midst of the People of God.

But we must define with greater precision the way in which the influence of the agricultural cults was exerted upon the Old Testament doctrines, and make clear whether a proclamation like that of Dan. xii is actually derived from Canaanite mysticism. Some writers, such as W. Baumgartner, A. Bertholet and E. Sellin hold that, while it may be maintained that Israel learned the idea of the rising god in Palestine, if it did not also discover the concept of personal resurrection there, the faith manifested by the *Ḥasidim* who died in the Maccabean period can scarcely be considered to have arisen under the influence of the indigenous cults; other events occurred to lead the Chosen People into the assurance that the Living God would recall His dead to life.

On the other hand, other Old Testament specialists attach the utmost importance to the myth of the dying and rising god and to the New Year festival which actualises it from year to year. They consider that the celebration of the death of the god and his return to life is at the core of the Old Testament, it affords an explanation of Israelite ritual as a whole, and of some of the greatest passages in the Old Testament Scriptures as well; Messianism along with the Jerusalemite cultus depend upon it, and by it both prophets and priests alike live; in short, from the Exodus to the persecutions of Antiochus, the theme of the divinity periodically descending into Hell and emerging again into the world of light—a divinity whose destiny is represented by the king, a sacral or even divine being from

---

[9] T. WORDEN, "The Literary Influence of the Ugaritic Fertility Myth on the O.T., ' *Vet. test.*, 1953, pp. 273-97.

whom flows the future of the whole nation, because he ensures
the continuance of Yahweh's blessing—is the key to the message
of the Old Testament; obviously, from this point of view, the
belief in the resurrection of the dead is quite naturally derived
from this theme. This opinion is more or less shared by a great
number of Anglo-Saxon and Scandinavian scholars, such as
S. H. Hooke, A. R. Johnson, S. Mowinckel, A. Bentzen,
I. Engnell, and others; but we need give no detailed examination of their theses here, nor indicate the particular standpoint
of each of these.[10]

During our exegesis of Ezek. xxxvii, Is. liii, and Ps. lxxiii
we have already come across this theory without adopting it;
in point of fact it seems to us, as it does to various Swiss and
German theologians, such as W. Baumgartner, W. Zimmerli,
G. von Rad, and J. J. Stamm, that the element of truth contained in this interpretation is at the outset in danger of being
falsified by its schematisation. It is on precisely this ground
that H. Frankfort contests the validity of a method which is
applied only to observing the resemblances between myths
and rituals, and to studying the supposed general culture
pattern of the Near East, while neglecting to lay stress upon the
diversity of the civilisations and mentalities involved in the
witnesses that it cites.[11] To compare is not to establish. It is
not enough to adduce some parallels between temporally and
spatially separated documents; every text and every practice
must be considered within its own cultural and religious
context. In opposition to the theses of S. H. Hooke and
I. Engnell, H. Frankfort recalls that kingship manifests itself
with peculiarly distinctive features in Egypt and in Mesopotamia, and even more so in Israel. Therefore attention

---

[10] We may cite some studies : S. Mowinckel, *Das Thronbesteigungsfest
Jahwes und der Ursprung der Eschatologie (Psalmenstudien II)*, Christiania
1922; S. H. Hooke, *Myth and Ritual*, 1933; A. R. Johnson, "The Role of
the King in the Jerusalem Cultus," *The Labyrinth*, ed. S. H. Hooke, 1935;
I. Engnell, *Studies in Divine Kingship in the Ancient Near East*, Uppsala
1943; etc.; cp. also the following recent works: W. Vischer, "La prophétie
d'Emmanuel et la fête royale de Sion," *Et. th. r.*, 1954, pp. 55-97; J. de
Fraine, *L'aspect religieux de la royauté israélite*, Rome 1954.

[11] H. Frankfort, "The Problem of Similarity in Ancient Near Eastern
Religion," *The Frazer Lectures*, 1950; *Kingship and the Gods*, Chicago 1948,
especially pp. 277 ff., 295 ff., 337 ff., and 405 (Ch. 21, n. 1).

ought to be devoted to the specific nature of each religion, and quite particularly to that of the Israelite faith.[12]

Moreover, in an interesting article, T. Worden has very ably demonstrated how literary dependence could be conjoined with an actual dogmatic independence; thus, although many epithets describing Baal were also applied to Yahweh, the latter's nature does not thereby become any less fundamentally different from that of the agricultural god.[13] For his part, A. Bentzen has several times laid stress on the fact that, in order to explain the Old Testament, it is not enough to cite some Near Eastern documents; in the final analysis these only concern the prehistory of the Old Testament text and are often more adequate to satisfy the curiosity of "antiquaries" than to the true exegesis of a Scriptural passage.[14]

Further, the interpretation of the texts, be they Sumerian, Accadian, or Phoenician, is difficult; J. J. Stamm, in a masterly summing-up of the subject,[15] counselled scholars to be cautious about basing themselves on the Ras Shamra documents, since they were still far from being agreed as to their exact significance.[16] Again, the principal element in the thesis maintained by the Scandinavian school, the existence of a New Year Festival at Jerusalem, similar to that which takes

---

[12] With others, Père Follet has protested against the exaggeration manifested by those scholars who find "patterns" everywhere. In criticising a work by T. H. Gaster, *Thespis, Ritual, Myth and Drama in the Ancient Near East*, New York, I, 1950, he declares: (not without malice) "Nothing is exempt from the imperialism of such expository ardour. By using these methods you could find all Gaster's 'patterns' and many others as well in today's newspaper. Why, for example, could not the Tour de France bicycle race be a 'seasonal ritual pattern'? All the ingredients are there: the beginning of summer (the month of Tammuz), a circumambulation, certainly of Canaanite origin, rituals of purification (the elimination of the unlucky), invigoration (a competition), and ululation (and how!) You see there the solar cult (sun-coloured jersey, bicycle wheels symbolising the sun), and the invocation of the gods above by the ascension of mountains . . . not even a 'hymnody' is lacking—the sporting press, etc. I am jesting, but not altogether." *Biblica*, 1952, pp. 141 f.

[13] T. Worden, *op. cit.* (above, n. 9), pp. 286, 296 f.

[14] Cp. especially: A. Bentzen, *Messias, Moses redivivus, Menschensohn*, Zürich 1948, pp. 53 f. (*King and Messiah*, London 1954, pp. 54 f.); "Der Tod des Beters in den Psalmen," *Festschrift O. Eissfeldt*, Halle 1947, pp. 59 f.

[15] J. J. Stamm, "Die Immanuel Weissagung, ein Gespräch mit E. Hammershaimb," *Vet. test.*, 1954, pp. 20-33. [16] Stamm, *op. cit.*, pp. 25 f.

place in Babylon in honour of Marduk, is, if not subject to suspicion, capable at least of different interpretations. Thus some critics, following S. Mowinckel, hold that it was primarily a cultic performance in which the mythological element predominated; others, such as A. Alt, G. von Rad, and H. J. Kraus, consider that it was determined rather by the history of the Chosen People, and was based on a series of events recorded in time and space, and not on a nature-mysticism, and was thus essentially distinguished from the Mesopotamian and Phoenician festivals.

Finally, it must not be forgotten that in extra-Israelite mythology, the divinity dies or succumbs to the weight of his enemies, and has to recover and rise again; the god, be he called Baal, Osiris, or even Marduk, is constrained by a law higher than himself to experience defeat or death regularly; the principal purpose of the New Year ritual is to ensure his return to life. Now, the point is that Yahweh does not die, and has therefore no need of being revived. As J. Pedersen writes: "The idea of a dying and rising god, so dear to the agricultural peoples, was incompatible with the nature of Yahweh." [17] On this capital point, the widespread theme of the whole of the Near East must have been modified; the Living God does not have to be reborn; it is only the bond that unites Him to His People that will be periodically remembered or renewed; the Israelite cult-practice ensures, not the revivification of a departed god, but, in some sense, the re-establishment or the maintenance of the Covenant between the God of Israel and His People.[18] The purpose of the New Year Festival is not to resuscitate the flagging powers of Yahweh, but to set Israel in the presence of the promises and the requirements of its God once more. The piety of Yahweh's subjects is therefore fundamentally different from Phoenician, Babylonian, or Egyptian religiosity; the latter is dependent on the operation of natural forces that are liable to all sorts of fluctuations which are quite inevitable; the former is based on Yahweh's creative and redemptive works in history, which reveal the true nature of the God of Israel.

In the warfare that He wages with Baal, Yahweh, as we have

---

[17] PEDERSEN, *op. cit.* (above, p. 2, n. 2), VOL. III-IV, p. 442.
[18] PEDERSEN, *ibid.*; T. WORDEN, *op. cit.* (above, n. 9), p. 286, etc.

seen, overcomes the agricultural god and despoils him of his prerogatives; He appropriates to Himself all that is not inconsistent with His own character, and therefore He takes the heaven, the tillage of the soil, and the land of Canaan itself, from Baal. But the God of Israel is careful not to become, after his rival's likeness, a mere expression of vital force; He eschews all sexual manifestation, and has neither father nor wife, which gives Him a unique position among all the divinities of the Near East. Yahweh rejects a dubious mysticism, born of the nature-cult, which easily degenerates into immoral practices; He is also fundamentally distinguished from death, into whose power Baal regularly falls, and who shares in this same equivocal reality. He confronts the indissolubly united partnership of Baal and Mot with His claim to be the sole sovereign of the world.

He stands over against the dominion of the dead, and in some sense imposes an interdict on Sheol and its inhabitants. In this trial that He makes of the attributes of the agricultural god, death, then, is condemned, and, with it, the resurrection is brought into jeopardy because it is associated with the operation of natural forces. Thus the myth of the dying and rising god, far from having led the Chosen People to faith in the return of the departed to life, appears rather to have removed it farther from it. W. Baumgartner justly writes that if this belief arose so belatedly in the midst of Israel, it was not because the Israelites did not know of it, but because, it was at first rejected as a mysticism incompatible with the holiness of the Living God; its connexions with condemned rituals and prohibited doctrines for long made it suspect in the eyes of the true worshippers of Yahweh.[19]

Israel, then, knew of the concept of resurrection long before the Exile, but, officially at least, rejected it. G. von Rad considers with good reason that it was one of the glories of the Chosen People that it refused it at that particular moment in its history.[20] The return of the dead to life, as it was conceived

---

[19] W. BAUMGARTNER, "Der Auferstehungsglaube im Alten Orient," Z. M. R., 1933, pp. 212 ff.; "Ras Shamra und das A. T.," Th. R., 1941, p. 179.

[20] G. VON RAD, "Gerechtigkeit und Leben in der Kultsprache der Psalmen," Festschrift A. Bertholet, Tübingen, 1950, p. 435.

by the agricultural cults, could not be admitted, such as it was, into the framework of the revelation of Yahweh; all the more so since the destiny of Baal or Adonis, though perhaps shedding some light on certain aspects of Is. LIII, Ezek. XXXVII, or Ps. LXXIII, does not explain their essential assertions, as we have already seen, nor does it necessarily give rise to the hopes and certainties expressed by the *Ḥasidim* in Maccabean times. It must, as a matter of fact, be observed that, at the period when the Old Testament was written, the resurrection of a divinity re-enacted from year to year by the king, is not in any way a guarantee of the return of the faithful to life, the actuality of which is not involved in its cultic symbolism. There is a world of difference between the mysticism of Baal-worshippers and the confidence of Maccabean martyrs; the transition from Hos. VI to Dan. XII was not effected by a natural process of evolution, but under the constraint of new forces which made themselves manifest in the course of the history of the Chosen People.[21] The underlying reasons for the gap between the representations in the Near Eastern cults and the reality of the expectation of the Jews whom Antiochus persecuted are the contacts that the Jewish community had with Iranian thought, as H. Birkeland holds, and even more, as we shall see, the important changes that will take place in the course of several centuries in both the life and the faith of Israel.

In conclusion, we must state that the People of Yahweh found the concept of resurrection in Canaan; but for a long time this formed part of a realm over against which Yahweh stood in His sovereign will, so that, with regard to the resurrection, the religion of the Canaanites played a negative part, by obliging the Israelites to make their stand against it; it had, nevertheless, a sort of indirect action, in making possible a sort of purification of this belief which, in another age and within another context, received a new content. The agricultural cults thus brought the Israelites face to face with an assertion which could not take its legitimate place within the framework of the Biblical revelation until once and for all freed from its ties with nature-mysticism; for the Canaanite belief to be accepted by the servants of the Living God, the Jewish community had to discover, in the midst of its sufferings, the

[21] BIRKELAND, *op. cit.* (above, p. 187, n. 5), p. 7.

extent of the reach of the power, and of the righteousness, and of the goodness, of its God.

CONCLUSIONS

In the course of this chapter we have studied the possibility of foreign influence on the formation of the Old Testament belief in the resurrection of the dead; we have endeavoured to define with precision the particular part played in this matter by Iran and Canaan. We concede that the heathen world made a real contribution to the development of the doctrine professed by the Old Testament believers: on the one hand, Persian thought, at the critical moment, was able to help towards a decision, in Israel, in favour of the return of the departed to life; on the other, the agricultural cults of Canaan provided the Israelites with a concept which, too much compromised by its provenance, for a long period of time was not accepted into the midst of the Chosen People. Thus the foreign contribution is incontrovertible; nevertheless, the determinative factor came from Israel itself, from its faith in the Living God as He revealed Himself, little by little, to His own; the worshippers of Yahweh were not content to copy the followers of Baal or Ahura Mazda, they thought for themselves, and out of their own experience the certainty that God would raise His dead was finally born. These assertions will be more precisely defined in the following pages.

CHAPTER II

OLD TESTAMENT BELIEF IN THE RESURRECTION OF THE DEAD
A CONSEQUENCE OF THE REVELATION OF THE LIVING GOD
TO HIS PEOPLE

Various writers consider that the faith in the resurrection
of the dead is, in Israel, primarily the result of an internal
development of its religion and that there is no need to have
recourse to the hypothesis of foreign influence for its explanation;
thus the part played by Canaan or by Iran tends to be diminished
or even denied. F. Baumgärtel declares that, although the
assertions contained in Is. xxvi and Dan. xii have the appearance of being alien intrusions into the Old Testament context
they were in reality prepared for by the evolution of Israelite
thought.[1] R. Kittel thinks that Persia hardly did more than
assist the Jews to admit of the return of the departed to life;[2]
W. Eichrodt and F. Nötscher both uphold the originality of
the Old Testament belief as against the Canaanite or Iranian
doctrines.[3] A. T. Nikolainen, for his part, considers that
Israel rejected resurrection as based on the natural scene, or on
the survival of the soul, to found it uniquely on the knowledge
of Yahweh as He revealed Himself in the course of its history.[4]
We concede the validity of these positions, in so far as they do
not claim to be exclusive and to eliminate entirely the possibility
of some Iranian or Canaanite influence, as defined in the
previous chapter.

We hold that, among the Chosen People, faith in the
resurrection of the dead is definitely based on the revelation of
Yahweh; it is, as we already have had occasion to observe,
fundamentally theological, in the sense that it begins from God
and ends in Him, it depends on what the Living God is and does

---

[1] BAUMGÄRTEL, Die Eigenart der alttest. Frömmigkeit, p. 20.
[2] R. KITTEL, Geschichte des Volkes Israel, 1929, VOL. III/2, pp. 745 f.
[3] EICHRODT, Theol. des A. T., VOL. III, pp. 160 ff.; NÖTSCHER, op. cit.
(above, p. 55, n. 5), pp. 173 ff.
[4] NIKOLAINEN, op. cit. (above, p. 131, n. 3), pp. 101 ff.

for Israel, since it is ultimately part of His purpose which is
to establish His kingship over the entire universe; in short, it
is what the believers know about their God that ultimately
enables them to assert that the perished will live again; the
God of Israel's actions in the past are the guarantee of the future
of the *Ḥasidim* who have died for His sake: Yahweh alone is able
to force Sheol to give up its captives, He wills the deliverance
of the dead to make His divinity manifest, He is, at one and
the same time, the source and the end of the Old Testament
hope of victory over death.

Though the People of God, in face of the powers of Hell,
bases its expectation on Yahweh as He made Himself known in
former days to the Fathers throughout the whole course of the
history of Israel, and as He reveals Himself today to the
believer's heart, other factors are not thereby precluded from
having been effective in leading the Jews to profess faith in the
resurrection of the dead; there is no doubt that, in this respect,
various influences were at work; for example, we must not
overlook the part played by the foreigner in an age when there
was such free circulation of new ideas from India in Greece,
from Egypt in Asia Minor; more personal interests could have
come in also, such as the individual's desire to see the divine
righteousness made manifest, sooner or later, on his behalf, but,
in the last resort, the particular character of the *Ḥasidim's*
certainty, prepared for by the previous generations, is essentially
derived from its theological foundation. Faith in the resurrection assumes definite form through Yahweh having revealed
Himself to His People as a powerful, just, and gracious God;
this threefold aspect of the God of Israel explains the formation
and development of the Old Testament belief in the return of
the departed to life; the resurrection of the dead, the Old
Testament's ultimate revelation regarding the God of Abraham
and of Isaac and of Jacob, confirms, at one and the same time,
His power, His righteousness, and His mercy alike.

YAHWEH'S POWER CAN DELIVER THE DEPARTED FROM SHEOL

From its infancy, Israel has learned to reckon with the power
of Yahweh, it owes its existence to Him; the Exodus, the

foundation of the whole history of the Chosen People, is the first of the mighty acts in which the Living God manifested Himself to the Israelite clans. By the same power He preserved their life throughout the centuries; the whole existence of Israel bears witness to His might, its disasters and triumphs alike show forth the wrath or the graciousness of a God whom nothing escapes. Moreover, in the eyes of His People, Yahweh's dominion has not ceased to spread, from the wilderness to the utmost ends of the universe; He finds Israel in an arid land and subdues the fertile and goodly soil of Palestine for it, He controls the greatest empires and creates the world in which the destiny of the Israelites is wrought out. His power is boundless and is particularly made manifest when He calls beings into life. He rules over all creation, He holds all things in His hand, and every creature is dependent on Him.

Especially in its Psalms, Israel sings of the creative and redemptive activity of its God, it knows unhoped-for deliverances, healings in sorest straits; because in bygone days Yahweh has mastered the forces of the *Nihil*, therefore He is able to break their power once again; since He has created all things out of nothing, He can make all things new.

It is upon this limitless power of the God of Israel that Ezekiel bases himself in inviting his brethren to hope; Yahweh is recalling His People to life even as He gives breath to the dry bones again. Deutero-Isaiah, in his turn, knows the unique destiny of the Servant to be the work of the Living God; his vindication and his suffering alike both form part of a plan whose accomplishment depends on Yahweh's omnipotent will. Later on, anonymous prophets proclaim the punishment of the powers, of the heavens as well as of earth, who dare to offer resistance to Israel's God; death itself, that casts its shadow over His creation, is doomed to disappear before Him, that it may no longer tarnish His glory; in the day when Yahweh establishes His Kingdom for the saints, the resurrection which allows the martyrs to share in the heavenly glory and the apostates to experience the divine judgment, makes the greatness of the God of the Jews manifest. It seems that, with the passing of the centuries, the more intense the pressure exerted by Yahweh upon Sheol becomes. The days of death are numbered; when the Old Testament comes to an end, death has virtually had to surrender to the God of Israel; a few more decades, and prophecy becomes accomplished fact.

In conclusion, the transcendence of the Living God over the infernal powers is apparent in every text that we have studied. A. T. Nikolainen justly writes that Yahweh's power over death is the presupposition of the resurrection of the dead.[1]

YAHWEH'S RIGHTEOUSNESS MUST ULTIMATELY PREVAIL

Though He is jealous, that is to say exclusive, the God of Israel is neither arbitrary nor capricious, He intends to remain true to Himself. He reveals Himself, from the beginning, of course, but especially in the period of the great prophets of the eighth century, as the Holy God, the God who founds and guarantees morality. Yahweh gives the Decalogue to His People, He reminds it, particularly by the voice of Hosea, Amos, or Isaiah, that He prefers mercy to sacrifice and righteousness to prayer. The Covenant which since the departure from Egypt binds Him to Israel is the foundation of the Law that governs the relationship between the Chosen People and its God and at the same time regulates the life of each of its members; the history of Israel is the history of this agreement continually jeopardised by the Israelites, but maintained and ultimately re-established by Yahweh, who makes His righteousness manifest by keeping His promise in every possible circumstance; His righteousness is an essential characteristic of the Living God who applies Himself not only to making it respected in the midst of Israel, but also to revealing it in every one of His interventions in this world. The acts of Yahweh are righteous works inasmuch as they are in conformity with the divine will as it is freely defined in the Covenant, and because they restore Israel to normal relationship with its God.

At first the righteousness of the God of Israel primarily concerns the Chosen People itself; it is the people as a whole that is punished or pardoned, the people and not the individual that experiences the justifiable wrath or the gracious forgiveness of the Lord. Israel does not constitute a mass in which the man is lost, and we must not overlook the part which, from the very

---

[1] NIKOLAINEN, *op. cit.*, pp. 113 ff.

dawn of its history, was (according to the best-known Israelite traditions) played by individuals such as Abraham, Moses, Elijah, and others as well: [1] yet, generally speaking, for centuries the Israelite, without being entirely identified with his people, experiences the righteousness of Yahweh through the community as a whole; he is conscious of his strict solidarity with a whole people, whose merits and faults he shares; his lot is dependent on the attitude of his family or nation towards God.

But the bonds uniting the individual to the group tend to relax more and more with the passing of the centuries, before and especially after the Exile, under the pressure of all kinds of events, political or economic as well as religious. The successive wars that the great Assyrian, Babylonian, Persian, and finally Greek conquerors waged in Palestine threw the country into complete confusion and destroyed the authority of the central power, promoting the emancipation of local communities; the establishment of the Chosen People in Canaan, the institution of the monarchy, the development of the great cities, and the enrichment of a whole class of Israelites, little by little destroyed the sentiment of solidarity binding the Israelite to his clan and put an end to the ancestral organisation of the Israelite tribes. Moreover the prophets, by their calling for faith and obedience, compelled their hearers to chose their own course themselves, to make a personally binding decision, and thus reinforced their consciousness of individual responsibility.

In short, after the Exile, but especially from the time of Alexander the Great's conquests, a process of disincorporation becomes apparent which affects not only the Chosen People but the whole of the regions subject to the Greeks. Israel then tends to be no longer an ethnic group but a religious community, to make use of the title of one of A. Causse's works. [2] At this period, man discovers his individuality in a very special way, he dissociates himself psychologically from the group, he seeks to distinguish himself from it. He means no longer to resign himself to the common lot, but to take his personal destiny upon himself; the God whom he seeks is no longer a

---

[1] On this point cp. the recent and precise summary by J. DE FRAINE "Individu et société dans l'A. T.," *Biblica*, 1952, pp. 324-55, 445-75.

[2] A. CAUSSE, *Du groupe ethnique à la communauté religieuse. Le problème sociologique de la religion d'Israël*, Paris 1937.

mere national divinity, but the Lord with whom he will be able to communicate in a sort of dialogue, in fellowship with whom he will be able to fulfil his life in this world, in short, the personal God, the God with whom he will have real personal relationship. Concomitant with this emergence of individualism, the problem of death assumes an increasing importance and tends to become the great anxiety of the living. As a matter of fact, as E. Morin has justly observed, there is a close connexion between the discovery of human personality and the question of death, the latter does not have the same sharpness as long as the individual is more or less identified with the group, it is urgent only for the man who is aware of his personal individuality.[3] In the same way the problem of the resurrection only actually arises in so far as the human being, becoming conscious of its personality, considers that its destiny is not automatically identical with that of its people and that its life has an intrinsic value which cannot disappear for ever in death. Like the Book of Job and Pss. XVI, XLIX, and LXXIII which we have studied, the anonymous oracles in Is. XXVI and Dan. XII thus presuppose that the lot of the believer has assumed a capital importance among the Chosen People.

In this process of disintegration in the midst of Israel the prophets played a major part not only by inviting every man to make his decision, but above all by making a distinction between the Chosen People as a whole and those whom Yahweh really recognises as His own. The concept of a "remnant" which alone will be spared by the divine judgment, is already discernible in Amos, it assumes a special importance with Isaiah, and we find traces of it in Zephaniah as well. Groups of the faithful gather themselves together round the messengers of the Living God, separating themselves from the mass of the nation; thus Isaiah is surrounded by a band of disciples who

---

[3] E. Morin writes: "Wherever death is not individualized, there is nothing but indifference and mere stench. No emotion is aroused by the sight of animal carrion, nor by that of the enemy or traitor . . . because he is not recognized as a human being. What is horrifying is not carrion as such but the carrion of an 'individual' . . . it is obvious that his obsession with personal survival reveals Man's agonising anxiety to retain his individuality after death." MORIN, *op. cit.* (above, p. 133, n. 7), pp. 20 ff.; cp. also LANDSBERG, *op. cit.* (above, p. 42, n. 33), pp. 26 ff.

doubtless continued his work; it is possible that communities
of the "pure" were formed before the Exile, which are to be the
ancestors of the *Hasidim* of Maccabean times. Be that as it may,
henceforth the true People of God is no longer absolutely
identified with the whole body of Abraham's descendants;
the latter enter into membership of the former by free choice
and personal obedience.

Similarly, the Prophets lay stress on the rigorous righteousness of Yahweh which is made manifest throughout the whole
of the history of His People; they recall that Yahweh does not
allow His guilty Nation to go unpunished; after them, the
Old Testament historians explain the ups and downs in Israel's
destiny by its attitude to the Living God; Yahweh makes His
law manifest in punishing His unfaithful partner as He also
does in pardoning the Israelites who repent; the failures and
successes of Israel in the course of the centuries show forth the
divine verdict upon the Chosen People.

In the days of Jeremiah and Ezekiel, the successive disasters
of the people of Judah, which are to culminate in the fall of
the Holy City, assume such a scale that the prophets concede
that their generation is paying for sins accumulated since the
Exodus; the patience of Yahweh is exhausted, and His chastisement, because long deferred, will be all the more fearful
(Ezek. xvi, xx). But the contemporaries of Jeremiah and
Ezekiel reject this argument, which to them appears grossly
unjust, they refuse to shoulder the responsibility of the crimes
of their fathers; the *libertins* (J. Chaine) dare to call the
justice of the Living God into question. Jeremiah answers them
by assuring them that a day is coming when no man will be
stricken for the sins of others (Jer. xxxi. 29 f.); Ezekiel, with
greater audacity and effect, proclaims that henceforth none
shall be punished except for his own faults (Ezek. xviii. 1 ff.)
With remarkable boldness he recalls that every human being
is directly dependent on Yahweh; he is to be judged in accordance with his own life; his personal attitude, and not that of his
father, will be decisive at the judgment seat of God. Even
the past will no longer determine the present, the sin of yesterday will not entail the condemnation of tomorrow; every
member of the Chosen People, declares the prophet, is free
to serve God and live; thus Ezekiel concludes his defence of the

divine righteousness by calling his brethren to be converted in order to escape death.

Doubtless this doctrine is not entirely original, but the way in which Ezekiel presents it brings it into peculiar relief. Moreover, it will become a fundamental dogma of Judaism: in this world, Yahweh renders to every man according to his works, He rewards the righteous and punishes the wicked during their earthly life.

After the Exile, the Chosen People believes more than ever in a strictly earthly retribution of human actions, and assesses the piety of men in terms of their prosperity or misfortune; like the Wisdom books, the Psalms are steeped in this notion, which ultimately results in God being conceived of as a master whose sole function is to mark the merits and misdeeds of every man and to mete out rewards and punishments accordingly. But this legalistic righteousness, which is belied every day, brings the believers into an impasse; the faithful comes up against the stumbling-block of the prosperity of the wicked and the suffering of the *Ḥasidim*; Jeremiah, in his day, is bold enough to call Yahweh to account for this (Jer. xii. 1 ff.); Pss. xxxvii, xlix, and lxxiii show us what difficulties beset believers who would find the divine righteousness manifested in this world.

The Book of Job shows us how great is the struggle of a believer who refuses to question the integrity and the justice of his God; Job wants his innocence to be acknowledged, he is aware that the God whom he serves will justify him sooner or later, only he does not know when and how the truth will be revealed, and feels that his time is short and that death is approaching, after which it will be too late. Sometimes his faith breaks through the limitations within which his friends' rigid orthodoxy has confined it; he appears to be certain that he will be vindicated sooner or later, tomorrow if not today and perhaps in the next world if not in this; for he knows intuitively that God would still be able to intervene though nothing were left to him but his bones . . . and even after that; are there any conceivable limits to what the Living God can do? Jerome and Luther after him took Job's words as being a prediction of his resurrection; doubtless they were wrong, but he does lead us in that direction; his faith, determined

P

by the revelation of God to Israel, ultimately raises this question: "Can death, this 'No' that God the Creator says to His creature, really be God's final word to the being that He has made and loves?" [4]

That one day or another Yahweh must necessarily make His justice manifest is also the assurance of the psalmists who wrote Pss. XLIX and LXXIII, although they are unaware of the precise manner in which the divine righteousness is to be fulfilled; they know that the prosperity of the wicked is an illusion and that their downfall is inevitable, and they themselves rely on the protection of Yahweh in the hour of judgment and dream of being for ever with the Living God, who alone is their joy; it may be that their convictions are bringing them to believe that the God of Israel will enable His servants to dwell with Him even on the other side of death.

The necessity of posthumous vindication is already apparent in the last Servant Song (Is. LIII), the same concern for righteousness is seen in the desire that Yahweh's dead should be raised from the dust while His enemies remain in Sheol for ever (Is. XXVI). His preoccupation that every man should receive his due leads the writer of Dan. XII to proclaim the resurrection of the *Ḥasidim* and the apostates; the former will obtain everlasting life, the latter will know eternal shame, while the mass of the Chosen People will doubtless remain in the dust.

Thus in the passages where the return of the departed to life is envisaged or affirmed, we constantly find this demand by the believer to see the realisation of the righteousness of God. In order to ensure this, the faithful, in some sense, threw open the gates of Sheol; because, as F. Schwally declares, "if it does not exist in this world, it has to be found elsewhere." [5] In its quest for divine retribution, the Chosen People discovered the resurrection, for the latter is a consequence of the former. [6]

In this perspective, its chief end is not so much to give satisfaction to the righteous as to safeguard the equity of Yahweh. The resurrection enables the *Ḥasidim* to keep their

---

[4] ZIMMERLI, *Das Menschenbild im A. T.*, Munich 1949, p. 22.

[5] SCHWALLY, *op. cit.* (above, p. 25, n. 2), p. 112.

[6] NIKOLAINEN, *op. cit.* (above, p. 131, n. 3), pp. 126 ff.; cp. also NÖTSCHER, who, with other specialists, lays stress on this close connexion between the resurrection and the righteousness of God: *op. cit.* (above p. 55, n. 5), pp. 215 ff.

vision of their Lord intact by confirming the revelation of the Living God to Israel. Believers do not ask vaguely for length of life, but first of all pray Yahweh to be faithful to His own word; they want to live again so that the divine righteousnes brought into question every day in this world, may be fulfilled at last, so that once again they may find the God who is represented to them as righteous by all their tradition.

The awakening of the dead makes judgment possible; its theocentric character becomes all the more apparent when, as W. Eichrodt observes, in the canonical texts the return of the departed to life is connected with the final establishment of the absolute sovereignty of the God of Israel.[7] The *Ḥasidim* are called to the light to share in the celestial glory of a kingdom founded on the righteousness of Yahweh victorious over all the powers of disorder and death (Is. xxvi; Dan. xii). Later on, in post-Biblical Judaism, interest will be primarily directed to the reward of the righteous and the punishment of the ungodly, Yahweh Himself being obliged to take strict account of the good or evil works of every man. This anthropocentric conception is utterly different from the main concern of those who are to discover that Yahweh would throw the gates of Sheol open so as to ensure the triumph of His justice at the Last Judgment.[8]

In conclusion, life is devoid of meaning for the believer if Yahweh be not righteous; thus he will demand that the divine righteousness, continually belied today, shall be fulfilled tomorrow; because he refuses to despair of it, he will dare to proclaim the return of the perished to life. His belief in the resurrection is the fruit of his faith in the God of Israel whose equity has been revealed to him by his fathers.

YAHWEH'S GRACIOUSNESS WILL CALL HIS OWN
TO DWELL WITH HIM FOR EVER

But Yahweh also and perhaps primarily reveals Himself to His People as a gracious God; His goodness stands at the beginning of Israel's history; it has been manifested since the

---

[7] Eichrodt, *Theol. des A. T.*, vol. iii, pp. 157 ff.
[8] Eichrodt, *ibid.*, p. 166.

Exodus; His care has watched over it from century to century, notwithstanding all the acts of ingratitude of which the Israelites have been guilty. His graciousness will continue to characterise the relationship of the Living God with His People to the end of time (Is. II. 2 f.; Jer. II. 2 ff.; Is. LV. 3, etc.)

חֶסֶד, *hesed*, "piety," defines Yahweh's attitude to Israel, His affection for the nation He chose for Himself. This term, which is especially employed by Hosea and Jeremiah, brings to mind the idyll of betrothal, the promises exchanged by the lovers, their mutual self-giving, in short, all the love that God feels for His People and all that He looks for from it in return.[1]

To this gracious, generous, welcoming attitude of Yahweh corresponds the piety of the *hasid*. This word, which is usually translated as "pious" or "faithful," involves more than the idea of devotion; it is frequently used by the psalmists,[2] and denotes the believers to whom Yahweh gives proof of His graciousness, the well-beloved of God, who by its agency enter into communion with Him, the faithful who live by the friendship of God and who, satisfied by His love, seek His presence and freely and joyfully respond to His welcome.

The *Hasidim* (in Greek, 'Ασιδαῖοι, 1 Macc. VII. 13) thus originally appear as Yahweh's companions, they are His clients, His Chosen.[3] They form special groups within the people of Israel, gathered together chiefly about the Temple, and their ideal is to live by Yahweh and for Him. B. D. Eerdmans thinks that he finds evidence of their existence before the Exile. In his opinion, Ps. XVI is a remarkable expression of the piety of the *hasid* who, as the favoured of God, is able to find his security in the divine graciousness; according to this same writer, Ps. LXXIII was the work of a *hasid*, doubtless a layman, belonging to the Temple circles, a confessor of the faith informed with a burning zeal for Yahweh; this commentator also finds a picture of a group of *Hasidim* in the description of

---

[1] STOEBE, *op. cit.* (above, p. 79, n. 6), pp. 244 ff.; A. R. JOHNSON, in a recent study, takes חֶסֶד in the sense of "loyalty" ("Ḥesed und Ḥāsîd," *Interpretationes*, S. Mowinckel, Oslo 1955, pp. 100-112).

[2] Pss. XVI. 10, XVIII. 25, XXX. 4, XXXI. 23, LXXXIX. 19, CXVI. 15, CXXXII. 9, 16, etc.

[3] STOEBE, *op. cit.*, p. 254; B. D. EERDMANS, "The Chasidim, Essays on Masoretic Psalms," *Oudtest. St.*, 1942, pp. 176-257.

the Servant of Yahweh, and, in particular, in the last Servant Song.

Whatever there may be in these various identifications, it seems to be the case that the party of the *Ḥasidim* was not an *ex nihilo* creation of Maccabean times; its foundation may go back to the period before the Exile when prophets like Isaiah are trying to gather a group of true Yahweh-worshippers about them. These men are characterised by their love for Yahweh and His gifts, especially His Law; they praise their God as the greatest of blessings (Ps. LXXXIV); they are athirst for the Living God (Ps. XLII); they find the fountain of life in His presence (Ps. XXXVI); they would dwell continually in the Temple to behold Yahweh (Ps. XXVII); they know that God leads them like a shepherd and satisfies them with His gifts (Ps. XXIII), and they find a blessing that is better than life in the goodness of God and inexpressible joy in His presence (Ps. LXIII).

G. von Rad [4] justly observes that these last-mentioned psalms sound a distinctive note in the Old Testament; they reflect a piety that is particularly intense and evidence a sort of mysticism which is quite unusual in the Old Testament. Their faith is, of course, wrought into the framework of the Biblical revelation, and is dependent on the Covenant sealed at the time of the Exodus which has become the permanent basis of the dialogue which, from century to century, the Living God sustains with His own; it is based, not on nature-mysticism, but on facts wrought out in the history of this earth, and it in no way aspires to some manner of absorption into the divine, nor to a loss of individual being in universal existence, but to a perfect communion with Yahweh. [5] Yet here we are probably concerned with one community or several within the Chosen People, whose spiritual life, highly developed and continually nourished and enriched by God's word to His People, became characterised by a rare intimacy. The *Ḥasidim*, among whom the writers of Pss. XVI and LXXIII are doubtless to be numbered, exalt the friendship of Yahweh and are aware that His presence confers an inestimable value upon their lives. They are unable to conceive of ever being deprived of it, their faith has brought

[4] G. VON RAD, *op. cit.* (above, p. 148, n. 1), 1950, pp. 429 ff.
[5] On this point cp. FRANKEN, *op. cit.* (above, p. 148, n. 1), esp. pp. 62 ff.

them a blessing more precious than life, a higher reality than
all that this world has to offer them; moreover, there is something unbreakable about the bonds that unite them to the
God of Israel; Sheol remains in some sense impotent against
Yahweh's well-beloved, for whom the principal problem
seems no longer to be that of attaining to the greatest
possible span of earthly days, but that of knowing henceforth
every grace that the fellowship of the Living God involves.
Similarly, from this point of view, their first concern is not that
justice may be granted them but that above all Yahweh may
be near them. Primarily they thirst, not for retribution, but
for the grace of the God of Israel, without which their existence
has no longer any meaning; they seek, above all, not the judgment of God, but His presence.

The piety of the *Ḥasidim* gives them a presentiment that
nothing can separate them from Yahweh and makes them
aware of the fact that the former Israelite beliefs are outmoded
by their knowledge of God, and thus it prepares the way for
faith in the resurrection. This faith is ultimately based on life
lived in communion with Yahweh; as A. T. Nikolainen writes,
"belonging to God is the motive for the conquest of death." [6]
Out of the heart of the union with God, living in the midst of
His own, broke forth the hope of the Hereafter; Hell was overcome by the *Ḥasidim's* faith; [7] because it created the desire to
be for ever with Yahweh in the hearts of believers, the love of
God showed itself to be stronger than death; the grace of the
God of Israel had both the first word and the last in the destiny
of His own.

YAHWEH GRANTS FAITH IN THE RESURRECTION TO HIS WITNESSING MARTYR PEOPLE

The piety of the *Ḥasidim*, those forerunners of the Pharisees,
does not consist in day-dreaming that allows the creature to
escape from the hard facts of earthly existence and attain to

[6] NIKOLAINEN, *op. cit.* (above, p. 131, n. 3), p. 125.
[7] SÖDERBLOM, *op. cit.* (above, p. 183, n. 1), pp. 342 ff., etc.; SELLIN,
op. cit. (above, p. 55, n. 5), pp. 266 f., 287; O. PROCKSCH, *Theologie des A. T.*,
1950, p. 502.

some intemporal reality; it is based on the revelation of Yahweh to His People and fashioned by the Covenant and the Law derived from it, and thus its end is strict obedience to the commandments of the God of Israel, apart from which it is impossible to live in His fellowship. Thus the *Ḥasidim*, far from being lost or taking refuge in another world, find themselves led by their convictions into struggling to keep the Chosen People true to the traditional way; by constraining them to resist the doctrines of the heathen world and the ruling powers of Palestine, their faith exposes them to persecution and even to martyrdom. A countless number of them pay for their devotion to Yahweh with their lives during the period which begins with the successors of Alexander the Great and ends with the Jewish Wars, in which, one after the other, Antiochus Epiphanes, the Hasmoneans, and the Romans made furious onslaughts upon the Jews. The spiritual life of the *Ḥasidim* dooms them to be the first victims of these persecutions of their people, and also makes them the first witnesses to the new faith in the resurrection of the dead; it is in point of fact to them that this will be primarily granted, for it is they who need it most of all.

A close relationship subsists between martyrdom and resurrection. This connexion is perhaps already apparent in the mysterious destiny of the Servant of Yahweh, the pitiful victim whom his God will vindicate gloriously; it is more evident in the hope of seeing the dead return to life on the day when Yahweh will arise to avenge the blood of the innocent that drenches the earth (Is. xxvi). Dan. xii, again, lays stress on the honours in store for the "teachers of righteousness" who perished in great numbers during the persecutions of Antiochus; the Second Book of the Maccabees expresses the martyrs' assurance that they will receive their broken bodies again, and that the only effect of their torture is to hasten the coming of the resurrection day.

Later texts confirm this connexion between the death of the witnesses in Israel and their return to life; it is reflected in the Book of Revelation (xx. 4 ff.), as it is by the testimonies of Josephus, Tertullian, and even Tacitus.[1]

---

[1] For example, JOSEPHUS emphasises the courage of the Essenes, who face death in the certainty that their life is immortal (*Bell. Jud.* ii. viii. 10, 11); cp. also TERTULLIAN, *De resurrectione carnis*, xliii; TACITUS, *Hist.* v. v.

It is an indubitable fact that faith in the resurrection of the dead established itself at a time when the Jewish People experienced an almost uninterrupted succession of difficulties and even persecutions; this period begins with the suffering of the *Ḥasidim* in Maccabean times and comes to its close with the execution of Rabbi Akiba. W. Bousset correctly characterises the Jewish religion of this age as the religion of martyrdom. In a world hostile to the witnesses of the Living God this appears as the normal end to a life devoted to Yahweh.[2] The suffering of the Chosen People then impelled it to discover, everywhere in its history, examples of faith strong enough to confess the God of Israel in times of torment.[3]

In this perspective, the resurrection is seen as God's answer to the man who sacrifices everything for Him. It is in some sense the sequel to martyrdom, the reward of the man who is willing to lose his life for Yahweh's sake. If the martyrs are making atonement for the sins of their People and are thus bringing the advent of the Messianic Age nearer, as the brethren butchered by Antiochus already believe, then it is only right that they should be the first to share in the glorious Kingdom of the God of the Jews.[4]

In these circumstances, we are not surprised to observe that the new and in some respects revolutionary belief in the return

---

[2] Bousset, *op. cit.* (above, p. 187, n. 3), 3rd edn., p. 374.

[3] Abel is the prototype of the martyr, the first witness to die for his faith; according to certain Palestinian traditions, Moses is to come back to this world and suffer; Elijah and Enoch endured martyrdom, destroying the power of the devil by their blood; Isaiah, according to the Ascension of Isaiah, was sawn asunder with a wooden saw in the reign of Manasseh (Heb. xi. 36); Job, according to the lxx, was a martyr, etc. These traditions referring to the persecutions endured by the faithful servants of Yahweh are to be found again in the New Testament (Mt. xxiii. 31 f.; Acts vii. 52; Heb. xi. 36 f.; 1 Thess. ii. 15). Cp. the articles in Kittel on Elijah, Moses, Enoch, etc.; H. Strathmann, s.v. μάρτυς, Kittel, vol. iv, 1942, pp. 477-520; E. Lohmeyer, "Die Idee des Martyriums in Judentum und Urchristentum," *Z. syst. Th.*, 1927, pp. 232-49; W. Surkau, "Martyrien in jüdischer und frühchristlicher Zeit," *Forsch. R. L. A. N. T.*, Göttingen 1936; H. J. Schoeps, *Die jüdischen Prophetenmorde*, Uppsala 1948; J. J. Stamm, "Das Leiden des Unschuldigen in Babylon und Israel," *Abh. Th. A. N. T.*, Zürich 1946, etc.

[4] According to Baumgartner, *Z. M. R.*, 1932, p. 214, the Resurrection was to ensure the martyrs' share in the Messianic Kingdom.

of the departed to life is welcomed with open arms by the *Ḥasidim* and their successors, the Pharisees, similarly exposed to persecution; on the other hand, the old priestly aristocracy, represented by the Sadducees, shows itself much more reserved and ultimately hostile towards it. Faith in the new life that God gives to His own is the gracious gift that Yahweh bestows only upon these who hazard their earthly existence for Him. "The real leaven of the belief in the resurrection," A. Causse justly writes, "was the persecution in the time of Antiochus Epiphanes." [5]

Thus the Old Testament believers did not arrive at the conviction that their God would raise the dead merely through their contacts with Canaan or Iran, nor by academic deductions from some doctrine unrelated to real life; what finally effected their adherence to the new creed was the bearing of the tormented *Ḥasidim* greeting the advent of the Messianic Age in advance. Thus the truth of Ernest Renan's dictum is established: "The martyr was the real creator of belief in another life." [6]

CONCLUSIONS

In concluding the third part of this study, we consider that although Persian and Canaanite doctrines fulfilled a certain role in the elaboration of the Old Testament belief in the resurrection of the dead, the essential element is nevertheless found in Israel itself. In the interventions of its God the People of Yahweh found assurance that, in His sovereignty, righteousness, and love, He would triumph over all the forces of evil and grant His faithful servants a share in His Kingdom. Yahweh cannot deny Himself; the faith of the *Ḥasidim*, based on the acts of the Living God in control of His People's history, did not falter in the face of persecutions; the sufferings of the Jewish martyrs rather led them to look to the day when God would crush His adversaries and call His own to life in a world made new.

[5] A. Causse, *Der Ursprung der jüdischen Lehre von der Auferstehung*, Cahors 1908, p. 36.

[6] E. Renan, *Histoire d'Israel*, vol. iv, p. 226.

Faith in the resurrection is thus definitely born of Yahweh's revelation to Israel, which, by making manifest His transcendence over the powers of destruction, His faithfulness to the Law on which the Chosen People's life is based, and His graciousness towards beings who were His debtors for all things, created this devotion of the *Ḥasidim*, who could give up their lives for the sake of remaining in communion with Him. The persecution of the Jews thus played a decisive part in promoting the relinquishment of the former Israelite conceptions of human destiny; out of the turmoil of the life of the martyr nation broke forth the good news that transcended the intuitions of the wise: "God restores life to the departed!" The assurance of the victory over death was veritably born in the pangs of the servants of the God of Israel; that is why we can conclude by adapting a famous saying of Tertullian's: the blood of the martyrs was a seed of immortality!

CONCLUSION

To complete this study we shall briefly recall the history of the belief in the resurrection of the dead among the Chosen People and the way in which its members reacted to the proclamation of the new faith professed by the *Hasidim*.

On its occupation of Canaan, Israel found the concept of the return to life there; Hos. VI vouches for that. The prophet rejects a belief connected with the agricultural cults, which, owing to its origin, will for long be suspect in the eyes of the fervent Yahwists. Even before the Exile, the Chosen People is exalting the power of its God over the powers of the nether world and is telling extraordinary stories about Elijah, Elisha and Enoch.

During the captivity in Babylon, Ezekiel bases his hope of the restoration of Judah on the Parable of the Dry Bones, which bears witness to the omnipotence of the God of Israel; Deutero-Isaiah proclaims the posthumous vindication of the Servant of Yahweh, whose death is thus seen as not the closing chapter of his destiny.

It is only after the Exile, or more exactly, immediately after the conquests of Alexander the Great, that the concept of resurrection takes definite form and becomes the expectation of the return of the departed to life on the last day. Then all things conspire to lead the People of Yahweh towards adopting a belief that overturns the conceptions by which it has lived for so long: the new ideas current in the world brought into being by Alexander's campaigns, the importance attached to the lot of the individual who is contending with sufferings incompatible with the righteousness of Yahweh, the yearning for a life lived in fellowship with God that will not sooner or later fall into the power of death, and the misfortunes of a community devoted to its traditions and led, by the enmity of the powers of the earth, to count more and more upon the coming of the Messianic Age; in short, faith in the resurrection is born in the sweat, tears, and blood of a people prepared to lose all to preserve its communion with Him who, from the dawn of its history, has revealed Himself as the sovereign, just, and gracious God.

The *Ḥasidim* and, following them, the Pharisees, profess the new faith; indeed it arises in their midst, and strengthens them in those centuries in which persecutions are unleashed against them; nevertheless the Jewish nation as a whole remains reserved about it for a long time; it will require long controversy and a succession of events, such as the capture of Jerusalem by the Romans, which marks the end of the priestly aristocracy, for it to become one of the fundamental dogmas of Judaism.

Thus the post-canonical writings, contemporary with or subsequent to Daniel, ignore all possibility of new life after death: Ecclesiasticus, for example, with the earlier Wisdom literature, continues to confine the destiny of man to his existence in this world and to connect retribution with earthly life.[1] Works like the Books of Judith, Tobit, Baruch, and even the First Book of the Maccabees [2] take no account of the resurrection; in other documents, it is sometimes mentioned and sometimes neglected; [3] in short, we can say with J. Bonsirven that "round about the beginning of the Christian era the thought of the resurrection has not yet taken possession of the minds of men as it will later on; it is not yet a fixed and familiar point on the eschatological horizon." [4] The certainty of the return of the dead to life, or at least of some of them, is, on the other hand, expressed not only in the Second Book of the Maccabees, but in general in the Enoch literature and the Psalms of Solomon, as well as in later writings such as, in particular, the Testaments of the Twelve Patriarchs, the Fourth Book of Ezra, and the Apocalypse of Baruch.[5] Alongside this peculiarly Semitic expectation of bodily revivification, a different interest is exhibited in other more or less Hellenistic

---

[1] Ecclesiasticus XIV. 16 ff., XXXVIII. 21, XLI. 4, etc.

[2] I Baruch II. 17, IV. 1; Tob. IV. 10, XIII. 2; I Macc. II. 49-70.

[3] Ps. Sol. XVII; the opening chs. of I Enoch; IV Ezra XIII, etc.

[4] J. BONSIRVEN (S.J.), *Le judaïsme palestinien au temps de Jésus-Christ*, VOL. I, Paris 1934, pp. 470 f.; cp. also SCHWALLY, *op. cit.* (above, p. 125, n. 2), pp. 131 ff.; VOLZ *op. cit.* (above, p. 126, n. 5), pp. 126 ff.; NIKOLAINEN, *op. cit.* (above, p. 131, n. 3), pp. 148 ff.; NÖTSCHER, *op. cit.* (above, p. 55, n. 5), pp. 245 ff.; A. LODS, "De quelques récits de voyage au pays des morts," *C. r. Ac. Inscr.*, 1940, pp. 434 ff., etc.

[5] II Macc. VII. 9, 11, 14, etc., XII. 43 ff.; I Enoch CII-CIV; Ps. Sol. III. 15 f.; II Bar. XXX; T. Levi XVIII; T. Judah XXV; T. Benj. X; IV Ezra V. 41, etc.

writings, such as the Book of Wisdom, the works of Philo, the Qumrân documents, and the Fourth Book of the Maccabees, which are devoted to the immortality of the soul.[6]

We are not going to refer here to everything in the post-canonical literature that deals with the lot of man after death; this study, which in any case is frequently undertaken and stands by itself, would lead us too far afield; let us, however, note that the acceptance of new doctrines concerning the destiny of the departed raised a whole series of problems, the answers to which, motivated perhaps rather by a desire to penetrate into the mystery of the Beyond than by a real devotion to the Living God, were as varied as they were confused.[7]

[6] Wis. I. 15 f., II. 1 ff., III. 2 f., IX. 15, etc.; Qumrân, Pss. נ, ה; JOSEPHUS, Bell. Jud., II. viii. 11; Antiq. XVIII. i. 5; etc.; cp. J. VAN DER PLOEG, "L'immortalité de l'homme d'après les textes de la Mer Morte," Vet. test., 1952, pp. 171 ff.; G. VERMÈS, Les manuscrits du désert de Juda, Paris 1953, pp. 121 f.

[7] Palestinian Judaism primarily regarded the resurrection as a means of ensuring the strict retribution of good and evil works and associated it with the end of the age. In the Diaspora, under the influence of Greek ideas, the soul, it is thought, goes to Heaven or to Hell immediately after death, and thus the separation of the righteous and the ungodly is effected at once. The two beliefs sometimes come to terms in a compromising formula; the faithful begin to enjoy some measure of bliss in Sheol, and the wicked start to pay for their sins while they are awaiting the resurrection and the final verdict of God.

The abode of the dead then tends to become the place in which sinners are punished, Gehenna; it is divided up into several sections, some being reserved for the martyrs and believers, others being set apart for the guilty (I Enoch XXII; Jub. XXIII; etc.)

Does the resurrection affect all the dead or only a certain number of them? Opinion is divided; the older writings, it would appear, reserve the return to life for the righteous only (II Macc.; Ps. Sol. III. 16; I Enoch XCI. 10, XCII. 3, c. 5), and thus it is a reward from which sinners are excluded. The resurrection is general in the more recent documents (IV Ezra VII. 29 ff.; II Baruch XXX. 1 ff.; L. 2 ff.; cp. also I Enoch XXII. 1 ff., LXI. 5; T. Sim. 6; T. Zeb. 10; T. Judah 25; T. Benj. 10); the Rabbinical writings reflect the same diversity, with some reservations regarding universal resurrection, since certain categories of the wicked are eternally excluded from it, for instance the Egyptians drowned in the Red Sea, the generations of the Flood and the Tower of Babel, Kings Jeroboam, Ahab, and Manasseh, the proud, and the heretics.

Cp. H. STRACK and P. BILLERBECK, Excursus, "Allgemeine oder teilweise Auferstehung?" Komm. N. T., Munich 1928, VOL. IV, pp. 1166-98.

Among the resolute opponents of belief in the resurrection are the Sadducees; Josephus tells us about the heated arguments they had with the Pharisees on this subject, the Gospel informs us of one of their principal objections, and the Book of Acts shows us that a mere reference to this question was enough to cause division among the Apostle Paul's enemies.[8]

As their conversation with Jesus indicates, the Sadducees claim to hold to the letter of Scripture; their objections emphasise the absurd consequences of the doctrine professed by the Pharisees; it may ultimately be the case, as F. Schwally thinks, that their hostility is motivated by political rather than by dogmatic considerations, and that, in point of fact, the Sadducees reject the Messianic hope with which the expectation of the resurrection is connected,[9] to avoid friction with the Romans. The Pharisees are going to prevail, their belief answers the deep longings of a martyr people; moreover, they alone will survive the destruction of the Temple. The Rabbis will then impose the dogma of retribution upon Judaism as a whole; as early as A.D. 90, Rabbi Gamaliel declares: "He who denies the resurrection has no part in the world to come . . . it is taught by all Scripture"; similarly from the first century, the ritual prayers lay stress on the power that God possesses of raising the dead. Henceforth the expectation of the return of the perished to life is going to be a fundamental characteristic of the Messianic hope, an essential article of the Jewish faith.

Along with a whole party among His contemporaries, Jesus

[8] JOSEPHUS, *Antiq.* XVIII. i. 3, 4; Mk. XII. 18 ff.; Mt. XXII. 23 ff.; Lk. XX. 27 ff.; Acts XXIII. 6 ff.; XXVI. 5 ff.; NIKOLAINEN, *op. cit.* (above, p. 131, n. 3), pp. 169 ff. The Sadducees are not alone in rejecting the doctrine of the resurrection; the Samaritans also condemn it, and the heathen scoff at it; thus a whole system of apologetics comes into being for the defence of the belief adopted by the Pharisees, which claims to be based, on the one hand, on the Scriptural revelation, and, on the other, on reason. All Scripture, according to the Rabbis, teaches the resurrection, which is necessary to make judgment possible and is not less credible than creation: BONSIRVEN, *op. cit.* (above, p. 224, n. 4), pp. 471 ff. These arguments will be repeated again and again by the Christian apologists. Cp. P. NAUTIN, *Je crois à l'Esprit saint dans la Sainte Eglise pour la résurrection de la chair,* Paris 1947; C. M. EDSMAN, "The Body and Eternal Life," *Mélanges J. Pedersen II,* Stockholm 1946; H. I. MARROU, "La résurrection des morts et les apologistes des premiers siècles," *Lumière et vie,* III (1952).

[9] SCHWALLY, *op. cit.* (above, p. 25, n. 2), pp. 163 f.

speaks of the resurrection as an accepted feature of the end of the age and defines His own position regarding it in the Sadducees' presence. To these interlocutors, who base themselves on one text in the Law in order to assail the Pharisees' belief, He replies by citing Scripture as a whole; He places His opponents at the heart of the Biblical revelation by bringing them into the presence of the Living God. Over against their legalistic, literal, and ultimately dead conception of Scripture, He sets His own dynamic, spiritual, and living understanding of the Word of God.

In agreement with the Old Testament He bases the certainty of the resurrection on God and on God alone; the sovereign and creative power of the God of Israel is the sole guarantee of the departed coming back to the light at the end of the age. God is the Living God, He cannot be the God of the dead, thus He will be the God of the living, the God of the resurrection. "Only on the ground of the reality of God can the reality of the resurrection be established" (J. Schniewind).

With the *Hasidim*, Jesus similarly connects assurance of the life to come with personal communion with His Father. Abraham, Isaac, and Jacob do not fall into the power of death for ever, for they were the servants of the Living God; those who, following the example of the patriarchs, devote themselves to Him and live by Him are called, not to disappear into nothingness, but to share in the glory of God. Eternal life does not begin in the Beyond, on the morrow of death or on the day of resurrection, but now, in the daily round of the believer's existence, for it is essentially life in which the presence of God dwells. Finally, in common with the Old Testament tradition, Jesus postulates a close connexion between martyrdom and the resurrection (Mk. viii. 35, 38); the future of man is dependent on the attitude that he adopts in this world towards the crucified Messiah; the disciple must follow in his Master's footsteps; the road to eternal life leads by way of the Cross; he who loses his life for the sake of the Son of Man shall find it again.

Thus Jesus repeats the essence of the fundamental Old Testament ideas about the resurrection; He emphasises, as does the Scriptural revelation, that the ultimate lot of every man is wrought out in this world, within the framework of his daily existence; the certainty of the Hereafter by no means diminishes the importance of earthly life, indeed it increases it, since the creature's ultimate salvation is being decided here and now in accordance with the attitude that it assumes towards the Son of Man.

Though Jesus is at one with the Pharisees in asserting the resurrection, He rebukes them for their materialistic conception of it; for them the re-awakening of the dead is, in point of fact, essentially no more than a mere re-animation of the corpse, a revivification which is tantamount to a mere return to life in its present dimensions. Jesus takes a serious view of the fact that the resurrection is connected with the coming of the Messianic Age; for Him, the Kingdom of God does not consist in a restoration of the former dispensation, but in its transfiguration. The ultimate life of the faithful is not a repetition of his present existence but its fulfilment under entirely new conditions determined by the Living God. "For in the resurrection they . . . are like angels in heaven" (Mt. xxii. 30).

Moreover, Jesus is not satisfied with merely proclaiming the resurrection to His People; like the *Ḥasidim*, He lives it; His destiny transforms it into more than a magnificent but far-off hope; through what happens to Him, it becomes a present reality to the joyful and confident believers whose faith from that time is founded on an accomplished fact. For with Easter, the Resurrection had come.

We have seen how in the Old Testament faith in the return of the departed to life ultimately rests on the revelation of Yahweh to His People; it was because the God of Israel revealed Himself as a powerful, just, and gracious God, that the *Ḥasidim* asserted the return of the departed to life. The event that Christians celebrate at Easter gives similar sanction in their eyes to the greatness, righteousness, and mercy of the God of Israel and of the Church: the resurrection of Jesus confirms the Living God's victory over the demonic powers (Acts iii. 15; iv. 10; x. 40, etc.); it bears witness to the divine righteousness that gives salvation to sinners and conforms them to the likeness of the Son of God (Rom. iv. 22 ff.; x. 9 f.); and it reveals to believers the love of the Father, from which nothing is able to separate them, and the care of Christ, who continually makes

intercession for them (Rom. VIII. 34 ff.)   Thus Easter is the
ratification of Yahweh's revelation to His People; the faith
of the Apostles becomes one with the hope of the *Ḥasidim*;
with Israel, the Church, then, bases itself on the promises of
God in its expectation of the death of death; yet only the
Church knows that death is already defeated, it exalts Jesus
Christ, against whom Hell has no more power, and who, once
and for all, has opened the way to eternal life to all mankind.

Q

BIBLIOGRAPHY

ABRAHAMSSOHN, H. *The Origin of Death, Studies in African Mythology*, Uppsala 1951.

ADDISON, J. T. *Life beyond Death in the Beliefs of Mankind*, London 1933.

ALBERT, A. *Die israelitisch-jüdische Auferstehungshoffnung in ihren Beziehungen zum Parsismus*, Königsberg 1910.

ALT, A. "Hosea 5. 8-6. 6: Ein Krieg und seine Folgen in Prophetischer Beleuchtung," in *N. k. z.*, XXX (1919), pp. 537-68, and *Kleine Schriften zur Geschichte des Volkes Israel*, VOL. II, Munich 1953.

AUBERT, L. *La vie après la mort chez les Israélites*, Lausanne 1902.

BARTH, C. *Die Errettung vom Tode in den individuellen Klage und Dankliedern des A. T.*, Basle 1947.

BAUDISSIN, W. VON. *"Adonis und Esmun," Eine Untersuchung zur Geschichte des Glaubens an Auferstehungsgötter und Heilgötter*, Leipzig 1911.

——. "Alttestamentliches 'hajjim' 'Leben' in der Bedeutung von Glück," in *Festschrift E. Sachau*, Berlin 1915, pp. 143-61.

BAUMGÄRTEL, F. *Die Eigenart der alttestamentlichen Frömmigkeit*, Schwerin i. Mecklenburg 1932.

——. *Der Hiobdialog*, Beitr. z. Wiss. vom A. N. T., Stuttgart 1933.

BAUMGARTNER, W. " Der Auferstehungsglaube im Alten Orient," in *Z. M. R.*, XLVIII (1933), pp. 193-214.

——. "Ras Shamra und das A. T.," in *Th. R.*, 1940, pp. 163 ff.; 1941, p. 1 ff., 85 ff., 157 ff.

——. "Zur Etymologie von Scheol," *Th. Z.*, 1946, p. 233.

BEER, G. "Der biblische Hades," *Festgabe H. J. Holtzmann*, Tübingen-Leipzig 1902.

BENTZEN, A. "Messias, Moses redivivus, Menschensohn," *Abh. Th. A. N. T.*, 1948; Eng. trans., *King and Messiah*, London 1954.

——. "Der Tod des Beters in den Psalmen, Randbemerkungen zur Diskussion zwischen Mowinckel und Widengren," in *Festschrift Otto Eissfeldt*, Halle 1947.

BERTHOLET, A. *Die israelitischen Vorstellungen vom Zustand nach dem Tode*, 2nd edn., Tübingen 1914.

——. "The pre-Christian Belief in the Resurrection of the Body," *Am. J. Th.*, 1916, pp. 1 ff.

——. "Zur Frage des Verhältnisses vom persischen und jüdischen Auferstehungsglauben," in *Festschrift F. C. Andreas*, Leipzig 1916, pp. 51-62.

BIEDER, W. "Auferstehung des Fleisches oder des Leibes? (Eine biblisch-theologische und dogmengeschichtliche Studie)," in *Th. Z.*, 1945, pp. 105 ff.

———. *Die Vorstellung von der Höllenfahrt Jesu Christi* (Beitrag zur Entstehungsgeschichte der Vorstellung vom sog. Descensus ad inferos), Zürich 1949.

BIRKELAND, H. "The Belief in the Resurrection of the Dead in the O.T.," in *St. th.*, III/I (1950), pp. 60-78.

BÖKLEN, E. *Die Verwandtschaft der jüdisch-christlichen mit der parsischen Eschatologie*, Göttingen 1902.

BONDT, A. DE. *Wat leert het Oude Testament aangaande het Leven na dit Leven*, Kampen 1938.

BOURGUET, P. *Problèmes de l'au-delà*, Paris 1947.

BOUSSET, W., and H. GRESSMANN. *Die Religion des Judentums*, 3rd edn., Berlin 1926.

BURNEY, L. F. *Israel's Hope of Immortality*, Oxford 1909.

CAUSSE, A. *Der Ursprung der jüdischen Lehre von der Auferstehung*, Cahors 1908.

———. *Israël et la vision de l'humanité*, Strasbourg-Paris 1924.

———. *Les dispersés d'Israël*, Paris 1929.

———. *Du groupe ethnique à la communauté religieuse: le problème sociologique de la religion d'Israël*, Paris 1937.

CHAINE, J. "Révélation progressive de la notion de rétribution dans l'A. T.," in *Rencontres*, IV (1941).

CHARLES, R. H. *A Critical History of the Doctrine of a Future Life in Israel and in Judaism*, London 1913.

———. *Religious Development between the Old and the New Testaments*, London 1914.

CONGAR, Y. "Le purgatoire," in *Le mystère de la mort et sa célébration*, Paris 1951, pp. 279 ff.

DANELL, G. A. "Psalm 139," in *Upps. U. Årsskr.*, 1951.

DELITZSCH, F. *Das Land ohne Heimkehr*, Stuttgart 1911.

DHORME, E. (P.) "Séjour des morts chez les Babyloniens et chez les Hébreux," in *Rev. bib.*, 1907, pp. 5 ff.

———. *L'emploi métaphorique des noms de parties du corps en hébreu et en accadien*, Paris 1920.

———. *La religion des Hébreux nomades*, Brussels 1937.

———. "L'idée de l'au-delà dans la religion hébraïque," *R. h. r.*, 1941, pp. 113-42.

DUBARLE, A. M. "Les sages d'Israël," in *Lectio divina*, Paris 1946.

DUCHESNE-GUILLEMIN, J. *Ormazd et Ahriman, Mythes et Religions*, Paris 1953.

DUPONT-SOMMER, A. "L'Iran et Israël," in *La civilisation iranienne*, Paris 1952, pp. 71 ff.

DÜRR, L. " Die Wertung des Lebens im A.T. und im antiken Orient," *Verz. Vorles. Ak. Braunsb.* 1926-7.

DUSSAUD, R. " La *nephesh* et la *rouach* dans le livre de Job," in *R. h. r.*, 1945, pp. 17 ff.

EBELING, E. *Leben und Tod nach den Vorstellungen der Babylonier* (i), Berlin 1931.

EDSMAN, C. M. "The Body and Eternal Life," *Mélanges J. Pedersen*, I-II, Stockholm 1946, pp. 33 ff.

EERDMANS, B. D. "The *Chasidim*," in "Essays on Masoretic Psalms," *Oudtest. St.*, 1941-2.

EICHRODT, W. *Theologie des A. T.*, Leipzig, VOLS. I-III, 1933-5; 2nd edn., Berlin 1948.

ELHORST, H. J. "Die israelitischen Trauerriten," in *Festschrift J. Wellhausen*, Beihefte z. *Z. A. W.*, 1914, pp. 117 ff.

ELIADE, M. *Le mythe de l'eternel retour*, Paris 1949.

——. *Traité d'histoire des religions*, Paris 1953.

ENGNELL, I. *Studies in Divine Kingship in the Ancient Near East*, Uppsala 1943.

——. "The 'Ebed Yahweh Songs and the Suffering Messiah in Deutero-Isaiah," *B. J. R. L.*, 1948.

FÉRET, H. M. "La mort dans la tradition biblique," in *Le mystère de la mort et sa célébration*, Paris 1951, pp. 15 ff.

FRANKEN, H. J. *The Mystical Communion with JHWH in the Book of Psalms*, Leyden 1954.

FRANKFORT, H. *Kingship and the Gods*, Chicago 1948.

FRAZER, J. G. *The Golden Bough*, 3rd edn., London 1915; abridged edn., London 1954.

——. *The Fear of the Dead in Primitive Religion*, London 1933.

FREY, J. *Tod, Seelenglaube und Seelenkult im alten Israel*, Leipzig 1898.

——. "La vie de l'au-delà dans les conceptions juives au temps de Jésus-Christ," in *Biblica*, Rome 1932, pp. 129-68.

GRESSMANN, H. *Der Ursprung der israelitisch-jüdischen Eschatologie*, Göttingen 1905.

——. *Der Messias*, Forsch. z. A. N. T., Göttingen 1929.

GRUNEISEN, G. *Der Ahnenkultus und die Urreligion Israels*, Halle 1900

GUILLET, J. "Les sources scripturaires de la foi en la résurrection de la chair," *B. v. c.*, 1953, pp. 40-56.

GUNKEL, H. *Schöpfung und Chaos in Urzeit und Endzeit*, Göttingen 1895.

HALDAR, A. "The Notion of the 'Desert' in Sumero-Accadian and West-Semitic Religions," *Upps. U. Årsskr.*, 1950.

HALÉVY, J. *La croyance à l'immortalité de l'âme chez les Sémites*, Mélanges de critique et d'histoire, Paris 1883.

HEIDEL, A. *The Gilgamesh Epic and Old Testament Parallels*, 2nd edn., Chicago 1949.

HERZFELD, E. "Die Religion der Achaemeniden," in *R. h. r.*, 1936, pp. 21 ff.

HUMBERT, P. *Recherches sur les sources égyptiennes de la littérature sapientiale d'Israël*, Neuchâtel 1929.

——. *Etudes sur le récit du paradis et de la chute dans la Genèse*, Neuchâtel 1940.

IMSCHOOT, P. VAN. *Théologie de l'Ancien Testament*, VOL. I, Paris-Rome 1954.

JENNI, E. *Das Wort "Olam" im A. T.*, Berlin 1953.

JEREMIAS, A. *Die babylonisch-assyrischen Vorstellungen vom Leben nach dem Tode*, Der Alte Orient, Leipzig 1887.

——. *Hölle und Paradies bei den Babyloniern*, Der Alte Orient, 2nd edn., Leipzig 1903.

JOHNSON, A. R. "The Role of the King in the Jerusalem Cultus," in *The Labyrinth*, ed. S. H. Hooke, London 1935, pp. 71-111.

——. *The Vitality of the Individual in the Thought of Ancient Israel*, Cardiff 1949.

KARGE, P. *Rephaim, die vorgeschichtliche Kultus Palästinas und Phöniziens*, 1st edn., Paderborn 1917.

KEES, H. *Totenglaube und Jenseitsvorstellungen der alten Aegypter*, Leipzig 1926.

KITTEL, R. *Geschichte des Volkes Israel*, esp. VOL. III(a), Stuttgart 1927, and VOL. III(b), Stuttgart 1929.

KLEINERT, P. "Zur Idee des Lebens im A. T.," *Th. St. k.*, LXVIII (1895), pp. 693-732.

KÖHLER, L. *Theologie des A. T.*, 2nd edn., Tübingen 1947; Eng. trans. by A. S. Todd, *Old Testament Theology*, London 1957.

KROLL, J. *"Descensus ad inferos," Verz. Vorles. Ak. Braunsb.*, 1922-3.

LAGRANGE (O.P), M. J. *Etudes sur les religions sémitiques*, 2nd edn., Paris 1905.

LANDSBERG, P. L. *Essai sur l'expérience de la mort*, Paris 1951.

LARCHER (O.P) "La résurrection dans l'A. T.," *L. v.*, 1952, pp. 11-34.

LEENHARDT, F. J. "La situation de l'homme d'après la Genèse," in *Das Menschenbild im Lichte des Evangeliums: Festschrift Prof. E. Brunner*, Zürich 1950.

LEEUW, G. VAN DER. *Religion in Essence and Manifestation: A Study in Phenomenology*, Eng. trans. by J. E. Turner, London 1938.

LINDBLOM, J. *Das ewige Leben*, Uppsala-Leipzig 1914.

——. "Die Jesaja-Apocalypse (Jes. XXIV-VII)," in *Upps. U. Årsskr.*, 1938.

——. "'Ich weiss, dass mein Erlöser lebt' (Zum Verständnis der Stelle Job XIX. 25)," in *St. th.*, 1940, pp. 65 ff.

——. "Die Eschatologie des 49. Psalms," *Horae Soederblomianae, Mélanges J. Pedersen*, 1/1, Stockholm 1944.

LIPPERT, J. *Der Seelenkult in seinen Beziehungen zur althebräischen Religion*, Berlin 1881.

LODS, A. *La croyance à la vie future et le culte des morts dans l'antiquité israélite*, Paris 1906.

——. *Le culte des ancêtres dans l'antiquité hébraïque et ses rapports avec l'orangisation familiale et sociale des anciens Sémites*, Paris 1906.

——. *Israël, des origines au milieu du VIIIᵉ siècle*, Paris 1932; Eng. trans. by S. H. Hooke, *Israel from its Beginnings to the Middle of the Eighth Century*, London 1932.

——. *Les prophètes d'Israël et les débuts du judaïsme*, Paris 1935; Eng. trans. by S. H. Hooke, *The Prophets and the Rise of Judaism*, London 1937.

——. *La religion d'Israël*, Paris 1939.

——. "De quelques récits de voyages au pays des morts," *C. r. Ac. Inscr.*, 1940, pp. 434-52.

——. "Notes sur deux croyances hébraïques relatives à la mort et à ce qui la suit: le sort des incirconcis dans l'au-delà et la victoire sur le Léviathan," *C. r. Ac. Inscr.*, 1943, pp. 271-97.

——. *Histoire de la littérature hebraïque et juive*, Paris 1950.

LOHMEYER, E. "Die Idee des Martyriums im Judentum und Urchristentum," *Z. syst. Th.*, 1928, pp. 232 ff.

MEHL, R. *Notre vie et notre mort*, Paris 1953.

MENOUD, P. *Le sort des trépassés*, C. th. (9), Paris-Neuchâtel 1945.

——. "La signification chrétienne de la mort," and "La victoire chrétienne sur la mort," in *L'homme face à la mort*, Paris-Neuchâtel 1952.

MOLIN, G. "Entwicklung und Motive der Auferstehung vom A. T. bis zur rabbinischen Zeit," *Judaica*. 9, Zürich 1953-4, pp. 225 ff.

MONNIER, J. *La descente aux enfers*, Paris 1905.

MORIN, E. *L'homme et la mort dans l'histoire*, Paris 1951.

NAUTIN, P. *Je crois à l'Esprit Saint dans la Sainte Eglise pour la résurrection de la chair*, Unam Sanctam, Paris 1947.

NIKOLAINEN, A. T. "Der Auferstehungsglaube in der Bibel und ihrer Umwelt," in *Ann. Acad. Sc. Fenn.*, 1944.

Nötscher, F. *"Das Angesicht Gottes schauen"* nach biblischer und babylonischer Auffassung, Würzburg 1924.

——. Altorientalischer und alttestamentlicher Auferstehungsglauben, Würzburg 1926.

Nyberg, H. S. *Die Religion des alten Iran*, Leipzig 1938.

Parrot, A. *Le "refrigerium" dans l'au-delà*, Paris 1938.

——. *Malédictions et violations de tombes*, Paris 1939.

Pedersen, J. *Israel, its Life and Culture*, 1st edn., Copenhagen-London, vols. i-ii, 1926; vols. iii-iv, 1940.

Pidoux, G. *L'homme dans l'A. T., C. th.* (32), Neuchâtel-Paris 1953.

——. " Encore les deux arbres de Genèse 3!," in *Z. alttest. W.*, 1954, pp. 37 ff.

Ploeg, J. van der. "L'immortalité de l'homme d'après les textes de la Mer Morte," in *Vet. test.*, 1952, pp. 171 ff.

Procksch, O. *Theologie des A. T.*, Gütersloh 1950.

Quell, G. *Die Auffassung des Todes in Israel*, Leipzig 1925.

Rad, G. von. "Alttestamtentliche Glaubensaussagen vom Leben und Tod," in *Allgemeine Evangelische Lutherische Kirchenzeitung*, 1938, coll. 826 ff.

——. "Gerechtigkeit und Leben in der Kultsprache der Psalmen," in *Festschrift A. Bertholet*, Tübingen 1950.

Renan, E. *Histoire du peuple d'Israël*, Paris 1887 ff.

Ringgren, H. "Einige Bemerkungen zum lxxiii. Psalm," in *Vet. test.*, 1953, pp. 265 ff.

Rost, L. "Alttestamentliche Wurzeln der ersten Auferstehung," in *Memorial E. Lohmeyer*, Stuttgart 1951, pp. 67 ff.

Scheftelowitz, J. "Der Seelen- und Unsterblichkeitsglaube im A. T.," in *Arch. Rw.*, 1916, pp. 210 ff.

——. *Die altpersische Religion und das Judentum*, Giessen 1920.

Schilling, O. *Der Jenseitsgedanke im A. T.*, Mainz 1951.

Schmidt, J. "Der Ewigeskeitsbegriff im A. T.," in *Alttest. Abh.*, 1940.

Schultz, A. "Der Sinn des Todes im A. T.," in *Verz. Vorles. Ak. Braunsb.*, 1919.

Schwally, F. *Das Leben nach dem Tode nach den Vorstellungen des alten Israel und des Judentums einschliesslich des Volksglaubens im Zeitalter Christi*, Giessen 1892.

Seligson, M. "The Meaning of נֶפֶשׁ מֵת in the O.T.," in *St. orient.*, xvi. 2 (1951).

Sellin, E. "Die alttestamentliche Hoffnung auf Auferstehung und ewiges Leben," in *N. k. Z.*, xxx (1919), pp. 232 ff.

——. *Theologie des A. T.*, Leipzig 1936.

SÖDERBLOM, N. *La vie future d'après le mazdéisme: etude d'eschatologie comparée*, Paris 1901.

SUKENIK, E. L. "Arrangements for the Cult of the Dead in Ugarit and Samaria," *Mémorial Lagrange*, Paris 1940, pp. 59 ff.

SURKAU, H. W. "Martyrien in jüdischer und frühchristlicher Zeit," in *Forsch. z. A. N. T.*, 1938.

SUTCLIFFE, E. F. *The O.T. and the Future Life*, Westminster 1946.

THIELICKE, H. *Tod und Leben, Studien zur Christlichen Anthropologie.* Oekuméné, Geneva 1946.

TORGE, P. *Seelenglauben und Unsterblichkeitshoffnung im A. T.*, Leipzig 1909.

TOUZARD, J. "Le développement de la doctrine de l'immortalité dans l'A. T.," in *Rev. bib.*, 1898, pp. 207-41.

VIROLLEAUD, C. "Les *Rephaïm*, fragments de poèmes de Ras Shamra," *Syria*, XXII, 1941.

VOLLBORN, W. *Studien zum Zeitverständnis des A. T.*, Göttingen 1951.

———. "Das Problem des Todes in Genesis 2 und 3," *Th. Lz.*, 1952, pp. 710 ff.

VOLZ, P. *Die jüdische Eschatologie von Daniel bis Akiba*, 1st edn., Leipzig 1903.

WIDENGREN, G. "The King and the Tree of Life in Ancient Near Eastern Religion," *Upps. U. Årsskr.*, 1951.

WORDEN, T. "The Literary Influence of the Ugaritic Fertility Myth on the O.T.," *Vet. test.*, 1953, pp. 273-97.

LIST OF ABBREVIATIONS

Abh. Th. A. N. T.	=*Abhandlungen zur Theologie des Alten und Neuen Testments.* Zürich.
Alttest. Abh.	=*Alttestamentliche Abhandlungen.* Münster.
Am. J. Th.	=*American Journal of Theology.* Chicago.
Ann. Ac. Sc. Fenn.	=*Annales Academiae Scientiarum Fennicae.* Helsinki.
Arch. Rw.	=*Archiv für Religionswissenschaft.* Leipzig-Berlin.
A. T. D.	=*Das Alte Testament Deutsch.* Göttingen.
A. V.	=Authorised Version.
B. Cent.	=*La Bible du Centenaire.* Paris.
B. Heb.	=*Biblia Hebraica*, ed. R. Kittel. Stuttgart.
B. J. R. L.	=*Bulletin of the John Rylands Library.* Manchester.
B. Jérus.	=*Bible de Jérusalem* (*i.e.* the Bible translated under the direction of the Ecole Biblique de Jérusalem). Paris.
B. v. c.	=*Bible et vie chrétienne.* Paris.
Beitr. z. Wiss. vom A. N. T.	=Beiträge zur Wissenschaft vom Alten und Neuen Testament. Stuttgart.
Beihefte z. *Z. A. W.*	=Beihefte zur *Z. alttest. W.*
C. r. Ac. Inscr.	=*Comptes rendus de l'Académie des Inscriptions et Belles-Lettres.* Paris.
C. th.	=Cahiers théologiques. Neuchâtel-Paris.
D.S. (Is.)	=Dead Sea Scroll of Isaiah, the Isaiah MS. of the Syrian Monastery of St. Mark.
Et. bib.	=*Etudes bibliques.* Paris.
Et. th. r.	=*Etudes théologiques et religieuses.* Montpellier.
Forsch. R. L. A. N. T.	=*Forschungen zur Religion und Literatur des Alten und Neuen Testaments.* Göttingen.
Hb. A. T.	=*Handbuch zum Alten Testament.* Tübingen.
Hk. A. T.	=*Handkommentar zum Alten Testament.* Göttingen.
I. C. C.	=*International Critical Commentary.* Edinburgh.
J. Bib. Lit.	=*Journal of Biblical Literature.* Newhaven.
J. Q. R.	=*Jewish Quarterly Review.*
K.-B.	=*Lexicon in Veteris Testamenti Libros.* Köhler-Baumgartner. Leyden.
K. H.-C. A. T.	=*Kurzer Hand-Commentar zum Alten Testament.* Tübingen.
KITTEL	=*Theologisches Wörterbuch zum Neuen Testament*, ed. Kittel. Stuttgart.
Komm. A. T.	=*Kommentar zum Alten Testament.* Leipzig.
Lunds U. Årsskr.	=*Lunds Universitets Årsskrift.* Lund.
L. V.	=*Lumière et vie.* St Alban-Leysse, Savoy.
LXX	=Septuagint.

M. T.	= Masoretic Text.
N. k. Z.	= *Neue kirchliche Zeitschrift.* Leipzig.
Oudtest. St.	= *Ondtestamentische Studien.* Leyden.
Rev. bib.	= *Revue biblique.* Paris-Rome.
Rel. G. G.	= *Die Religion in Geschichte und Gegenwart.* 2nd edn. Tübingen.
R. h. p. r.	= *Revue d'histoire et de philosophie religieuses.* Strasbourg.
R. h. r.	= *Revue de l'histoire des religions.* Paris.
R. th. ph.	= *Revue de théologie et de philosophie.* Lausanne.
Schr. A. T.	= *Die Schriften des Alten Testaments in Auswahl.* Göttingen.
Svensk Ex. Årsb.	= *Svensk Exegetisk Årsbok.* Uppsala.
St. orient.	= *Studia orientalia.* Helsinki.
St. th.	= *Studia theologica.* Lund.
Syria	= *Syria.* Paris.
Th. Lz.	= *Theologische Literaturzeitung.* Leipzig.
Th. R.	= *Theologische Rundschau.* Tübingen.
Th. St. Kr.	= *Theologische Studien und Kritiken.* Stuttgart-Gotha.
Th. Z.	= *Theologische Zeitschrift.* Basle.
Upps. U. Årsskr.	= *Uppsala Universitets Årsskrift.* Uppsala.
Voc. bib.	= *Vocabulaire biblique.* Neuchâtel-Paris.
Vet. test.	= *Vetus testamentum.* Leyden.
Verz. Vorles. Ak. Braunsb.	= *Verzeichnis der Vorlesungen an der Akademie zu Braunsberg.* Braunsberg.
Z. alttest. W.	= *Zeitschrift für die alttestamentliche Wissenschaft.* Giessen.
Z. D. M. G.	= *Zeitschrift der Deutschen morgenlandischen Gesellschaft.* Leipzig.
Z. M. R.	= *Zeitschrift für Missionskunde und Religionswissenschaft.* Berlin.
Z. neutest. W.	= *Zeitschrift für die neutestamentliche Wissenschaft.* Giessen.
Z. syst. Th.	= *Zeitschrift für systematische Theologie.* Gütersloh.